LONDONERS' LARDER

LONDONERS' LARDER

English Cuisine from Chaucer to the Present

Annette Hope

MAINSTREAM
PUBLISHING
EDINBURGH AND LONDON

First published in Great Britain in 2005 by
MAINSTREAM PUBLISHING COMPANY
(EDINBURGH) LTD
7 Albany Street
Edinburgh EH1 3UG

ISBN 1 84018 965 7

A catalogue record for this book is available
from the British Library

Typeset in Baskerville Book and Goudy Catalogue

Printed in Great Britain by
Antony Rowe Ltd, Chippenham, Wiltshire

NOTHING CONDUCES MORE TO THE HAPPINESS OF
MANKIND THAN TO HAVE FOOD SERVED UP IN A
DIGESTIBLE AND ATTRACTIVE FORM.
THE LORD MAYOR OF LONDON, C.1880

CONTENTS

INTRODUCTION

Among the most memorable phrases heard in my childhood was the one used by the BBC Overseas Service to announce its broadcasts: 'London calling'. For my parents, listening daily in South Africa during the Second World War, the words were an important link with a life left behind. But I had never been to London, and in my imagination it became a mythical and extraordinary place – the largest city in the world (as it then was), the hub of the Empire (I pictured a great wheel), the home of a discordant cracked bell they called Big Ben which was somehow very important since one heard it at the beginning of every broadcast.

As I grew older, I discovered another London through reading: Dickens came first, and then *Punch* and *The Listener*, which my grandmother sent out week by week. Other writers followed, from Dornford Yates to Charles Lamb, Agatha Christie to William Thackeray, Chaucer to Virginia Woolf. At last, when I myself stood on the platform at Victoria Station, it was with the excitement of someone coming home. I was not disappointed. For London is not, like some other ancient cities, a collection of beautiful or historic buildings. Much more it is a place of people and events; ghosts walk every city street and haunt the flyovers and office blocks just as much as they do the parks and churchyards, the Tower or the Abbey. This is a romantic approach, and if I were a Londoner myself, I should probably be impatient with it; but I am not, and in any case romantics do much to keep the past alive.

There is no better way of getting to know people than over a meal. For that reason, studying London's food brings us closer to the city and its inhabitants. As a capital city, a big port, a centre of trade, London has acted both as a magnet and the opposite, drawing people and goods but also sending them far and wide. It has special needs, special privileges and special problems. These have been my interest and, I hope, will be the reader's. As guides, we are lucky enough to have writers who, besides being good companions, themselves enjoyed a well-cooked meal and pleasant conversation. In *Londoners' Larder* only three – Chaucer, Samuel Pepys and Virginia Woolf – are Londoners born. Shakespeare, Sam Johnson and Oscar Wilde spent their working lives in London; it is impossible to imagine them writing anywhere else. Dickens and John Evelyn are the exceptions, for they were neither born in London nor did they do all their writing there. But Evelyn lived very near, and his concern for the pollution of the city by smoke from coal fires, his plan for rebuilding it after the Great Fire, his devoted work during the plague and the fact that his estate at Deptford is now part of Greater London would qualify him for inclusion, if his booklet on vegetable growing and eating did not. Dickens, of course, knew London more intimately than anyone before or since; of all our guides, he and Johnson are most part of the city's intellectual fabric.

At the end of each chapter, I have given recipes drawn from cookery books of the period. The earlier ones have been rephrased in modern English to save work for the reader, and I have given approximate quantities and cooking times which are lacking in the originals. 'From' – as in 'from Elizabeth Raffald' – indicates that a recipe has been thus adapted. Later recipes are quoted verbatim, sometimes with a gloss. Choosing recipes has been difficult – I wanted dishes people could cook (therefore with accessible ingredients and methods suitable to the modern kitchen) and enjoy eating (therefore not too extreme in flavour) but which were both representative of the period and not too similar to what we eat today. A few recipes are clearly impractical. They are included for interest alone. Those for use should feed four to six people except where otherwise indicated.

Many people were thanked in the introduction to the first edition. For help in the preparation of this new edition, I especially wish to thank Dr Elizabeth Chase, who most insistently urged its usefulness and who gave me valuable encouragement and information; Andy Faulds, who should have been thanked first time around and whose excellent photo of Robert Cooke is in this edition; Jonathan Meades, who took the trouble to share with me thoughtful reflections on London food today; Roger Nobbs, another Londoner who also responded generously to an appeal from a complete stranger; and Julian Payne, of Rules restaurant, who kindly answered my questions for over an hour on a dark December evening. The editorial team at Mainstream were as always kind, patient and cheerful. My husband was all of these; but only he knows how much more besides.

Annette Hope
May 2005

Chapter 1

GEOFFREY CHAUCER

Baked meat was never wanting in his house,
Of fish and flesh, and that so plenteous,
It seemed to snow therein both food and drink,
Of every dainty that a man could think.

The Canterbury Tales, Prologue

The place we call London has a population of more than 7 million, and extends over 610 square miles. When Chaucer was alive, its population numbered below 60,000, it covered just one square mile, and the city still sat snugly within its Roman wall, as it had done for centuries. For all that, and despite being smaller than Paris and Florence, smaller even than Ghent, the capital was still the largest and wealthiest city in England. No one lives now where once stood wooden houses each with its kitchen garden; instead you will find office blocks. Modern Londoners live outside the City – London has swallowed its surrounding villages and turned them into suburbs.

There are other differences too. Chaucer's London was not a capital in the modern sense of the word. The King did not live there (though the Tower was an awesome symbol of his existence) nor was it the immutable seat of government. Its growing importance lay in its position on the Thames, which reached deep into the heart of England and was navigable by merchant ships much of the way; and also in the close proximity of another city, Westminster, where the royal palace and that great ecclesiastical showpiece, the Abbey, asserted the power of Monarch and Church. London's first role may have been as a trading centre, but her function as supplier of goods and services to the City of Westminster was almost equally important to her development.

In many ways, Chaucer was a typical upper-middle-class Londoner of his time. His father was a wine merchant, his mother a merchant's daughter. When their son was born in 1340 they were probably living in a house on Thames Street, backing onto the west bank of the little stream called Walbrook near where it flowed into the river at Dowgate. Thames Street today is practically impassable to pedestrians; even then it was a busy thoroughfare, running parallel to the river and its wharves. The nearest wharf was Queenhithe, which, as well as being the principal landing-place for fish, was used by the wine ships from Rouen, so that the Chaucer house was conveniently placed. Many vintners made their homes in this district, which is still known as Vintry.

To a child, Vintry's cosmopolitan atmosphere must have made it an exciting and stimulating place. The ships which brought wine from France, Italy and Spain carried other cargoes too – spices from Venice, cotton and flax from Greece, sugar, soap, dried fish, raisins and figs from Syria or Cyprus or Alexandria – all in barrels brought ashore at Queenhithe and the other wharves, to be rolled or carted to warehouses throughout the city.

The merchants who imported these goods controlled London. They were grouped together in Guilds, some of which, such as the Fishmongers, the Pepperers (later to become the Merchants in Gross, or Grocers) and the Vintners, had great wealth. It was from their leaders that the powerful Lord Mayor was most often chosen – it had been said in King John's time that 'come what may Londoners would have no other King but their Mayor'. In 1374 it was a fishmonger, William Walworth, who was elected. After two years he was succeeded by another, Sir Nicholas Brembre. John Philpot, a grocer, held the post in 1378. Thus, at his birth, Chaucer joined the most influential group of people in the city. He knew Walworth and Brembre, and Philpot may have been a particular friend. (It was Walworth who killed Wat Tyler, the leader of the Peasants' Revolt. The dagger he is said to have used can still be seen in Fishmongers' Hall.)

But although all his life Chaucer had friends in the merchant community, his chosen profession was outside it. He began his career at fourteen as a page in an aristocratic household. After a brief spell as a soldier, during which he was captured in France and ransomed for sixteen pounds, he may have been sent on minor diplomatic missions; a Spanish museum holds a safe conduct from the King of Navarre for 'Geoffrey Chaucer and three companions', dated 1366. The following year he was back in England on the King's payroll, on the strength of which he married Philippa Roet, a lady-in-waiting to John of Gaunt's wife Duchess Blanche. For some years the couple continued at Court, but in 1374 they moved to London, where Chaucer became Comptroller of Customs and Subsidy of Wools, Skins and Hides in the Port of London.

It was the Chaucers' first opportunity to set up house on their own, and they moved into a government-owned house over Aldgate, an easy walk from the Wool Wharf and Custom House. Westward the apartment overlooked busy Leadenhall Street and Fenchurch Street, but from the east windows they could see the tranquil fields and green woods of Essex, for in the fourteenth century the country still lay very close to the city wall.

The peaceful outlook was dramatically disturbed in June 1381, when a mob of tenant farmers and labourers, brandishing scythes and hoes, encamped in the fields outside the wall. The cause of their fury was a new tax levied to pay for the war with France. On the night of Wednesday, 12 June, someone opened the Gate. The crowd streamed in – Chaucer and his wife, if at home, must have been very much afraid – and terrorised the city. From Kent, other peasants swept across London Bridge to join them. The Chancellor and the Treasurer, hiding in the Tower, were found and decapitated. A wave of xenophobia seized the populace, and there was a great massacre of Flemings. Then the rioters went outside the walls to the Strand, which at that time was lined with fine houses and beautiful gardens. There they ransacked and set on fire the Savoy, John of Gaunt's magnificent palace. As the building collapsed, thirty-two looters sleeping off the effects of the Duke's wine were trapped where they lay by fallen beams and stones; for several days people heard their desperate cries, but when help finally arrived all were dead.

On the fourth day the Peasant's Revolt ended as suddenly as it had begun when Richard II, supported by the Lord Mayor, rode to confront the rebels at Smithfield. As their leader, Wat Tyler, stepped forward threateningly, Walworth stabbed him. The crowd hesitated. Richard immediately took the initiative and spoke, promising to put things right; such was his air of authority that the people dispersed. The tax was revoked, and Walworth was knighted. But the incident left behind many unpleasant memories, and may have been partly responsible for Chaucer's decision not long after to put his post into the hands of a deputy and move to Kent.

In November 1386 his wife died, from a cause unknown to us. A few days later he resigned his various posts (he was by now both a Justice of the Peace and MP for Kent), and dropped out of sight for three years. He was still only in his forties.

He returned to public duty in 1389 as Clerk of the King's Works, charged with maintaining all the royal properties, and also with responsibility for the scaffolding and seating at the courtly tournaments which were held periodically at Smithfield ('smooth field'). The entire Court attended these events; for a week the place became a chivalric venue alive with colour and noise, each silken tent decked with a fluttering pennant, each knight in gleaming armour, each lady wearing her gayest robes. When all the jousting and feasting were over, the scaffolding came down and Smithfield returned to its normal function as a cattle and hay market. Chaucer may also have had a hand in arranging an event which took place on London Bridge on St George's Day, 1390. On that occasion a huge crowd watched Sir David Lindsay, later Earl of Crawford, defeat Sir John de Welles in a contest to settle whether Englishmen or Scots were the more valiant.

In 1390 Chaucer took on yet another job, as member of a commission to survey London's drainage system; this involved inspecting walls, bridges, sewers and ditches, and serving orders for repairs to be carried out by the landowners. How, one wonders, did he ever find time to write? Yet by this time he had produced all his major work – *The Book of the Duchess, Troilus and Cressida, The Parliament of Fowls* and *The Canterbury Tales*. He may well have felt the strain, for in 1391 he resigned the Clerkship of Works and became a minor administrator for a private estate. In 1399 he took a fifty-three-year lease on a little house in the garden of St Mary's Chapel, at Westminster, on the site now occupied by Henry VII's Chapel. Ten months later – on 25 October 1400 – he died, aged fifty-six. The cause of his death is not recorded, but he may have had the plague.

To picture life in fourteenth-century London we must hold firm to one central concept: that of a medium-sized market town with a busy port. An early map shows that within the Roman wall the city's east district was separated from the west by the Walbrook. Each side had its major shopping centre: East Cheap and West Cheap took their names from the Anglo-Saxon word for market. West Cheap, now called Cheapside, was predominantly a food market, and some of the streets roundabout still bear names indicating their former function. In an attempt to control quality and price Bread Street, for example, was designated by royal edict of 1300 the only street in which bakers might sell bread. Near it we find Milk Street and Wood Street. Once there was a Fish Street; that became, within Chaucer's lifetime, Old Fish Street, for a new fishmarket was set up closer to the Thames, near Billingsgate, which soon ousted Queenhithe as the major fish-landing wharf.

As with fish, so with meat. East Cheap had originally been where the butchers pursued their bloody trade, with Pudding Lane – 'pudding' originally meant offal – providing handy access to the river. But by the fourteenth century they had moved their shambles (stalls with benches for cutting up the meat) much nearer to Newgate, conveniently close to Smithfield. The cattle were bought live and driven to the shambles to be slaughtered. A large open gutter designed to carry away refuse ran all the way down to the Thames, causing distress and annoyance – even illness – to unfortunate citizens living nearby.

Poultry too had its specific points of sale, the main one being outside the Church of St Michael on Cornhill, a popular area which became increasingly congested with other traders. As a group the poulters, as they were called, seem to have had rather anti-social tendencies: they insisted, for example, on arranging cages and pens of live birds in the street outside their tiny shops, thus hindering the free passage of pedestrians – despite repeated representations from the Common Council. In 1366 they had to be ordered not to pluck birds in the street. And a century later there was a public petition against 'the grete and noyous and grevous hurt' caused to the inhabitants of the city by the presence of swans, geese, young herons, and other live birds 'whereof the oordure and standing of hem is of grete stenche and so evel savour that it causeth grete and parlous infecting of the people and long hath done'.

Contrary to general belief, medieval people greatly valued vegetables and herbs, and many London houses, even small ones, had their own gardens. Worts (root vegetables) and pot-herbs (onions, parsley, spinach, sorrel, leeks) were eaten at most meals but rarely mentioned by name. Cabbage and lettuce were likewise taken for granted. Plants like daisies, dandelions, nettles, roses, violets, mint, hyssop, all had their place in the garden and at table. If you did not grow your own vegetables, you might perhaps walk towards Westminster, and shop at the convent garden on the north side of the Strand; but within the city there was a vegetable and fruit market at the gate of St Paul's churchyard, near St Austin's Church. Its source was the well-stocked kitchen gardens of the great secular and ecclesiastical palaces nearby. Because it was the custom for aristocratic households to travel from one home to another, when a great lord was elsewhere his gardeners might legally sell their surplus produce. In a document dated 1372, we read that Nicholas Gardiner was to receive two pence per day for his labour: he was to till and work the gardens of the Savoy at his own charge, but 'we will that he have for his own use all manner of fruit and herbs growing therein to make his profit thereof, saving to us what we shall expend for the expences of our household at our comings.' The market by the churchyard was well frequented; the 'scurrility, clamour, and nuisance of the gardeners and their servants there selling pulse, cherries, vegetables, and other wares to their trade pertaining' upset not only the priests celebrating their office, but also the 'reputable persons' who lived nearby. In 1345, despite petitions from the gardeners and much discussion, the reputable persons won the day. The gardeners were moved away from St Austin's to beyond the south gate of the churchyard.

Chaucer was more interested in people than places, and it is no good turning to him for a description of the London scene. Fortunately for us, a vivid picture exists in an early fifteenth-century ballad, 'London Lickpenny'. The narrator is a young countryman visiting the bright lights. In Westminster he spends all his money and has his hood stolen:

> Then unto London I did me hie,
> Of all the land it beareth the prize.

'Hot peascods,' one began to cry;
'Strawberries ripe,' others coaxingly advise.
One bade me come near and buy some spice,
Pepper and saffron they gan me bid.
But for lack of money I might not be sped.
. . .
Then went I forth by London Stone,
Throughout all Canwick Street;
Drapers much cloth offered me anon.
Then met I one, cried 'Hot sheep's feet.'
One cried 'Mackerel', 'Rushes green' another gan greet.
One bade me buy a hood to cover my head;
But for want of money I might not be sped.

Then I hied me into Eastcheap;
One cried 'Ribs of beef and many a pie;'
Pewter pots they clattered on a heap;
There was harp, pipe, and minstrelsy.
'Yea, by Cock!' and 'Nay, by Cock!' some began cry;
Some sang of Jenken and Julian for their meed,
But for lack of money I might not speed.

The ballad ends with the young man finding his own hood for sale at Cornhill, 'But for lack of money I could not speed.'

Chaucer's writing does supply us with some details to fill in the blank spaces in the picture. From 'London Lickpenny' street vendors to the Cook in *The Canterbury Tales* is but a short step. Using the host of the Tabard Inn as mouthpiece, Chaucer spells out the risks involved in buying takeaways:

. . . many a pasty have you robbed of blood,
And many a Jack of Dover have you sold
That has been heated twice and twice grown cold.
From many a pilgrim have you had Christ's curse,
For of your parsley they yet fare the worse,
Which they have eaten with your stubble goose;
For in your shop full many a fly is loose.

Clearly, such establishments, from which you could expect only a dried-up pasty or an old tough goose served with gritty parsley sauce full of dead flies, or a reheated meat pie, were not rare. But equally obviously, cookshops were a very important part of city life. Part of the explanation can be found in the twelfth-century writer William FitzStephen's description of the single public cookshop then serving the needs of the city:

> There . . . you may find viands, dishes roast, fried and boiled, fish great and small, the coarser flesh for the poor, the more delicate for the rich, such as venison, and birds both big and little. If friends, weary with travel, should of a sudden come to any of the citizens, and it is not their pleasure to wait fasting till fresh food is bought and cooked . . . they hasten to the river bank, and there all things desirable are ready to their hand.
>
> (*Description of London*, William FitzStephen, *c*.1174)

There were other reasons for the popularity of the cookshop. Fuel was expensive. Many town-dwellers lacked cooking facilities. Only the very rich had properly equipped kitchens, with an oven, a spit, pot-hooks for hanging pots above the fire, and a chimney-crane to move them horizontally or vertically over the heat. Also necessary were a tripod or two and a variety of cooking pots, cauldrons and baking pans which the poor could not afford. For the majority of citizens, therefore, the cookshop was an essential adjunct to daily life.

But not all professional cooks were like Hodge of Ware in *The Canterbury Tales*, and possibly Chaucer was alluding to a current scandal which his readers would recognise. We know that great efforts were made to protect customers from unscrupulous food merchants. Bakers were forbidden to bake rabbits, geese or the entrails of poultry in pasties because of the risk of food poisoning; it was illegal to bake beef in a pasty and sell it as venison – a common dodge for getting rid of meat that was high. The penalties inflicted on sellers of unfit goods would have gladdened W.S. Gilbert's Poo-Bah: John Welburgham, a cook in Bread Street who had sold pieces of conger eel 'rotten and stinking and unwholesome for man', was put in the pillory for an hour and his fish burned under his nose, as well as having to return their money to the complainants. A like punishment was imposed on a man who offered for sale thirty-seven pigeons described as 'putrid, rotten stinking, and abominable to the human race'.

Cookshop prices were also controlled, as can be seen from a detailed list issued by the Mayor and Aldermen in 1378. A roast pig cost eight pence, roast goose seven pence, roast hen four pence. All kinds of birds are named, from larks, thrushes and pheasant to bittern and heron. Clearly, the waters of the Thames and the surrounding woods were well stocked with wildlife. If you brought your own bird, a cookshop would cook it for a fixed price 'for the paste, fire and trouble'.

Naturally, wealthy people made less use of the cookshops. We know something of their diet because a few cookery books of the period have survived. Sample menus for banquets suggest that the rich ate copiously and ostentatiously, and it is not unusual to find two or three courses listed, each comprising twenty dishes and a 'subtlety' – an elaborate creation made from coloured marzipan or pastry, served between courses and designed to amuse or amaze the guests rather than be eaten. We have a relic of 'subtelties' today, as Constance B. Hieatt and Sharon Butler point out in their book *Pleyn Delit*, in the little figures of bride and groom surmounting so many wedding cakes; but the Middle Ages were less romantic and more down-to-earth than we are – the most suitable subtlety for a wedding feast was considered to be 'a wyf lying in childe-bed'. At other times, a besieged castle, birds or animals, the Virgin and Saints, or a gaily bedecked warship might appear to delight the diners. In contrast to this kind of extravagance, devout people like Princess Cecil, the mother of Edward IV, who was famous for her piety and frugality, ate from only two or three simple dishes twice a day. But even at banquets, people were not expected to eat everything on the table. As with Chinese or Indian meals nowadays, people took small servings from several dishes, helping themselves and their neighbours to whatever lay within reach.

One of the best-known contemporary recipe books is *The Forme of Cury*, compiled by his Master Cooks in about 1391 at the request of 'the best and royallest vyaundier [provider of food] of alle cristen kynges', Richard II. Its 196 recipes are an unexpected mixture of the very simple and the highly elaborate, ranging from homely cabbage soup ('caboches in potage') to the fantastic 'cokagrys', in which a cock and the hindquarters of a pig were sewn together and stuffed before being parboiled and roasted. Recipes like the latter are in the minority. On the whole, they are straightforward and practical, though we would be hard put today to find some of the ingredients, such as peacocks and porpoises.

Excluding the most ostentatious dishes, it is possible from this and other recipe books to see what someone of the status of Chaucer's Franklin might have eaten. The Franklin was a country squire; his partridges came from the estate, his pike and bream were caught in his own fish-ponds. In other respects, he was much like any wealthy Londoner who loved good eating. He was so generous, says Chaucer, that he might have been St Julian (the patron saint of hospitality) himself. In his house it almost snowed meat and drink, and the table in the hall was always set ready for a meal. But his standards were high, for 'he was Epicurus' very son', and intolerant of the second-rate: 'Woe to his cook, except the sauces were / Poignant and sharp, and ready all his gear.'

Fundamental to the nature of the Franklin's meals are two facts: table forks were unknown, and the custom of eating off individual plates had barely begun. Dishes therefore had one of two consistencies: they were either spoonmeat or trenchermeat. Pottages – soupy stews – and broths were spoonmeat, eaten from a bowl usually shared by two people. Trenchermeat was firmer – roast or grilled meat, fish or vegetables which could be cut and put onto a thick slice of four-day-old bread known as a trencher, from the French *trencher*, to slice. In households like the Franklin's, the trenchers would be gathered in a basket after the meal and given to the beggars crowded round the kitchen door; in poorer houses they were probably eaten. Trenchermeat was held in the fingers and, not surprisingly, many instructions on etiquette attached to the care of your hands and their use at meals: don't scratch your head, pat the dog, pick your nose, pick your teeth.

Not surprisingly also, the carver's art was much esteemed, assuming a ritualised complexity. It had its own vocabulary: 'Tyere that egge – chynne that salmon – splat that pyke – side that haddock – tayme that crabbe – lift that swan – spoil that henne – dismember that heron – disfigure that peacocke.' (John Murrell, *A new Booke of Cookerie and Carving*)

One may doubt whether swans and peacocks often appeared on the Franklin's menu. These were in the main ceremonial foods. Their size was appropriate to a banquet, their beauty and dignity gave them symbolic value at the nobleman's table. Another of Chaucer's pilgrims, the Monk, loved a fat swan 'best of any roast', and a contemporary reader would at once have understood that the Monk lived in unimaginable luxury, ignoring the rule of his Order.

Peacocks held the same attributes. Both birds were commonly skinned unplucked, then roasted and reassembled to be served in all their feathered beauty, with the added glory of gilded beak and feathers.

The average Londoner, naturally, was more modest in his poultry. It may seem strange to us, but almost no bird in the airspace above the city or in the woods roundabout was deemed inedible, from larks and curlews to thrushes and herons. The fact is that however small, birds were a year-round source of fresh meat. In winter, estate owners like the Franklin probably ate venison, but although the forests around London were well stocked, all game in them was the king's and could only be hunted under licence. A day's hunting seems to have been for the medieval Londoner what a weekend's skiing is for today's young executive, but poaching was severely punished. In the thirteenth century, Henry III gained some popularity by granting London citizens one free day's hunting at Easter each year, within a twenty-mile radius of the city.

Far more important than meat to the medieval Londoner was fish. The wealth and power of the Fishmongers' Guilds – in Chaucer's day there was one for sellers of salt fish and another for fresh fish vendors – is less surprising when we remember that more than half the days in the Church's calendar were meatless. When other protein was scarce, salt fish and stockfish (fish dried on sticks without salt) were the great staple for rich and poor alike. Both were sold by the saltfishmongers and eventually the word stockfish was used of either.

The freshfishmongers might not sell dried fish. Their clientele was usually better off, if smaller, than that of the saltfishmongers, and they benefited too from the convention that any animal living in salt water qualified as fish. There was, for instance, no ban on barnacle geese during Lent, since they were thought to breed in shells attached to trees standing in tidal waters. A clear-headed visitor to London, writing in about 1467, thought barnacle goose tasted like wild duck: 'We had to eat it as a fish, but in my mouth it turned to meat, although they say it is indeed a fish because it grows at first out of a worm in the sea.' Similarly with seals, whales and porpoises. Salted whale, called 'craspois', was imported from France, especially during Lent. Porpoises may have been the 'fat fish' referred to on the bills of lading of the wine ships coming from Rouen. (An eighteenth-century antiquarian, noting the number of fifteenth-century recipes for porpoise, concluded that they must have been something of a delicacy. Great was his disappointment when a friend who had eaten porpoise in Portugal told him that the flesh was 'intolerably hard and rancid'.)

The sale of fresh fish was very strictly controlled. Much of it was caught locally – the Thames itself was a source of supply, and people set nets near London Bridge. Even at that early date, the size of the mesh was regulated in an attempt to conserve stocks and, as always, infringement was appropriately punished: the offender was condemned to ride through the streets wearing a garland made from his undersized catch. Fresh fish could be bought in the open market or at stalls in certain streets but, as a concession to its perishable nature, it could also be hawked through the city. Mackerel, which loses its freshness particularly quickly, could even be sold on Sundays. It was strictly forbidden to offer for sale any unpreserved fish over two days old.

Among the most popular fish were herring (fresh, salted or smoked), plaice and whiting. Sole, salmon and halibut were enjoyed by wealthier people. Pickled salmon was a major import from Scotland and, despite the frequent wars with England, seems to have reached London without hindrance.

Shellfish, abundant round the south coast, were cheap enough to be eaten even by the poor. In 1298, oysters were two pence a gallon – it is difficult to make comparisons with twentieth-century prices, but two pence was the price cooks charged to roast a goose. Eels and elvers were another good buy; they could be gathered locally in season, but were often imported by the barrel from the Netherlands.

Chaucer's Franklin was fussy about sauces, and these were most important to the medieval diner. They might be sweet – we still serve apple sauce with roast pork – or strongly flavoured, like the mint sauce many people today enjoy with lamb; or they could be rich and spicy. Usually, but not invariably, they were cooked with the food they accompanied. A sage sauce for pork contained parsley, sage, breadcrumbs, the yolks of hard-boiled eggs, and vinegar. A 'green sauce' to be served with fish was made up of a variety of pulverised herbs with breadcrumbs, garlic, pepper, and vinegar or ale. Boiled capons were served with a white almond-based sauce, but roasted birds had a spicy black sauce of which the chief ingredient was the capon's liver. Another peppery sauce, pevorat (French: *poivre*), was a standard accompaniment for roast veal or venison.

Spices are common in medieval recipes. There is nevertheless a misconception in the idea that all food was heavily spiced in order to conceal the nasty taste of rotting ingredients. For one thing, those who could afford spices were precisely those who, as landowners, had most access to year-round fresh meat. Secondly, fifteenth-century recipes rarely indicate quantities, although quite often they describe the effect desired ('loke that it be poynant and doucet' – sharp and sweet – is a frequent injunction). Again, a great number of recipes use no spices at all. Finally, medieval forms of transport were slow and unpredictable; travelling by camel or mule and then by sailing ship, spices took many months to reach London. Packed in containers which were far from airtight and exposed to many variations of climate, by the time they arrived, they might well have lost much of their flavour. One possible explanation for the popularity of spiced food is that to palates accustomed to the salt meat and fish which most people ate during winter, unseasoned dishes would have tasted very bland. There is little doubt also that spices were a part of ostentatious living – a useful demonstration of status. The richer you were, the more spices figured at your table.

Britain's only native spice is mustard. If contemporary account books can be relied on, most households used enormous quantities, although recipe books hardly mention it. *The Forme of Cury* calls for mustard once, the *Liber Cure Cocorum*, also written in the fifteenth century, refers to it three times: it is always to be offered with herring, and there are two recipes, one for 'pykulle', the other for mustard sauce. It is not, of course, a cooking spice, and, having made your mustard sauce, you might eat it with all sorts of dishes without needing a recipe. With boiled salt meat its attractions are immediately apparent. Nevertheless, its major role may have been in the medicine chest, for there is evidence that it was used widely to treat such disparate ills as constipation, epilepsy, colds, chilblains and rheumatism.

Another spice, not native to Britain but whose cultivation was beginning in Chaucer's day, was saffron. Tradition has it that a bulb was brought to England hidden in the hollow staff of a fourteenth-century pilgrim returning from Tripoli. Since it was one of the dearest spices, many people must have blessed him, although because of the cost of harvesting – the stigmas of the saffron crocus must be carefully hand-picked – it never became cheap. Saffron Walden in Essex was the centre of cultivation, and it is pleasant to think that Chaucer in his travels may have seen and marvelled at the fields of purple blooms.

Too much has perhaps been made of the frequency with which spices were used in the Middle Ages. It is easy to disparage medieval cooks, but I believe a walk round supermarket shelves will show parallels between their tastes and our own, though now sugar and monosodium glutamate are more frequent additives than ginger and cubeb.

The parallel with our tastes extends also, perhaps, to a liking for coloured food. How medieval cooks would envy twenty-first-century Britons their dyed carrots, kippers and oranges, the unnatural green of their tinned peas and the whiteness of their flour! The Middle Ages differed only in changing rather than emphasising colours. Saffron turned things yellow or golden – the technical term was 'to endore'. White dishes were easily made from ingredients such as fish, chicken and almonds. (Blancmange simply means 'white food'.) Green was derived from spinach or parsley, and red from sandalwood or alkanet, a form of borage. Purple could be made from indigo, black from dried blood. For banquets, very elaborate colour-combinations of food were designed, and one cannot escape the feeling that some dishes must have looked much better than they tasted.

A more fundamental difference than texture, flavour or colour between the food of Chaucer's day and our own is that of seasonal variation. For fourteenth-century cooks without benefit of refrigerator or deep-freeze, the permanent problems were how to keep food from going rotten in summer, and how to have any at all in winter.

More seasonal even than meat were vegetables, yet surprisingly they figure quite substantially in medieval diet, often in a form which we would today find unfamiliar. Root vegetables which store well were standard ingredients of most broths and stews. Cabbages, leeks and onions were also much used. In summer, there were spinach, lettuce, radishes and peas. Large households with no problems of space or labour preserved vegetables and fruit for winter by drying, pickling or bottling. But there was much less variety than there is nowadays. Of the seventy-eight plants for the kitchen garden listed in a fifteenth-century gardener's manual, most are culinary or medicinal herbs. By early spring, before new crops were ready, many people suffered from minor scurvy, showing itself in skin ailments and 'loose teeth'.

Milk was another seasonal food. It came from farms just outside the city, in unsterilised, unrefrigerated wooden churns bumping along muddy and deeply rutted roads. This accounts for the expensive but reliable alternative so much used, almond milk, made by grinding almonds very fine and simmering them in water until the required consistency was obtained. Butter and cheese were also seasonal and rarely used in cooking, although *The Forme of Cury* has several cheese dishes, including 'macrows' (macaroni cheese) and 'rauioles' (ravioli). Another dish called 'tart de Bry' uses 'cheese ruayn', which may have been Brie imported from Rouen.

If milk, only seasonally available, was relatively rarely drunk in towns, water-drinking was hardly less uncommon, for water was quite untreated and often polluted. While for centuries the effects of contaminated water on public health went unguessed, foul-tasting or muddy water was obviously rejected; it is noticeable how often medieval recipes recommend the cook to use only 'sweet' or 'fayre' water. Outside the walls of London, there existed wells and springs whose sweet water was brought by carrier into the city; place names such as Sadler's Wells and Clerkenwell testify to the importance attached to these sources. Of the two, Clerkenwell is the older, dating back to at least 1140, when the parish clerks of London performed plays near the site. The well was given to the people of London in 1673 and was used until 1856, when it was closed after an epidemic of cholera. It was rediscovered in 1924 during renovation work on a building in Farringdon Lane.

What then did Londoners drink? The most popular beverage was ale, often home-brewed, for most people were particular about its flavour and strength, the weakest brew being given to children. Chaucer's Franklin insisted on good bread and good ale; the Cook too could 'tell a draught of London ale'. It was taken at every meal, and when the Pilgrims set out on the first morning of their journey, the Miller had already drunk so much that he could hardly sit on his horse and was inclined to be quarrelsome, as he himself acknowledged:

> . . . I'm quite drunk, I know it by my sound:
> And therefore, if I slander or mis-say,
> Blame it on ale of Southwark, so I pray;

In London, the commercial production of ale was strictly controlled both as to quality and price. From 1267, an ale-conner, or taster, was appointed to assess all ale destined to be sold to the public. Anne Wilson tells us, in *Food and Drink in Britain*, how the ale-conner carried out his duties:

> Tradition has it that the ale-conner spilt a little of the liquor on a bench, sat on it for a time, and then made his assessment by whether his leather breeches had stuck to it or not. If they had, the ale had not fermented long enough, for it contained too much unconverted sugar and not enough alcohol.

Often, herbs and spices were used to flavour the ale and conceal any sourness, and it could also be mixed with honey and spices to make a sweet drink, called bragot, or used to curdle spiced milk for posset, a favourite supper food.

Beer was still very much a foreigner's drink in Chaucer's day; in London it was brewed by Flemish immigrants from imported hops, for the plant was not grown in Britain until the sixteenth century.

Wine was the other major beverage. Chaucer's Prioress, well born and carefully educated, drank it as a matter of course, wiping her lips daintily before they touched the cup so that no trace of grease should sully the liquid within. Probably the Knight also drank more wine than ale. More ordinary folk reserved wine for special occasions, and Chaucer tells us that when the pilgrims had their first meal together at the Tabard, 'Strong was the wine, and pleasant to each guest'. Strong it most certainly was, for wine-making was not the exact science that it is now. Fermentation was but imperfectly understood, and corks had not yet been invented. Any wine over a year old was therefore apt to turn to vinegar; this explains perhaps why so much wine was spiced or had herbs added to it. It also accounts for the ubiquity of verjuice, that sour liquid made from unripe grapes so readily used in medieval cooking.

The nineteenth-century view that medieval food was coarse and without sophistication has been refuted by the research of later writers. Nevertheless, it has to be acknowledged that the dishes in Richard II's kitchen were more highly flavoured, and more adulterated, than the food characteristic of Britain from the eighteenth to the early twentieth centuries. We do not today serve golden cabbage seasoned with nutmeg, cinnamon and mace. Nor do we habitually cook fish or chicken with sugar and almonds. But now that the thraldom in which French haute cuisine held the British imagination for so long is at last broken, many of us seek out Indian, Greek, Moroccan, Chinese or Thai restaurants in London and appreciate their food, perhaps the closest our age can get to medieval gastronomy. The gap between what we enjoy and what was eaten by Chaucer and his contemporaries may be less wide than we imagine. I hope you will be pleasantly surprised by some of the recipes which follow.

RECIPES

GREEN PEA SOUP

This simple soup is especially good. You can use frozen peas, but fresh mint is essential to give it a real taste of summer. Parsley is another essential herb – vary the others according to preference and availability.

2 lb (1 kg) young green peas, frozen or fresh
1 pt (600 ml) good beef or chicken stock
2 slices white bread, crusts removed
selection of fresh herbs – mint, parsley, sage, savory, tarragon
salt and pepper

Bring the stock to the boil and cook the peas until just tender. With a slotted spoon, remove two cupfuls and put them in the blender or food processor with the herbs, bread, and 1 cup of the stock. When blended, return the mixture to the pan, season with salt and pepper, reheat, and serve.

(from Warner, *A Book of Ancient Cookery*; *c.*1381)

FENNEL SOUP

A good way to cook this under-used vegetable.

1 bulb of fennel
1 large or 2 medium onions
1½ pts (900 ml) chicken broth or water
2 tbsp olive oil
small pinch saffron
1 tsp sugar
½ tsp ground ginger
salt
1 slice bread per person

Slice the fennel bulb into half-inch slices. Mince, grate or finely chop the onions. Heat the oil in a pan and sweat the vegetables in it with the lid on for about 5 minutes. Then pour in the broth, and the spices, sugar and salt, and simmer for about half an hour. Toast the bread and put a piece in each soup plate. Ladle the soup over it and serve.

(from *The Forme of Cury*; *c*.1390)

ONION SOUP

The real name of this soup is Sowpys Dorry. It may or may not derive from the French word *doré*, meaning 'golden', since some of the recipes use saffron. This version does not, but the flavour is sumptuous for all that.

1 lb (500 g) onions
2 tbsp olive oil
½ pt (300 ml) dry white Spanish wine (or use 1 large wineglass dry sherry and increase the amount of stock)
½ pt (300 ml) chicken stock
2 oz (60 g) ground almonds
1 slice rye bread per person
salt

Chop or slice the onions finely and put in a heavy-bottomed pan with the oil. Cover and cook over very low heat, shaking occasionally, for 10 minutes. Mix the wine and stock. Reserve one cupful and add the rest to the onions and bring to the boil. Reduce the heat and allow to simmer gently for 45 minutes. Meanwhile, mix the almonds with the reserved liquid and toast the bread. When the onions are cooked pour in the almond milk and cook for a few minutes. Put a slice of toast in each plate, check the broth for seasoning, and pour over the toast.

(Warner, *A Book of Ancient Cookery*; appended to *The Forme of Cury* in early printed editions)

Blancmange of Fish

Chaucer's Cook made blancmange with the best of them, according to the Prologue to the *Tales*. There were two versions of this popular dish in Chaucer's day, one made with fish and the other with capon or chicken. Though somewhat unexpected to a modern palate, both are well worth reviving.

½ lb (250 g) white fish (cod, haddock, John Dory, hake are all good)
1 cup easy-cook rice
4 oz (120 g) ground almonds
1 tsp sugar
½ tsp ground ginger
salt, pepper
½ tsp anise seeds (easily available by mail order if you cannot get them locally)

Put the fish in a pan with water to cover and bring to simmering point, then cook gently for 5 or 10 minutes. Drain off the liquor, reserving 1 cup and making up the remainder to 2 cups with cold water, adding salt. Place the almonds in a bowl and as soon as the reserved cup of liquor is cool, stir it in. Put the rest of the liquid into a clean pan with the rice and bring it to the boil, then cover and cook over gentle heat until the liquid is nearly all absorbed. Turn off the heat and keep the pan covered. Add the sugar, ginger and anise seeds to the almond milk and pour into the rice, stirring very gently with a fork. Then flake the fish and add it. Season with salt and pepper to taste. Oil the inside of a ring mould or other shape, and put the blancmange into it. Cover with greased foil and heat in a pan of simmering water or in a moderate oven for about 20 minutes. Turn out and garnish with fresh fennel or coriander.

Chicken blancmange may be made the same way, substituting two chicken breasts, cooked and cut into small pieces, for the fish. For added effect, turn it out onto a dark green dish or a bed of spinach purée.

(from *Liber Cure Cocorum* in Austin, Thomas, *Two Fifteenth-Century Cookery Books*)

CABOCHES IN POTAGE
(Stewed Cabbage)

1 head of cabbage (summer cabbage or winter white)
1 medium onion
1 large leek
½ pt (300 ml) beef stock
pinch saffron
½ tsp sugar
½ tsp ground ginger
salt, pepper

Cut the cabbage into sections (quarters or eighths) and put them in the pan with the chopped onion and the white of a leek, chopped. Boil gently in the beef stock until tender, then drain off the liquid, cut the cabbage into smaller pieces, and add the spices and sugar. Taste and season with salt and pepper as you think fit, then serve.

(from *The Forme of Cury*)

SPYNOCH YFRYED

I have had spinach cooked in a similar way in the Pyrenees. There the cook added a handful of raisins plumped up in boiling water and a scattering of pine kernels before serving. Although the recipe below does not specify these embellishments, they are typically medieval and if you wish to use them your dish would be no less authentic.

2 lb (1 kg) fresh spinach, or 1 lb (500 g) frozen spinach
3 tbsp olive oil
salt and pepper
raisins and pine kernels (optional)

If using fresh spinach, wash it very well and chop it roughly, then put it in a heavy pan without water over very low heat. Cover and stew for about 10 minutes, shaking occasionally. If using frozen spinach, dispense with pre-cooking. Take a heavy frying pan and heat the oil in it. Add the spinach, salt and pepper, and turn it over and over in the pan until well coated with oil and dark green. Mix in the raisins and pine kernels and serve.

(from The Forme of Cury)

EMBER DAY TART

Ember Days were days of prayer and fasting during Ember Week, one of which occurred in each season of the year.

**4–6 ozs (125–175 g) shortcrust pastry for 1 9-inch tart dish
2 large onions
2 slices white bread with crusts removed
1 tbsp melted butter
4 medium-sized eggs
pinch saffron
salt
1 handful currants
½ tsp sugar
pinch cinnamon
pinch ground coriander or cumin seed**

Roll out the pastry and fit it into the dish. Put into the refrigerator. Slice the onions, boil in a little water for about five minutes, then drain well and chop. Grate the bread into crumbs or make crumbs in a blender. Mix them in a bowl with the beaten eggs, butter, saffron and salt. Add the currants, sugar and other spices, and mix in the onions. Pour into the pie shell. Bake at 350°F/175°C/Gas Mark 4, for 30–40 minutes until the filling is firm.

(from The Forme of Cury)

PIGGES IN SAWSE SAWGE
(Pork in Sage Sauce)

This is meant to be served cold. I think it is equally good hot, with a hot sauce. Watch the vinegar content of the latter. If you find it too strong, dilute it and add a pinch of sugar.

1 lb (500 g) boneless pork (loin or fillet)
1 tbsp chopped parsley
6–7 leaves of fresh sage, or 1 tsp dried sage
yolks of 2 hard-boiled eggs
1 slice white bread
4–5 tbsp vinegar or vinegar-and-water
salt, pepper

Put the meat in salted water to cover and bring to the boil, then simmer for about 20 minutes. Remove from the water and allow to cool. Meanwhile, put the egg yolks, decrusted bread and chopped herbs in a blender. If you want to use diluted vinegar, use some of the water in which the chops have cooked for extra flavour. Mix the liquid with the ingredients in the blender and check the seasoning. When the meat is cold, arrange it in a dish and pour the sauce, which should be 'sumwhat thyk', over it. Serve with cold diced boiled potatoes and beetroot.

(from *The Forme of Cury*)

ROAST CHICKEN WITH BLACK SAUCE

I am afraid this sauce comes out dark grey, not black. But it is very good, and seems to bring out the flavour of the chicken to maximum advantage. As with the sauce which accompanies the pork, do not be afraid to dilute the vinegar to your own taste.

1 roasting chicken
¼ lb (125 g) chicken livers
1 tsp anise seeds
¼ tsp ground ginger
¼ tbsp cinnamon
3–4 cardamom seeds

1 slice decrusted rye bread (white bread will do, but the sauce will be paler)
1–2 tbsp vinegar
¼ cup chicken stock
drippings from the chicken

Roast the chicken according to your favourite method. Fry the livers in butter until well cooked, then allow to cool. Grind the cardamom seeds with the other spices, grate or process the bread into breadcrumbs, grate or process the chicken livers and put all together in a bowl. Add the vinegar and thin with the stock. When the chicken is ready to carve, pour off the drippings and add them to the sauce, and reheat gently while you carve the bird.

(from *The Forme of Cury*)

Chapter 2

WILLIAM SHAKESPEARE

. . . give them great meals of beef, and iron and steel,
they will eat like wolves, and fight like devils.

Henry V Act III Sc vii

Of all our London guides, Shakespeare will prove to be the most impersonal. The creator of characters so familiar that we use their words and imagery every day of our lives – as the schoolboy said, *Hamlet* is full of quotations – himself wears a mask. His tour is comprehensive, showing us royalty at Westminster and Windsor, tavern life at the Boar in Eastcheap, and the merchants (thinly disguised in Venetian dress) buying and selling at Sir Thomas Gresham's grand new Royal Exchange. Yet he is like a bus conductor whose face no one notices, and we know as little of his life as if he were the man who gives out tickets on the No. 23. No matter; using eyes and ears, consulting his friends and listening carefully to what he tells us, we may catch unexpected glimpses of the man. And though his London has now largely vanished, we should be able in some part to reconstruct it.

When, in 1587, the twenty-two-year-old Shakespeare arrived in London seeking work, it was still a city in which Chaucer might have felt at home. Nearly two hundred years had gone by since his death. London was experiencing a period of prosperity, and the population was fast increasing, but so far this had only slightly extended the built-up area outside the walls. Inside the city, Henry VIII's dissolution of the monasteries had released land for housing, and new money was beginning to construct buildings in stone and brick, with glazed windows, but many people continued to live in flimsy wooden houses with walls of fireprone lath-and-plaster. Changes to the street-plan were minimal. The city walls still stood; to the six gates existing in the fourteenth century, a seventh, Moorgate, had been added, leading to what is now the City Road. Many streets now extended some distance beyond the old wall, especially to the north and west; here, little enclaves of Protestant refugees from the Continent were forming, for Londoners were still hostile to foreigners, despite, or perhaps because of, the skills they brought with them. To the west, the little Walbrook had been covered over, but the Fleet remained an important landmark. South of the river, Southwark had prospered, maintaining its dubious reputation for brothels and low pubs. It also had a cemetery tactfully known as the Single Woman's Graveyard, and five prisons: the Clink, the Marshalsea, the Counter, the King's Bench and the White Lion.

Both inside and outside the walls there was plenty of open space, some occupied by the gardens of the monasteries, some of it green fields and woods. Just outside the walls, one might hear the horn of the huntsmen and their cry, 'Soho!'. As late as 1562, a sportsman could write: 'After dinner to the hunting of the fox, and there was a goodly cry for a mile and after the hounds killed the fox at the end of St Giles.' Hard to imagine: standing today in New Oxford Street looking up St Giles High Street, not the faintest echo of thundering hooves penetrates the rush-hour din.

Between Moorgate and Bishopsgate Street, in the area now largely occupied by Liverpool Street Station, lay a swamp which each winter became an icy lake. This was Moorfields, where from earliest days the city's youth had gone for its winter sports. There was sliding and skating, and what might be called skate-skiing, to go by the description of a contemporary chronicler: '. . . some tie bones to their feet and under their heels; and shoving themselves by a little picked staff, do slide as swiftly as a bird flieth in the air, or an arrow out of a cross-bow'. But in 1576, it was not the prospect of this fascinating pastime which brought the crowds streaming through Bishopsgate along the road to Shoreditch. It was something altogether new: a theatre. Like the taverns of the day, it consisted of wooden walls with galleries built round a central space, and the audience sat in the galleries or stood round the stage, which jutted into the arena. The resemblance to an inn was hardly accidental, for previously the only choice for actors had been taverns or open spaces, and for long years they were at the mercy of a landlord's forbearance or the whim of the elements. These difficult conditions and a vagabond way of life had inhibited developments in playwriting and acting techniques. Now, an impresario, James Burbage, had designed a special building and put it up just north of Moorfields in Holywell Lane. It was called, with superb simplicity, 'the Theatre', and so great was its success that within a year a competitor, the Curtain, opened almost opposite it.

But the theatres were far from being universally popular. By the late sixteenth century the English Reformation was gathering religious momentum. London's City Council, composed largely of Puritans, was becoming hostile to the ungodly pleasures of the populace. This was the reason for the choice of Holywell Lane for the site of the Theatre – it lay outwith the jurisdiction of the City Fathers.

Southwark too was outside the city boundary (hence the brothels). Before long it had two theatres, the Rose (rediscovered in 1989 during excavations for the foundations of a new office block and now lying submerged in the basement of that block beneath a protective pool of water) and the Swan. The Globe was to follow. They were handsome buildings, lavishly decorated. Their owners were as keen to put on the latest plays as audiences to watch them, despite Puritan condemnation. Within the city, acting companies were still using makeshift venues. At times, the London Council succeeded in banning all 'profane spectacles' for short periods, but the only long-term bans it dared impose were when the city was struck by plague or the sweating sickness. Then the companies of actors were forced to leave London and take their plays on tour.

Shakespeare joined a company which was first under the patronage of the Lord Chamberlain and later of the King. When not performing in private houses or before the Court, its main venue was the Theatre, and probably Shakespeare took his first London lodgings nearby. At any rate, a William Shakespeare is inscribed in the parish token books of St Helen's Church, just off Bishopsgate, for the year 1598. (All adult male taxpayers were given tokens when they paid their taxes and required to attend church each Sunday, handing in one token at the communion table each time.)

He next appears in Southwark, near the new theatre in which he had a part-share. This was the famous Globe, described in a contemporary survey as a new building owned by 'William Shakespeare and others'. Here the parish church was St Saviour's, formerly St Mary Overie. With three theatres close by, it was very much an actors' church, and when Shakespeare's youngest brother, Edmund, also an actor, died in December 1607 at the age of twenty-seven, he was buried in its churchyard. St Saviour's was damaged and restored many times before eventually becoming Southwark Cathedral. Edmund Shakespeare is commemorated by an inscribed stone in the paving of the choir, and in the south aisle there is a memorial, dedicated in 1911, to his famous elder brother. Above, a window designed in the 1950s depicts characters from the plays.

But Shakespeare had left Southwark by 1603 (some say his frequent changes of lodging were attempts to evade local taxes) and moved to Silver Street at the junction with Monkwell Street. This is the part of the Barbican now redeveloped as Monkwell Square. It is possible that he remained there until he finally retired to Stratford. He only appears once more in London records. The Globe syndicate had been very successful, and when the Blackfriars theatre (somewhere near the present junction of Queen Victoria Street with New Bridge Street) fell vacant, the Globe decided to take it over. After extensive repairs, it reopened in 1610, and in March 1613 Shakespeare bought a house and yard nearby. He had probably already returned to live with his family in Stratford, but he knew the investment value of London property and rented out the premises. When he died in 1616, they were inherited by his eldest daughter, Susanna.

The character of London, if not its shape, had altered considerably since Chaucer's time. With domestic peace had come prosperity and leisure for the middle and upper classes. In the country, on the other hand, agrarian reforms had dispossessed many peasant smallholders and forced them to look for work in the towns, thus creating a new class of London poor. While many found only casual labour, some at least were adapting, apprenticing themselves with a view to becoming craftsmen.

Because the aristocracy preferred to live on their estates, merchants still formed the richest class of Londoner. One of the principal sights of the city was the new Royal Exchange, built in 1567 by the mercer Sir Thomas Gresham at his own expense so that merchants could meet and do business under one roof. They sold their wares to the public in the shops on the first floor, and Londoners were proud of this early shopping complex, which offered an international array of goods. More than ever the city was one of Europe's major ports, and the Thames, which had been deepened and widened in the 1540s, was choked with ships. 'A man would say,' wrote an observer, 'that it is, as it were, a very wood of trees disbranched to make glades and let in light; so shaded is it with masts and sails.' Though still small in comparison with Naples, Venice and Paris, there was no question but that London was wealthy. In 1497, even a Venetian stood amazed at the quantity of silverware on sale. 'In one single street,' he wrote, 'there are fifty-two goldsmith's shops, so rich and so full of silver vessels great and small, that in all the shops in Milan, Rome, Venice and Florence put together, I do not think there would be found so many of the magnificence that are to be seen in London.'

The prosperity of the merchants could be seen inside their tall wood-framed houses. Cramped for space they might be – sometimes even wealthy families slept six to a room – but in the principal apartments silver and pewter vessels, Venetian glass, carpets from Turkey and clocks from Germany, furs from the Baltic and stoneware from the Rhine, furniture from Spain and embroidery from Nantes, all contributed to comfort and well-being. In the presses and chests where they kept their clothes were furs and silks, fine lawn and cambric and embroidered linen, heavy brocades and soft woollen cloth. Wool was the clue: English wool had never been in such demand, and for it the world brought its goods to London's door. No wonder Londoners marvelled at their own city:

> She is growne so Great, I am almost affraide to meddle with Her; She's certainly a great World, there are so many little worlds in Her: She is the great Bee-hive of Christendome, I am sure of England: Shee swarmes four times in a yeare, with

people of al Ages, Natures, Sexes, Callings: Decay of trade, the Pestilence, and a long Vacation, are three scar-Crowes to her . . . She seemes contrary to al other things, for the older she is, the newer and more beautifull . . . I am sure I may call her a gally-mophrey of al Sciences, Arts, and Trades.

(*London and the Countrey Carbonadoed*, D. Lupton, 1632)

Lupton's little volume is a frivolous offering, relying heavily on simple puns, designed to amuse the contemporary reader for an hour or two. But his 'Table of Contents' lists the principal sights of the town Shakespeare knew: the Tower, St Paul's, the Bridge (London Bridge – there was as yet no other), Cheapside, the Exchange, Turnbull Street (a prostitutes' quarter – 'their chiefest desire is to bee well mann'd . . . It is hazardable to trust them because they are much addicted to Lying'), Paris gardens (an animal show, on the South Bank, very close to the Swan theatre), Artillery (the military training ground), Bedlam (the Hospital of St Mary of Bethlehem for the care of the insane), Play-houses, Fencing schools, Dancing schools and Fisherwomen.

It is interesting that the fisherwomen should be listed among the sights. According to Lupton:

These Crying, Wandring, and Travailing Creatures carry their shops on their heads, and their story-house is ordinarily Billingsgate or the Bridgefoot, and their habitation Turnagaine-land, they set up every morning their Trade afresh. They are easily set up and furnished, get something, and spend it jovially and merrily: Five shillings a Basket, and a good cry, is a large stocke for one of them. They are merriest when all their ware is gone: in the morning they delight to have their shop full, at Even they desire to have it empty: their Shop's but little, some two yards compass, yet it holds all sorts of Fish, or herbs, or Roots, Strawberries, Apples, or Plums, Cowcumbers, and suchlike ware: Nay, it is not destitute some times of Nuts, and Oranges, and Lemons. They are free in all places, and pay nothing for shop-rent, but only find repairs to it. If they drinke out their whole Stocke, it's but pawning a Petticoat in Long-lane, or themselves in Turnbull-street for to set up againe. They change every day almost, for She that was this day for Fish, may be tomorrow for Fruit; next day for Herbs, another for Roots: so that you must hear them cry before you know what they are furnished withall.

Here we encounter for the first time the itinerant street vendor, whose cries were to become so characteristic of London in later centuries. The stringent medieval rules had so far relaxed as to allow hawkers to sell wares other than fish, but hawking food was still the fisherwomen's prerogative.

If Lupton's sightseers wanted a snack, nothing was easier; more cookshops than ever before ministered to hungry wanderers, especially in the little lanes around St Paul's and those leading off Fleet Street. An innovation since Chaucer's day was the 'ordinary', serving set meals at a fixed time on its own premises. Like the Temple in Jerusalem, St Paul's was used less for devotions than as a meeting place for businessmen and people of fashion, who would take a turn or two among the aisles while discussing affairs of moment; but at the stroke of noon the hubbub stopped and the church emptied. Those too poor to visit an ordinary 'dined with Duke Humphrey', for an imposing tomb in the cathedral was thought (wrongly) to be that of Humphrey, Duke of Gloucester. Ordinaries varied in quality and clientele. The playwright Thomas Dekker defined the customers of a threepenny ordinary as London usurers, stale bachelors and thrifty attorneys. The company, and doubtless the food, were of a higher order in places where one paid a shilling.

London's taverns had by now established a special role. The most famous was the Devil and St Dunstan in Fleet Street, where Ben Jonson presided over the Apollo Club. In the Directors' Room of Child's Bank, which now occupies the site, the Club rules written out by Jonson on a board in gold letters in 1624 are still preserved. Jonson's physical life was as robust as his intellectual achievements. Who but he could have written a 'Hymn to the Belly' ('First father of sauce and deviser of jelly')? What guest could resist his 'Invitation to Supper'?

> Tonight, grave sir, both my poor house and I
> Do equally desire your company;
> . . .
> It is the fair acceptance, sir, creates
> The entertainment perfect; not the cates.
> Yet you shall have, to rectify your palate,

An olive, capers, or some better salad
Ush'ring the mutton; with a short-legged hen,
If we can get her, full of eggs, and then
Lemons and wine for sauce; to these a coney
Is not to be despaired of, for our money;
And though fowl now be scarce, yet there are clerks,
The sky not falling, think we may have larks.
. . .
And I'll profess no verses to repeat;
To this, if aught appear which I not know of,
That will the pastry, not my paper, show of.
Digestive cheese and fruit there sure will be;
But that which most doth take my Muse and me
Is a pure cup of rich Canary wine,
Which is the Mermaid's now, but shall be mine;
Of which had Horace or Anacreon tasted,
Their lives, as do their lines, till now had lasted.
. . .
Nor shall our cups make any guilty men,
But at our parting we will be as when
We innocently met. No simple word
That shall be uttered at our mirthful board,
Shall make us sad next morning, or affright
The liberty that we'll enjoy tonight.

Jonson, unlike Shakespeare, enjoyed the conviviality of taverns, and is associated with several. The Sun in New Fish Street, the Dog, the Three Tuns in Guildhall, the Mitre in Cheapside, the Swan in Dowgate, the King's Head, and the Mermaid all had his custom. Herrick wrote a little poem about it, and Beaumont, another playwright, also celebrated Jonson's inspired leadership at tavern meetings:

. . . What things have we seen
Down at the Mermaid! heard words that have been
So nimble and so full of subtle flame
As if that everyone from whence they came
Had meant to put his whole wit in a jest
And had resolved to live a fool the rest
Of his dull life.
('Master Francis Beaumont to Ben Jonson')

Elizabethan London provided entertainment for everyone, and the classes mixed freely in most of their amusements. One of the great London events which Lupton does not mention was the annual fair held at Smithfield, which lasted three days. Shakespeare does not speak of it either, but Jonson wrote a whole play about it, which might be described as the Elizabethan equivalent of 'London Lickpenny'. *Bartholomew Fair* is interesting not least for its references to real streets and pubs. Among the minor characters are Leatherhead, a toy-seller, Trash, whose gingerbread is made of 'stale bread, rotten eggs, musty ginger and dead honey', and Ursula, the fat pig-woman, who sells bottled ale as well as roast pork and who knows all the ways there are to diddle a customer. A travelling pedicure makes an appearance, and a tinderbox man; there is a seller of ballads and, naturally, a group of pickpockets, in league with Ursula and the ballad-singer. The country bumpkin who strays into this thieves' kitchen, like the central character in 'London Lickpenny', discovers to his cost the danger of trusting streetwise Londoners.

But there were of course more bourgeois aspects to city life. Home-making and gardening were important to the Elizabethans, whose creative energy was released by the years of prosperity and political stability. Even actors had settled homes – Shakespeare seems to have been an exception – and domestic cares. When Edward Alleyn, a leading actor in a rival company to Shakespeare's, left home to go on tour in 1593, he wrote instructions to his wife:

> . . . remember this in any case, that all that bed which was parsley in the month of September, you sow it with spinach for then is the time. I would do it myself but we shall not come home till All Hallows tide and so, sweet mouse, farewell, and brook our long journey with patience.

The new trends are clearly reflected in the proliferation of educational material. Publishers could now make a great deal of money from moral discourses and 'how to' books. The two sometimes combined: how to be a good housewife, husband, mother, child, Christian. At a more practical level, books explained how to build a house, how to plan and plant a garden, how to cook . . .

The verse which introduces Sir Hugh Platt's *Delightes for Ladies* (1609) perfectly expresses the mood of the time:

> Empaling* now adieu; tush, marchpane walls
> Are strong enough and best befits our age;
> Let piercing bullets turn to sugar balls,
> The Spanish fear is hushed and all their rage.
> Of marmelade and paste of Genoa,
> Of musked sugar I intend to write,
> Of leach, of Sucket and Quidinea,
> Affording to each Lady, her delight.
> * defence fortifications

Another much-studied manual was Gervase Markham's *The English Hus-wife*, first published in 1615. Here the moral sentiments and practical advice were sometimes tinged with a touch of chauvinism. Women were exhorted to grow their own vegetables, for example, so that their food would be liked for its 'familiar acquaintance', rather than for the 'strangeness and rarity it bringeth from other countries'.

Markham need not have worried. Although, as we shall see later in this chapter, there was great interest in what was being brought from the New World, vegetables in the average kitchen were practically the same as in Chaucer's day: onions, leeks, roots, peas and beans, pumpkin, spinach, cabbage and salad greens. This conservatism was nevertheless accompanied by a marked revival of interest in health through diet. One popular moralist wrote that no young woman should loathe the name of kitchen, for there lay the power whereby 'sick folk can mend' and 'whole folks live'.

Dietetically speaking, this was above all the age of the herbal. Within a space of fifty years three important works had been published: Gerard's *Historie of Plants*, 1597 (better known as *Gerard's Herbal*), John Parkinson's *Paradisi in Sole Paradisus Terrestris*, 1629, and Nicholas Culpeper's *English Physician*, 1652. If Gerard's is the most often quoted, it is probably because of the three it reveals most of its author; if it is also the least scientific, that adds to its charm. He had his own garden at Holborn, in which he grew over 1,000 different plants, including among the many imported rarities both the sweet and what he called the Virginian potato – indeed a portrait of him in the posthumous edition of 1636 shows him holding a flowering sprig of the potato plant. Gerard knew the botany of the London area well; he gathered bugloss in 'Piccadilla', lily of the valley and cotton grass on Hampstead Heath, mallow near Tyburn and the pimpernel rose near Knightsbridge village. He was as interested in these wild plants as in cultivated ones, for almost all plants, he believed, possessed 'vertues' for man's use and happiness. But never before or since has the kitchen garden held such importance; for it was thought that vegetables and fruit as well as herbs could influence man's physical and moral character. Fennel was very good for the eyes; leeks, garlic and parsnips were not, but were sustenance for a strong stomach. Radish refreshed the 'cloyed stomach'. Onions snuffed up into the nose 'purged the head', and their juice 'anointed upon a pild [shaven] or bald head in the Sun, bringeth the hair again very speedily'. Garlic was a laxative, lettuce a soporific, as well as being useful in poultices. Gerard tells us that though lettuce was usually eaten at supper before any other food, there was now a fashion for ending a meal with it:

> Notwithstanding it may now and then be eaten at both those times to the health of the body: for being taken before meat it doth many times stir up appetite: and eaten after supper it keepeth away drunkennesse which commeth by the wine; and that is by reason that it staieth the vapours from rising up into the head.

Gerard seems to have been especially fond of beets, describing them as 'great and beautifull . . . not only pleasant to the taste, but also delightfull to the eie', making 'a most excellent and delicat sallad'. Markham recommended beet juice squirted up the patient's nostrils for the 'frenzy', which he describes as 'an inflammation of the cauls of the brain'. Gerard also liked turnips and praised those grown by market gardeners on the sandy ground near Hackney: 'those that are brought to Cheapside market from that village are the best that ever I tasted'.

Chauvinism apart, more food was being imported than ever before, almost all of it via London. To the capital came all the luxuries; people living in other parts of Britain had either to travel there or wait in hope that a visitor or travelling pedlar would bring the longed-for article. As in the fourteenth century, spices, almonds and dried fruit – especially currants ('raisins of Corinth') – were among the major imports. Clown's shopping list in *The Winter's Tale* shows how popular these ingredients still were:

> Let me see; what am I to buy for our sheep-shearing feast? 'Three pound of sugar; five pound of currants; rice,' what will this sister of mine do with rice? . . . I must have saffron, to colour the warden pies; mace, dates, – none; that's out of my note; nutmegs seven; a race or two of ginger, – but that I may beg, – four pounds of prunes, and as many of raisins o' the sun.
>
> (*The Winter's Tale*, Act IV, Sc ii)

Sugar, which the Venetians had for years imported from the East, was becoming cheaper. Columbus had discovered that it would grow in the New World, and Vasco da Gama, by discovering a sea route to the East, had ended the Venetian monopoly. The Spaniards and Portuguese planted sugar cane wherever it would grow, and the increased supply brought the price down. The Elizabethans loved it. 'If sack and sugar be a fault, God help the wicked,' wrote Shakespeare in *Henry IV, Part 1*; and in *Richard II*: 'Your fair discourse hath been as sugar, / Making the hard way sweet and delectable.' Most people thought it beneficial to health, especially for children.

Other foods came from Europe. From Flanders arrived Greek olives, French capers, and live quails (the latter in wicker baskets furnished with water and hempseed to keep the birds healthy for the London market). From Spain came quantities of oranges and lemons, popular as never before, bought by the sackful and used in puddings and cakes, candies and jams, or eaten fresh with a lump of sugar, for they were not sweet, but bitter like the Seville oranges of which we make marmalade today.

Almost all the material illuminating the domestic life of Shakespeare's contemporaries comes from the archives of great families and the landed gentry, whose homes were outside London. Life in an Elizabethan country house did not have the restrictions of space and labour imposed on city dwellers, and it would be misleading to base any account of sixteenth-century London on these records. There is, alas, no London equivalent of *Elinor Fettiplace's Receipt Book*, so evocative of the life of an Oxfordshire household. However, one group of letters which survives sheds a tiny ray of light on urban housekeeping.

The Johnston letters were exchanged between three brothers, John, Otwell and Richard Johnston, who had set up a trading firm to export wool and cloth from Britain and to bring back various goods, especially wine, from the Continent. In time, John settled with his wife Sabine at Glapthorn, near Oundle, but Otwell remained in London, living first in Lime Street and then in Lombard Street. Richard married and established a branch of the business in Calais. Their correspondence gives an excellent insight into the domestic affairs of Elizabethan merchants, and through Otwell's letters in particular we get just a glimpse of life in London.

One of the most fascinating discoveries is how much food *travelled* in those days, despite the bad roads. We who are accustomed to eating raspberries grown in Scotland, cheese pressed in Wales, meat pies made in Melton Mowbray and scallops from Orkney take for granted the container lorries which transport all sorts of food to all sorts of places. In Shakespeare's England roads were dusty in summer, muddy in winter, rutted and potholed at all times; horse-drawn transport was slow and unreliable. Yet Otwell Johnston was forever sending down luxuries from London to Glapthorn – two loaves of sugar and a bag of spices, confits for his sister-in-law, dates, prunes, raisins, a whole sack of oranges, sugar-coated caraway and coriander seeds, a 'pot with succat' (a kind of conserve), pickled eels in vinegar, stockfish, samphire, even early green peas. In return, Sabine would pack up and dispatch butter, game (especially venison, killed under special licence – the Johnstons were keen hunters), pork, bacon and brawn, poultry, pigeons both raw and cooked, and fresh fruit – even, on occasion, home-baked bread. That this was not unusual is confirmed by the little scene at the beginning of *Henry IV, Part 1*, Act II, where two carriers in a Rochester inn-yard are waiting for their horses: one has 'a gammon of bacon and two razes of ginger, to be delivered as far as Charing-Cross', and the other is taking a pannier of live turkeys up to London.

The advantages and disadvantages of living in London are made obvious in the Johnston letters. Londoners had easy access to imported goods, some of which never reached rural dwellers. For home-produced food, however, people without country connections had to depend on what was brought in to market, competing with other shoppers for whatever was on offer. Occasionally, as with the early peas, they benefited from being at the centre of a wide network. Market and nursery gardens at Houndsditch, Brompton,

Brentford, Lambeth and Whitechapel could supply high-quality fruit and vegetables. Strawberries grown in London soil were said to be particularly good. The Duke of Gloucester in *Richard III* refers to the Bishop of Ely's famous garden:

> My Lord of Ely, when I was last in Holborn,
> I saw good strawberries in your garden there,
> I do beseech you, send for some of them.

But food sent in from the country, however experienced the dispatcher, must often have arrived in less than perfect condition.

The Johnston letters show that Sabine was a competent, forceful woman capable of running the estate when her husband was away. In general, Elizabethan women were more assertive than their Continental counterparts. (Perhaps this is why contemporary moralists stressed the desirability of docility and submissiveness in wives.) An Antwerp merchant who spent much time in London observed with surprise that 'wives have free management of the house', and that their husbands allowed them to go on their own to market 'to buy what they like best to eat'.

For these privileges, women worked hard. A good wife was expected to be thrifty, but encouraged to take a keen interest in cookery and keep a good table. If it was impossible to grow her own vegetables, she must still preserve, pickle or dry whatever she could buy at market for use during the winter. The produce must be bought early in the day, when it was still fresh, and be quickly processed. Onions, garlic, leeks and herbs were dried; cucumbers, peas, beans and artichokes were pickled; apples and other fruit had to be bottled, dried or made into jam. A certain kind of apple was grown especially for its keeping qualities. The fruit were called apple-Johns and were kept until the Michaelmas Day two years after picking; they were then supposed to be at their best. Shakespeare described them as 'dry, round, old, withered knights' (*Henry IV, Part 2*, Act II Sc iv) and has Prince Henry insult Falstaff by comparing him to an apple-John.

Meat required equal thought and attention. The poor still relied for their protein chiefly on 'white meats' – that is, milk, butter and cheese – with dried or salted fish and an occasional egg, but for those who could afford it, there was plenty of meat and fresh fish to be had. Indeed William Harrison, in his *Description of England* published in 1587, wrote that the nobility ('whose cooks are for the most part musical-headed Frenchmen and strangers') ate so much meat that 'for a man to dine with them . . . is rather to yield unto a conspiracy with a great deal of meat for the speedy suppression of natural health than . . . to sustain his body withal'. It appears that he was right, for a modern scholar, Susan Maclean Kybett, believes that Henry VIII's medical record proves him to have been suffering from scurvy, caused by eating too much meat and too few fresh vegetables. Ms Kybett thinks that Mary I, Cardinal Wolsey, Elizabeth I and James VI also exhibited symptoms of the disease.

For whatever reason, the authorities too agreed that meat consumption was too high. Consequently, although the Reformation had abolished the old religious fast-days, secular ones were designated 'to the end,' says Harrison, '[that] our numbers of cattle may be better increased and that abundance of fish which the sea yieldeth [be] more generally received'. There was another motive which perhaps Harrison did not perceive: higher fish consumption employed more men in the fishing fleets, reducing the number out of work and ensuring a large reserve of sailors available to the Navy in time of war.

Even so, after 1595, meatless days were fewer and less strictly observed, and fish lost ground as a staple food. Fish recipes of the period lack the feeling of desperate contrivance evident in medieval attempts to offer variety, luxury and interesting dishes for fast-days. Whales disappear from the menu, porpoises are less frequently mentioned. Freshwater fish like carp and pike appear more often, for the monastic stewponds were now in private hands. Shellfish were still popular. Less stockfish was eaten (except by the poor), but potted fish, sealed into stoneware pots with melted butter or lard, was something of a delicacy. Sousing, that is, cooking in vinegar or wine and water flavoured with various herbs and spices, was another method of keeping fish good for a few days. The soused herring we buy or make today uses a recipe which, sugar and all, harks straight back to Tudor cooking.

The first anchovies came to Britain at this time. Pickled in brine, they were used as they are today at cocktail parties – to stimulate thirst. Only during the next century was it discovered that they have the valuable characteristic of melting when cooked, leaving behind only their flavour.

In the kitchen, the consistency of dishes was still governed by the fact that table-forks, although not unknown, were despised. Thomas Coryat, an English traveller who returned from Italy in 1611, described how Italians held meat with a fork while they cut it. No civilised man, he declared, would endure to have his food touched with fingers, 'seeing all men's fingers are not alike clean'. But his contemporaries considered such sentiments an affectation, and not until late in the century did forks come into general use. Consequently, meat was cooked and presented much as it had been in medieval times.

In the opinion of many, venison was the best English meat. In *The Merry Wives of Windsor*, Justice Shallow makes a present of venison to the Pages, apologising for it being 'ill-killed'. Hunting was a popular Elizabethan sport (in a contemporary book there is a delightful woodcut of the Queen and her courtiers enjoying a forest picnic while hunting), and people could get a special licence to kill deer. But poaching was common.

At this time it became fashionable to 'carbonado', or grill, meat. The word comes from the Spanish, although Gervase Markham (reluctant perhaps to acknowledge that anything good could come from the enemy) attributed it to France. Whereas the old method of spit-roasting dealt with large joints which by constant turning were exposed to the heat of the fire on all sides, the carbonado was suitable for more shallow cuts. Markham recommended parboiling the meat first, then scoring it on both sides, sprinkling it with salt and pouring melted butter over it before putting it on a special metal gridiron which could be held over the coals. The meat which in his opinion responded best to this treatment was breast or shoulder of mutton, and poultry joints.

Other foreign terms which had entered culinary vocabulary were *fricassées* and *quelquechoses*. The former consisted of several ingredients cooked in a frying pan – Markham gives as an example a simple fricassee of egg and fried collops (which might be bacon but could equally well be beef, fish or pork). Quelquechoses were mixtures of many things all beaten together before being fried in butter.

One of the excitements of exploration was the discovery of new foods as well as new lands. Hakluyt wrote in 1587 that:

> In time of memory things have bene brought in that were not here before, as the Damaske rose by Doctour Linaker king Henry the seventh and king Henrie the eights Physician, the

Turky cocks and hennes about fifty yeres past, the Artichowe
in time of king Henry the eight, and of later time was
procured out of Italy, the Muske rose plant, the plumme
called the Peridigwene and two kindes more by the Lord
Cromwell after his travell, and the Abricot by a French Priest
one Wolfe Gardiner to king Henry the eight . . .

(*Principall Navigations, Voiages, and Discoveries of the English
Nation*,

Richard Hakluyt, 1589, quoted in *Food in England*, Dorothy
Hartley, 1954)

The turkey had actually reached Europe from America via Spain in
the first quarter of the sixteenth century. Its English name probably
reflects the fact that it arrived on ships carrying spices from the
Middle East; in France it was called *Poulet d'Inde* for the same reason.
Turkeys had been domesticated by the Aztecs and were instantly
successful in Europe. By Shakespeare's day their strutting gait was
familiar enough for him to write of Malvolio in *Twelfth Night*:
'Contemplation makes a rare turkey-cock of him: / how he jets
under his advanced plumes!'

Another new food was the potato, which may have been brought
to Ireland by Raleigh in 1586, or may have come with Drake on his
return from Colombia in 1587. Through a misunderstanding about
Drake's itinerary, Gerard called it the Virginia potato to distinguish
it from the better-known sweet potato, which had reached Europe
some time earlier. When Falstaff exclaims in *The Merry Wives of
Windsor*, 'Let the sky rain potatoes', it is the sweet potato that he
means, for it was already famous as an aphrodisiac: the scene is that
in which, disguised as Herne the Hunter, he sets out to seduce Mrs
Ford and Mrs Page in Windsor Park. According to Harrison's
Description of England, sweet potatoes and 'such venerous roots' were
among the delicate and exotic dishes consumed at the great feasts of
the Merchant Companies of London.

The potato was by no means the only new arrival to be found in
the English garden, where heated walls and hot beds allowed the
cultivation of plants undreamt of in Chaucer's day. In Holborn,
Gerard experimented with aubergines ('madde apples')
unsuccessfully, though he says a friend living in Lime Street got his
plants to bear fruit; he had better luck with 'Apples of Love', known
to us as tomatoes, which he grew in a bed of hot horse-dung but

thought not worth the trouble. And in *A Midsummer Night's Dream*, Titania orders for Bottom's delight 'apricocks and dewberries, / With purple grapes, green figs, and mulberries'. Grapes had been grown since medieval times, but apricots, figs and mulberries were recent imports. Requiring at the very least the shelter of a walled garden, their subtle colouring and velvety sweetness made them definitely a nobleman's luxury, appropriate food for the lover of a fairy queen.

Despite these introductions, there had been fewer changes in the food of London over two centuries than perhaps one might expect. In cooking, spices and herbs were still used in almost every dish, and the mingling of sweet and savoury or sweet and sour flavours was still common. But the composition of meals was not what it had been in Chaucer's time. Dinner often began with a salad. Just as today in France one may be served a plate of crudités before the main courses, so Elizabethans might begin with lettuce, or spring onions served without dressing on a fruit dish, or boiled onions, asparagus, cucumber or samphire served with a French dressing. Samphire, incidentally, was at the height of its popularity. Gerard described its taste as 'spicie with a certain saltinesse', and it was often pickled as an accompaniment to meat. It grew on the steep cliffs at Dover, and also at Rye, where Shakespeare must have seen it when he was touring with the Chamberlain's company. The famous set piece in *King Lear*, when Edgar pretends to the blind Gloucester that they are standing on the edge of a cliff, may well have been inspired by direct recollection:

> . . . half way down
> Hangs one that gathers samphire, dreadful trade!
> Methink he seems no bigger than his head.
> The fishermen that walk along the beach
> Appear like mice.

At fashionable tables, roasts and grills, fricassees and hashes were ousting the medieval potages, though these did not altogether disappear. And although the Elizabethans, like their ancestors, loved food to be visual, there was a freshness about its presentation which had been lacking before: the violent, crude colours were being replaced by more natural tones, garlands of flowers and leaves garnished the table, and the object was to delight or amuse rather than overawe the guests. Pasteboard cakes and pies might contain live frogs or birds, or a paste stag would be brought to the table, an arrow in its side. When the arrow was pulled out, claret flowed from the wound. If the conception was medieval, a certain playfulness about the execution was not. And to end the meal, a new course had been invented. For this, guests left the table and moved to another room, or perhaps to the garden if the weather was fine. On a board or table – the banquet – they found sweet wines and dishes of 'marchpane' (marzipan), little fruit tarts and cakes, conserves, jellies, and crystallised fruits and flowers.

Despite condemning the passion for meat, Harrison defended the English diet in general. On the whole, he thought, changes were for the better:

> Heretofore there hath been much more time spent in eating and drinking than commonly is in these days; for whereas of old we had breakfasts in the forenoon, beverages or nunchions after dinner, and thereto rear-suppers generally when it was time to go to rest . . . now these odd repasts . . . are very well left, and each one in manner (except here and there some young hungry stomach that cannot fast till dinner-time) contenteth himself with dinner and supper only . . .
>
> With us the nobility, gentry and students do ordinarily go to dinner at eleven before noon, and to supper at five or between five and six at afternoon. The merchants dine and sup seldom before twelve at noon, and six at night, especially in London . . . As for the poorest sort they generally dine and sup when they may.

Drinking habits also were changing. In Britain generally, home-brewed ale was still the staple drink. Sometimes it was flavoured with rosemary or other herbs, sometimes it was spiced with cinnamon, pepper and nutmeg, sweetened with honey and heated for a comforting drink on a chill winter's day. Cider from apples, and mead and metheglin from ale fermented with honey, were country drinks. In London, though, beer was gaining ground. 'Turkeys, Heresies, Hops and Beer, / All came to England in one Year' says the old jingle. The year was probably 1524, and beer-drinking increased as locally grown hops brought the price down.

The preservative effect of hops made beer popular with commercial brewers who no longer needed to worry about ale going sour. Anne Wilson (*Food and Drink in Britain*) says that by Elizabeth's reign even ale was beginning to be lightly hopped, to help it keep better. Both ale and beer could be made very strong, and London alehouses, where the 'ale-knights' sat all day, drinking until they fell from their stools, were a byword.

The taverns catered for what is sometimes called a better class of person, serving wine and simple food. What wines were served is not entirely clear. There is much evidence that the English enjoyed the wines of Spain, Madeira and the Canary Islands as much as they did claret (an English generic term for the light red wines from the Bordeaux region), but the nature of these wines is far from established. The 'sherris-sack' drunk by Falstaff (*Henry IV, Part 2*) came from Jerez in Spain but was probably not fortified; Falstaff, praising its many virtues, speaks of it ascending into the brain and warming the blood, but this was because like most of the dry white wines of southern Europe it had a higher alcohol content than Bordeaux. (The tavern bill found in Falstaff's pocket in *Part I* shows that he had washed down a capon, a little bread and some anchovies with more than two gallons of sack – no wonder he was 'fast asleep behind the arras and snorting like a horse'.) The term 'sack' seems to have been no more than a generic term for strong dry white wine, for Canary sack (Sir Toby Belch's favourite tipple) and Malligo (Malaga) sack are also sometimes mentioned in contemporary documents. Red wines from Spain were known as 'tent', from the Spanish for red, *tinto*. There was also malmsey (a corruption of *malvoisia*, the name of the grape which originated at Monemvasia in the Peloponnese). It was sweeter but unfortified and came mainly from Madeira. Portuguese wines were not much drunk, for at this period they did not travel well. (Port, so fashionable in England in the nineteenth century, had yet to be invented.) French wines, despite the Hundred Years' War, had never lost their appeal and were used for cooking as well as drinking, as *Elinor Fettiplace's Receipt Book* shows. German wines, however, had lost some ground.

Sixteenth-century London water seems to have been unfit for drinking. Although some citizens had Thames water specially pumped through lead pipes to their mansions, it was, in the words of an Italian visitor, 'hard, turbid, and stinking'. Even clothes washed in the river smelt unspeakably nasty. And the old wells were inadequate. Wooden conduits brought sweet water from springs at Tyburn and Islington, but it was stored in street cisterns which were too small and too old. What was needed was a radical solution. On 29 September 1613, Sir Hugh Myddelton's New River first flowed to its reservoir near Sadler's Wells along a channel stretching for almost forty miles. The sweet sparkling water, from springs in Hertfordshire, was fresh and clean. Myddelton, a private citizen, was never adequately recompensed, but for a time at least, Londoners north of the river had water that was fit to drink.

For our last sight of Elizabethan London, it is not Shakespeare but William Harrison, whose *Description of England* has already been referred to, who takes us by the hand. Going quietly with him up to the window of a merchants' hall – the Mercers', it may be, or the Master Butchers' – we look through and see them at their annual feast. We stand amazed at such extravagance, such luxury, such wealth. Ornate and heavy silverware decks the tables at which sit the merchants, clad in their best furred robes, and servants move quietly and efficiently to place or remove immense dishes covering the table from end to end. For the food:

> . . . it is a world to see what great provision is made of all manner of delicate meats from every quarter of the country . . . In such cases also geliffes of all colors, mixed with a variety in the representation of sundry flowers, herbs, trees, forms of beasts, fish, fowls, and fruites, and thereunto marchpane wrought with no small curiosity, tarts of divers hues and sundry denominations, conserves of old fruits, foreign and home-bred, suckets, codiniacs, marmelades, marchpane, sugarbread, gingerbread, florentines, wild fowl, venison of all sorts, and sundry outlandish confections, altogether seasoned with sugar . . . do generally bear the sway . . . of the potato and such venerous roots as are brought out of Spain, Portingale and the Indies to furnish up our banquets, I speak not.

As for drinking manners:

> . . . each one, as necessity urgeth, calleth for a cup of such drink as him listeth to have, so that when he hath tasted of it, he delivereth the cup again to one of the standers-by, who,

making it clean by pouring out the drink that remaineth, restoreth it to the cupboard . . . By this device . . . much idle tippling is furthermore cut off.

But Harrison thought that on the whole the behaviour of Londoners had altered for the worse: they had acquired the big-city mentality. In the country, he says, visitors were made as welcome every day of their stay as when they first arrived. But in London, lack of room was often given as an excuse not to put up friends and relatives; what was worse, instead of a fat capon or plenty of beef and mutton generously dispensed, 'a cup of wine or beer, with a napkin to wipe their lips and an "You are heartily welcome", is thought to be great entertainment'.

RECIPES

AN ENGLISH POTTAGE

Sir Kenelm Digby, from whose collection of recipes this is taken, was a writer, patron and friend of Ben Jonson, diplomat and traveller, described as 'the Ornament of England'. He died in 1665, and his sons submitted his recipes for publication in 1669.

1 pt (575 ml) strong beef or mutton stock
1 boiling chicken
½ cup fresh white breadcrumbs
1 bundle herbs – parsley, thyme, tarragon, marjoram
1 onion
1 pinch ground mace
3 eggs
3 tbsp white wine
1 slice white bread per person
salt and pepper

Put the chicken into the broth – Digby suggests, if it is a fat bird, that it be first parboiled 'to take away the Oyleness'. Bring to the boil and reduce the heat. When it has simmered for about an hour, put in the herbs, onion, mace and breadcrumbs, and cook for another half-hour. Beat the yolks only of the eggs with the wine. Take the bird out of the pan and put into a covered dish in a warm place. Gradually add a ladleful of the broth to the beaten egg, beating all the time, then transfer this mixture to a small heavy saucepan and heat gently. It should be like a thin béchamel; if it is too thick, add more broth. Correct the seasoning. Toast the slices of bread. Arrange the bird on a dish, with the toast round it, and pour the sauce over.

Digby suggests serving this with boiled marrow-bones and tender boiled white endives.

(from *The Closet of the Eminently Learned Sir Kenelm Digby Knight Opened*, 1669)

To hash a Leg of Mutton in the French Fashion

This was an economical recipe, providing both stock for broth and a meat dish. Elinor Fettiplace has a similar, but grander, version which uses wine, spices and the juice and rind of an orange for the sauce. Compare this hash with that enjoyed by Dickens (p. 170).

2 lb (1 kg) leg of lamb or mutton if you can get it
1 good bunch of sweet herbs – parsley, thyme, marjoram, rosemary, lovage, a very small quantity of mint, chervil – whatever you can find
about 1 oz (30 g) butter
1–2 tbsp lemon juice or cider vinegar
salt and pepper

Put the meat in a pot with water just to cover, and bring to the boil. Skim the liquid and reduce the heat until you have the merest simmer. Cover the pot and cook for about 1 hour. Then take out the meat and, over a soup plate or some such dish, cut the number of slices you are going to need, saving the juice which runs out. Prick holes in the remaining meat and add its juice to what you have already saved. Chop your herbs very finely and then pound them with the butter. Add a ladleful of broth, the meat juice, salt and pepper, and lemon juice or vinegar to taste. Put this sauce into a pan and cook fiercely until it is reduced by half. Lower the heat, add the slices of meat and let them heat gently. Serve in a warm dish with the sauce poured over.

(from John Murrell, *A new Booke of Cookerie*, 1638)

POACHED TROUT

This simple dish looks attractive and tastes good too. Trout from the Berkshire rivers reached London quickly and was very popular.

4 trout, gutted but with the head left on (this improves the flavour)
2 oz (60 g) butter
approx. ½ pt (275 ml) dry white wine
1 good handful herbs – parsley, savory and thyme, the parsley predominating
½ tsp ground mace
yolks of 2 hard-boiled eggs

Wash and dry the trout. Mince or chop the herbs and mix them well with the butter and the mace, then put some of this stuffing in the belly of each fish. Pack the trout into an oval saucepan that fits them neatly or, failing that, a deep frying pan, then pour over the wine. Bring slowly to the boil, then lower the heat immediately and cover the pan. Poach very gently – the liquid should be just moving – for 10 to 15 minutes. Remove the fish to a serving dish and garnish with minced egg yolk and sprigs of parsley. If you wish to be truly Elizabethan, sprinkle a pinch of granulated sugar over all. This can be served either hot or cold.

(from Gervase Markham, *The English Hus-wife*, 1675 edn)

TO BOIL CHICKENS, OR PIGEONS, WITH GOOSEBERRIES OR GRAPES

This dish, like most of these in this chapter, crops up in a number of recipe books of the period. Markham has one and Lady Fettiplace's manuscript book gives another version, without the hard-boiled eggs. Gooseberries, like grapes, do not ripen to the same degree of sweetness in England as on the Continent; they are therefore very suitable to add the touch of tartness so much liked in medieval and Tudor cookery.

1 boiling chicken
½ pt (300 ml) mutton or beef stock

½ pt (300 ml) white wine
herbs – thyme, tarragon, sage or marjoram, a lot of parsley
½ tsp ground mace
salt and pepper
yolks of 2 hard-boiled eggs
2 slices of white bread, crusts removed
1 tbsp vinegar or lemon juice
1 oz (30 g) butter
1 tbsp sugar
4 oz (125 g) gooseberries

Stuff a handful of herbs into the chicken and simmer it gently in the mutton broth and white wine. When it is cooked, keep it covered in the pan but pour some of the broth over the bread and leave it until soft. Use more of the broth, about a cupful, to cook the topped and tailed gooseberries until they are very soft and mushy. Season this sauce with sugar, mace, vinegar and a pinch of salt and pepper, and stir in the butter. Put the sauce, with the soaked bread and the egg yolks, into a liquidizer or through a sieve. Reheat it while you carve the bird. Arrange the meat on sippets (small pieces of toasted bread) or a layer of rice and pour the sauce over.

(from John Murrell, *A new Booke of Cookerie*, 1638)

To farce [stuff] a Leg of Lamb

This, again, is a dish found in a number of cookbooks of the period. Sir Hugh Platt suggests serving the broth and meat separately, the meat garnished with sliced boiled carrots sprinkled with ground black pepper.

4–5 lbs (2–2½ kg) leg of lamb
mutton or beef stock, or water, to cover
½ lb (225 g) suet
herbs – two handfuls parsley, half a handful mixed winter savory and thyme
¼ tsp ground cloves
¼ tsp ground mace
1½ tsp sugar
1½ tsp salt
1 tbsp currants

1 small egg
2 tbsp lemon juice
sippets of bread

Take the joint and, with a sharp knife, scrape out as much of the meat between the bone and the skin as you can, taking care not to break the skin; mince the meat and mix with half the herbs and all the other ingredients except the lemon juice, sippets of bread and half a teaspoon of the sugar. Then put half the mixture back into the leg and sew or skewer up the skin at the end to make sure the meat does not come out while it is cooking. Put the leg of lamb into a pot with the stock or water (if using water, remember to salt it) and the rest of the herbs. Bring to the boil, skim, and simmer gently. Shape the rest of the meat mixture into little round patties and add to the broth when it has been cooking for half an hour or so. After another half-hour take out the meat, put it on sippets of bread in a deep tureen and keep warm. Reboil the stock fiercely until it has reduced by half, then add the lemon juice. Taste and correct the seasoning. Pour the broth over the meat and meat patties, sprinkle on the remaining half teaspoon of sugar and serve hot.

(from John Murrell, *A new Booke of Cookerie*, 1638)

A Fregesey of Egges

This is a good recipe for a simple dessert. You should find rosewater at the chemist, but specify that it is for cooking purposes. The apples originally called for, Pomewaters, are no longer available, but Cox's or Granny Smith should do equally well.

4 large eggs
2 tbsp thick cream
2 tbsp caster sugar
pinch ground nutmeg
pinch ground mace or cinnamon
1 tsp rosewater
3 large juicy apples
3 oz (90 g) butter
½ an orange

Beat the eggs with the cream, sugar, spices and rosewater. Peel and slice the apples transversally. Melt half the butter in a large frying pan and put in the apples. Fry them gently for a few minutes, then turn them and cook on the other side, trying to keep the slices whole. Slide them out of the pan and put aside in a warm place. Rinse and dry the pan and put back over the heat with half the remaining butter. When the butter is about to change colour, pour in half the egg mixture and cook it like an omelette, lifting it at the edges and letting the liquid run underneath to cook. Then remove it from the pan, put it in a warm place and repeat the process with the remaining butter and eggs. Spread the apple slices on top of this omelette and cover with the first one, like a sandwich. Sprinkle with freshly squeezed orange juice and serve at once.

(from John Murrell, *A new Booke of Cookerie*, 1638)

Spinach Tart

As usual, there are various versions. This recipe, from Gervase Markham, emphasises the nice green colour (he goes on to say that if you want a black tart you should use prunes, if red, apples coloured with sandars, if yellow, egg custard, if white, whites of egg beaten with rosewater and cream). Elinor Fettiplace's version, adding egg yolks as well as currants and ginger, sounds delicious but the colour would be rather dull. Sir Kenelm Digby suggests filling little pasties with a similar spinach mixture and deep-frying them in butter.

2 lb (1 kg) spinach
2 tbsp white wine
1 tsp rosewater
3 tbsp sugar
½ tsp cinnamon
6–8 oz (175–225 g) shortcrust pastry

Wash the spinach and drain it very well, then put into a heavy pan with the white wine over low heat and cook until very tender. Drain it; put into a processor or mouli to purée it. Add the sugar, rosewater and cinnamon, put it into a saucepan and boil it 'till it be as thick as marmalade'. Allow to get cold.

Roll out the pastry to fit in an 11-inch (28-cm) tart tin, fill it with dried beans or crumpled foil and bake blind at 400°F/200°C/Gas

Mark 6, for 10 minutes, then remove the beans or foil, reduce the oven heat to 350°F/175°C/Gas Mark 4, and bake a further 10 minutes. When the pastry is cool, pour in the spinach and garnish it – I suggest sliced toasted almonds or other nuts.

(from Gervase Markham, *The English Hus-wife*, 1675)

AN ELIZABETHAN SALAD 'AS USED AT GREAT FEASTS'

almonds
raisins
dried figs
capers
stoned olives
currants
fresh sage leaves
fresh spinach, washed and drained
sugar
oil and vinegar
oranges and lemons
red lettuce (radicchio)
pickled cucumber or gherkin
a lettuce with a heart such as Webb's Wonderful or Iceberg

Take equal quantities (by volume not weight) of blanched, shredded almonds, seeded raisins, shredded dried figs, and capers. Add twice the quantity of olives and currants, a good handful of small tender sage leaves and spinach, mix all together with a 'good store of sugar' and lay in the bottom of a great dish. Sprinkle with oil, vinegar and more sugar. Cover all with thin slices of orange and lemon, then 'fine thin leaf of red colefloer' – you could substitute radicchio – then another layer of olives and slices of pickled cucumber or gherkin, then 'the very inward heart of cabbage lettuce cut into slices'. Garnish the edges with more orange and lemon slices.

(from Gervase Markham, *The English Hus-wife*, 1675)

TO MAKE MARMELADE OF QUINCES OR DAMSONS

Quinces were a favourite Elizabethan fruit, golden and delicious, with a quite unmistakable fragrance. Sweet, sticky quince jams, pastes and cheeses are hardly seen here nowadays, although they are still popular on the Continent. *Marmelo* is the Portuguese for quince, so your marmalade will have all possible authenticity if you use quinces; but damsons are good too.

Put the fruit into a large covered pot and bake them without water in a slow oven for about an hour, or until soft. Strain off any juice and put the pulp in a thick-bottomed pan over a low heat. Stir constantly until the mixture is stiff and dry. Cool it slightly and weigh it, and to every 3 lb (1½ kg) pulp, mix in 2 lb (1 kg) sugar. Then return to the pot and let the sugar dissolve slowly over the heat. When it is dissolved, test it by putting a little in a saucer and letting it cool. If it is nice and stiff, it is ready for putting into clean warm dry jars and covering with waxed paper and cellophane. If you want a darker colour, add the sugar before you dry the pulp and boil as for conventional marmalade or jam.

(from Sir Hugh Platt, *Delightes for Ladies*, 1609)

THE MOST KINDLY WAY TO PRESERVE PLUMS, CHERRIES, GOOSEBERRIES, ETC.

'You must first purchase some reasonable quantity of their own juice, with a gentle heate upon embers between two dishes, dividing the juice still as it cometh in the stewing, then boil each fruit in his own juice, with a convenient proportion of the best refined sugar.'

This comes from Sir Hugh Platt, and needs no translation. I cite it because the method is interesting and one I have not seen elsewhere. The effect of drawing off the juice as it comes from the fruit is that the fruit is slowly dried instead of cooking in its own juice. Only at the last stage are the two reunited. If you wish to try the recipe, you could put the fruit in a covered dish in the oven at low heat. When it has yielded up its juice, mix juice and sugar together in a heavy pan, stirring constantly until the sugar dissolves, then bring to the boil and put in the fruit.

Chapter 3

SAMUEL PEPYS AND JOHN EVELYN

Strange to see how a good dinner and feasting reconciles everybody.

Diary, 9 November 1665, Samuel Pepys

There is a short space of time – some fifty years – between the age of Shakespeare and that of Evelyn and Pepys. But while the Elizabethan period seems remote to us and in some respects still medieval, in the Restoration city we observe the beginnings of early modern London.

One reason for this is that major events during those years caused fundamental political, economic and religious changes which created a society more like our own. Then again, much more of Restoration London has survived. And thirdly, we know a great deal about it, not only from the literature of the period but also through the diaries of two gifted men who were ideally placed to observe and describe important events as they affected the city.

Samuel Pepys and John Evelyn first met in 1665, when Pepys was thirty-two and Evelyn forty-five. As far as is known, neither ever knew that the other kept a diary. Pepys's journal is the more personal, Evelyn's the more dignified and reflective. Pepys wrote for ten years; Evelyn continued writing his memoirs (in some cases entries were made long after the event) until a few weeks before his death. Between the two, we have material covering the entire second half of the seventeenth century. Taken in conjunction, they present a London which we can picture in vivid detail.

John Evelyn was born in 1620, the son of a country gentleman. After leaving Oxford, he studied law in the Middle Temple in London, but when his father died he gave up his studies and travelled abroad for a period coinciding more or less with the worst years of the Civil War. While in Paris, he married the daughter of the English ambassador, a firm Royalist, through whom he met the exiled Charles II. It was an encounter which was later to be useful. In 1652, he decided to return to England, bought back from the state his father-in-law's sequestrated property, Sayes Court near Deptford, and settled there with his young wife.

Life under the Protectorate was not easy, but after Cromwell's death in 1658, the hated Rump Parliament was dissolved (Londoners made little gibbets and roasted rumps of mutton and beef in the streets while they drank the health of Charles II) and the King was recalled. From now on, Evelyn was seldom away from Whitehall, first as informal courtier and adviser on matters scientific (he was a Fellow of the Royal Society) and later in various official capacities. In the early years, he travelled the five miles to Whitehall regularly on horseback or by boat. Later, he found it convenient to take winter lodgings in London.

He and his family lived in Deptford for more than forty years, but in 1694 they moved to Wotton, Evelyn's birthplace. Now in his seventies, he was still active and still writing, but Charles II (whom he had both liked and admired despite totally disapproving of his morals) had been dead for eleven years. James II had been replaced by William of Orange and his wife Mary. Younger men than Evelyn were on hand to offer advice and service to the new monarchy. The old courtier withdrew entirely from public life, occupying himself with the education of his grandson and regular church attendance, and deploring the fact that, increasingly, he was apt to fall asleep during sermons. He died on 27 February 1706, aged eighty-five.

In social origin, Pepys was inferior to Evelyn; his father was a tailor, his mother had been a domestic servant. But the Pepys family came from yeoman stock, and a great-aunt had married the well-known Royalist Sir Sidney Montagu. Their son, Sir Edward Montagu, who was first cousin to Pepys's father, later became Earl of Sandwich, proving to be a connection of the utmost importance.

Samuel was born on 23 February 1633. Bright and ambitious, he was educated free of charge at St Paul's School in London before winning a scholarship to Magdalene College, Cambridge, where he took his degree in 1653. Two years later, he married the fifteen-year-old daughter of a French Protestant émigré, Elizabeth, and almost immediately entered the service of his cousin, with the job of looking after that gentleman's affairs and family when he was at sea in joint command of the Commonwealth fleet.

It was through Montagu that Pepys then entered the civil service. The *Diary* opens on 1 January 1660, shortly before his move to the Navy Office, in which he eventually reached a high position. We first meet the Pepyses living in a garret in Axe Yard (destroyed in 1767), dining on the remains of (the Christmas?) turkey; when Samuel casts up his accounts, he is satisfied to find himself 'worth £40 and more'. By 31 May 1669 – the date of the last entry – the Pepyses are living in or adjacent to the Navy Office in Seething Lane near Fenchurch Street. They worship in St Olave's Church (badly damaged during the Blitz, but the memorial tablet to Elizabeth which Samuel put up survives), have several servants and their own coach, and his assets are worth over £7,000.

But his life was not to be entirely a progression from one pleasant event to another. For one thing, his eyes troubled him much, and eventually were the cause of his giving up his diary, though he did not, despite his fears, go blind. Secondly, his wife died soon after the *Diary* closes. She was twenty-nine, and he only thirty-six, but he never remarried.

His professional life also had rough patches. He was promoted to the post of Secretary to the Admiralty in 1673, but six years later enemies in Parliament were attacking both his supposed Papist sympathies and the integrity of his administration. Forewarned, he resigned his position just as the warrant for his arrest was put out. He was imprisoned in the Tower for six weeks, then released on bail; a year later the attorney-general's case collapsed before ever coming to court, and Pepys returned to public life.

After five years away from public office, he was recalled by

Charles II, who made him Secretary for the Affairs of the Admiralty of England, a post which he continued to hold after the King's death, supporting James II in his efforts to restructure the administration of the Navy. But after James's abdication Pepys, like Evelyn, felt it was time to retire. He remained in London in the fine house in Buckingham Street which he shared with his friend and former clerk Will Hewer, surrounded by his collection of books (including at least one fifteenth-century recipe book), manuscripts and engravings, and was frequently visited by fellow members of the Royal Society. Many honours came his way, including election as Freeman of London in 1699. He and Hewer moved to Clapham in 1700 and he died there on 26 May 1703, receiving a last visit from John Evelyn twelve days before his death.

For London and Londoners, the Stuart era was traumatic, and Evelyn and Pepys witnessed many of the more dramatic moments. By mid-century, block and gibbet dominated political life as they had done in Chaucer's day. Evelyn was present at the trial and execution of Charles I's friend, the Earl of Stafford, but he refused to watch the 'murder' of the King himself, writing afterwards that he 'could not be present at that execrable wickedness'. A few years later, with different feelings, he saw the magnificent funeral of 'that arch-rebell Ireton' and in 1659, the even grander obsequies for Cromwell. For him, as for many others, it was 'the joyfullest funerall that ever I saw, for there was none that Cried, but dogs, which the souldiers hooted away with a barbarous noise; drinking, and taking Tabacco in the streetes as they went'.

Pepys was one of the party which went to Holland to fetch the new king in 1660, but because he was still aboard ship with Montagu on 29 May, he missed Charles's triumphant entry into London. Evelyn, however, 'stood in the strand, and beheld it, and blessed God', noting the flower-strewn streets, the pealing bells, the City dignitaries in their liveries and gold chains, the ladies crowding at windows and balconies, the lords and nobles richly clad in cloth of silver, gold and velvet, and the thronging, rejoicing populace.

However, the Restoration could offer its own grisly sights: the King's revenge began with the public execution of the man who had signed his father's death warrant, and the same month the bodies of Cromwell, Bradshaw and Ireton were dug up, hanged on the gallows at Tyburn for a day and then buried in a deep pit. As Evelyn rode one day through the city he encountered the corpses 'mangled and cutt and reaking as they were brought from the gallows in basketts on the hurdle'. It was at about this time that Pepys suddenly remembered his own schoolboy ardour for the Roundhead cause; it caused him some anxious moments – did anyone else recall what he had said when Charles I was beheaded?

The general emotion, however, was joy. London relaxed, and its inhabitants once more took up the pursuit of happiness and innocent pleasure. In a reaction to the violence of the Civil War and the subsequent sobriety of the Protectorate, fashionable Restoration life revolved much around playhouses, alehouses and taverns. Here our diarists part company. Evelyn did not entirely disapprove of the theatre, but much of it was not to his refined and intellectual taste. He disliked alehouses, describing their clientele as generally forsaking ale for beer (of which he disapproved) and 'universally besotted by tobacco'. As for taverns, he thought them no more than a venue for 'bestial bacchanalia' conducted under the influence of Spanish wine. By contrast, Pepys, the modern man, loved the theatre almost to addiction and considered alehouses and taverns convenient and often pleasant meeting-places. He took his father to Standing's to drink a cup of ale and hear the news from home, and went to the Dog with Dr Thomas Fuller, author of *The Worthies of England*, to learn all about Fuller's newest book. In taverns, besides a glass of wine or spirits you could get a meal, and he often went with colleagues or friends for an informal dinner at the Dolphin, Tower Street, which seems to have been a popular eating-place for the men of the Navy Office. On one occasion, a manufacturer of sails entertained Pepys, his two bosses and their wives to dinner at the Dolphin:

> where a great deal of mirth, and there staid till eleven o'clock
> at night; and in our mirth I sang and sometimes fiddled. At
> last we fell to dancing, the first time that ever I did in my life,
> which I did wonder to see myself do.

Another visit to the Dolphin led to a reflection on the less acceptable effects of alcohol:

> . . . strange how these men, who at other times are all wise
> men, do now, in their drink, betwitt and reproach one

another with their former conditions and their actions as in public concernments, till I was ashamed to see it. But parted all friends at twelve at night after drinking a great deal of wine.

By this time the 'ordinary', which had first appeared in Shakespeare's day, was a familiar part of the London scene. As Pepys explains, 'it is very convenient because a man knows what he hath to pay' i.e. it had a set menu. But its character was changing. Pepys's entry dated 12 May 1667 refers, possibly for the first time in English writing, to something very like a modern restaurant. On the morning of that day, Pepys and his wife 'had words' over her wish to wear the fashionable 'white locks' in her hair and his obvious enjoyment of the company of Mrs Knipp, an actress. At noon, matters being amicably settled, they went to visit friends, hoping to be invited to dinner. When they arrived, however, they found that the family was already at table. Embarrassed, they turned their coach for home.

> And in our way bethought ourselves of going alone, she and I, to go to a French house for dinner, and so enquired out Monsieur Robins, my perriwigg-maker, who keeps an ordinary; and in an ugly street in Covent Garden did find him at the door, and so we in; and in a moment almost had the table covered, and clean glasses, and all in the French manner, and a mess of potage first, and then a couple of pigeons à la esterve, and then a piece of boeuf-à-la-mode, all exceeding well seasoned, and to our great liking; at least it would have been anywhere else but in this bad street, and in a perriwigg-maker's house; but to see the pleasant and ready attendance that we had, and all things so desirous to please, and ingenious in the people, did take me mightily. Our dinner cost us 6s.

Here we have evidence of direct French influence on the gastronomic life of middle-class London. With the Restoration, French manners and style had become particularly fashionable, and some wealthy aristocrats went out of their way to procure French cooks. Those who could not afford to do so encouraged their employees to learn the French approach and were helped in this by the publication of an English translation, one year after its appearance in France, of *Le Cuisinier français* by the celebrated cook La Varenne. But it was after 1685, when Louis XIV revoked the Edict of Nantes by which France had had a measure of religious toleration, that the French presence in Britain became more marked. Some 50,000 Huguenots, among them many craftsmen and artisans, settled in England. Pepys's wife was the daughter of such a man.

The wig-maker's little restaurant was obviously not owned by someone who had been master of a great kitchen, although he may well once have worked in such a place. The dishes he offered were in no way exceptional. They are significant, however, in the context of a public eating-house in England. One has only to contrast with this entry a later one chronicling a visit to another ordinary, Cary House, where 'we, after two hours' stay sitting at the table with our napkins open, had our dinners brought, but badly done', to understand that it was the style of the 'French house', more than its dishes, which the Pepyses appreciated.

The next gastronomic innovation to reach London also came from abroad. As a student at Oxford, Evelyn had seen the exiled Chaplain to the Patriarch of Constantinople making coffee in his room, and about twelve years later in that same town, the first public coffee-house in England was opened. For once, London was behindhand; but within a few years, a merchant returning from the East set up his Greek servant, by the name of Pasqua Rosee, in St Michael's Alley in Cornhill. Rosee's coffee-house provided a real alternative to the tavern, where men could meet and debate the issues of the day, or simply gossip, without encountering contentious drunks. Very soon, coffee-houses appeared like mushrooms all across central London. At the end of the seventeenth century, there were more than 2,000 establishments, many offering, according to a Florentine diplomat, chocolate, sherbet, tea, ale, cock-ale (made by boiling or grinding a cock in ale, then straining off and flavouring the resultant broth with spices and sugar – supposed to be a sexual pick-me-up) and beer according to season. (If the sign swinging above the door showed a woman's hand holding the cup, you could buy her as well.) And they were inexpensive: 'In winter to sit round a large fire and smoke for two hours cost but 2 soldi; if you drink you pay besides for all that you consume.' Best of all perhaps, coffee-houses were completely democratic, requiring only prompt payment and good manners from their customers. Most had a list of rules pinned up somewhere:

First, gentry, tradesmen, all are welcome hither,
And may without affront sit down together:
Pre-eminence of place none here should mind,
But take the next fit seat that he can find:
Nor need any, if finer persons come,
Rise up for to assign to them his room;
To limit men's expense, we think not fair,
But let him forfeit twelve-pence that shall swear;
He that shall any quarrel here begin,
Shall give each man a dish t'atone the sin;

There was to be no gambling, no blasphemy and no speaking of affairs of state 'with irreverent tongue'. This last rule may have been more honoured in the breach than in the observance, for coffee-houses very quickly became 'nurseries of sedition and rebellion', largely because they supplied their customers with all the latest pamphlets and broadsheets. So formidable did the government find them, in fact, that in 1675 the King issued a Proclamation for the Suppression of Coffee-houses. Public uproar forced a retraction of the edict within eleven days.

There were others who disapproved of the coffee-house atmosphere. In 1674, *The Women's Petition against Coffee* appeared anonymously. Nothing if not outspoken, it complained that there had been:

> . . . a very sensible Decay of that true Old English Vigour . . . Never did Men wear greater Breeches, or carry less in them of any Mettle whatsoever . . . The Occasion of which Insufferable Disaster, after a serious Enquiry . . . we can Attribute to nothing more than the Excessive use of that Newfangled, Abominable, Heathenish Liquor called COFFEE, which Riffling Nature of her Choicest Treasures, and Drying up the Radical Moisture, has so Eunucht our Husbands, and Crippled our more kind gallants, that they are become as Impotent, as Age, and as unfruitful as those Desarts whence that unhappy Berry is said to be brought.

And so on, over several pages.

It was, clearly, the exclusion of women from coffee-houses to which the pamphlet objected, and it was precisely this which men

74

most enjoyed. Coffee-houses provided the perfect atmosphere in which good friends might meet without interference. Pepys, going home late one night in 1664, stopped in Covent Garden at the Great Coffee-House (later known as Will's), where he had never been before. Dryden was the attraction here – Pepys had known him at Cambridge – and 'all the wits of the town' were gathered round his table. Pepys, too tired to stay on that occasion, made a mental note to come again. Dryden had a chair permanently reserved for him, near the fireplace in winter and on the balcony in summer; all aspiring young beaux and wits made a point of being seen at least once a day going into Will's.

Some shops sold the raw material as well as the finished product. Such a one was the Turk's Head in Change Alley, which advertised 'the right Coffee-powder' at from four shillings to six shillings and eight pence per pound. Pounded in a mortar, coffee cost two shillings; East India berry sold at one shilling and sixpence, and 'the right Turkie berry', well garbled (sorted), at three shillings. Also on sale were chocolate, sherbets and Chaa (tea).

In time, coffee-houses took over from the taverns the role of venues for clubs and became a feature of fashionable life. Then suddenly, just as seventeenth-century London seemed set for its Swinging Sixties, a double blow closed theatres, alehouses, taverns, coffee-houses and ordinaries for almost two years. In the summer of 1665, the city was ravaged by the Great Plague, and barely had it begun to recover when the Great Fire of September 1666 destroyed almost the whole area between Pudding Lane in the east and Pie Corner, just beyond St Bride's Fleet Street, in the west. (Literal-minded preachers claimed it was a judgement on Londoners' greed.) Both Evelyn and Pepys wrote detailed accounts of these tragic events, whose horror owed much to the cramped and unsanitary conditions in which many people lived.

What impressed Evelyn when the plague was at its worst was the absence of the very city noises which he had once found intolerable: 'so many cofines exposed in the streetes and the streete thin of people, the shops shut up and all in mourneful silence, as not knowing whose turn it might be next'.

Pepys saw it in more personal terms. The illness had begun in Drury Lane, but the first person to get it in the City was a good friend and neighbour, and on 17 June he felt he had had a close brush with death when the driver of his hackney coach:

come down hardly able to stand, and told me that he was suddenly struck very sicke, and almost blind, he could not see. So I 'light and went into another coach with a sad heart for the poor man and trouble for myself lest he should have been struck with the plague, being at the end of the towne that I took him up, but god have mercy upon us all!

Like Evelyn, he carried on working. He had sent his wife and mother away and continued an attempt at daily routine although, much troubled by the constant ringing of the toll bell, he took care to set all his papers in order. In August, the Mayor ordered a curfew to be imposed at nine each night, so that infected persons might go out of their houses to get a little air. By September, the weekly count of the dead in London was roughly 7,000. In the unweeded courtyards of Whitehall, the grass grew green. When the weather turned cold and the plague slowly, almost grudgingly, abated, even recovery offered painful experiences. As people moved back to London, the only talk was of who and how many in each family had died. In Westminster, not one doctor, and only one apothecary, had survived. That area, and others outside the city walls – Holborn, Finsbury, Shoreditch, Southwark and Whitechapel – had long been notorious for its filthy and overcrowded slums where vermin bred unchecked.

Just over a year later, on Sunday, 2 September, the Pepyses were woken at three with the news that there was a great fire in the City. Again Pepys makes a marvellous eyewitness, describing how people fled from the flames, dragging the mattresses of bedridden relatives through the streets, flinging belongings into boats or carts, clambering from one pair of waterside stairs to another. He himself ran from friend to friend helping to move furniture, plate and other valuables. At one point, he met the Lord Mayor:

> . . . like a man spent, with a handkercher about his neck. To the King's message he cried, like a fainting woman, 'Lord! What can I do? I am spent: people will not obey me. I have been pulling down houses, but the fire overtakes us faster than we can do it.'

When Pepys's own house was threatened, he put his money and iron chests into the cellar, got his bags of gold and his office papers ready to carry away and dug two pits in the garden. Into one he lowered his wine, into the other 'my Parmazan cheese as well as my wine and some other things'. In the end, after three days of makeshift meals and sleeping on the floor of the office, the danger passed and the household returned to normal. But almost all the city north of the river to Cheapside and Cornhill, and west as far as the Inner Temple had been destroyed. St Paul's lay in ashes. When Evelyn visited the area three days after, the heat from the stones was still so intense that his feet were almost burnt and his hair felt singed.

Within two years, London had lost thousands of inhabitants to the Plague and almost as many buildings to the Fire. Now, if ever, was an opportunity to start afresh and create a model city. Evelyn, Christopher Wren and others made suggestions and drew up schemes. In the end, the difficulty of establishing property rights, and the need to rehouse people quickly took precedence over imaginative schemes. London was rebuilt of stone rather than wood, but its basic plan was little changed.

A more immediate issue even than rebuilding was how to feed the survivors. Just before the Fire, Parliament had been debating whether to continue to allow the importation of live Irish cattle to the possible detriment of the English cattle farmers. In this light, the offer by the Duke of Ormond and others to give 20,000 Irish cattle to feed the poor of London was regarded in some quarters with deep suspicion. Was this not just a devious ploy of unscrupulous importers to bring in 'many 20,000s'? If the cattle were killed and salted up in barrels, would they be as useful as if they had been brought in alive and sold, and the money used for the benefit of the homeless? Not until December did Parliament make up its mind that the beef should come into London salted in barrels. But before that time, ordinary people all over the country were coming to the relief of those worst affected, with money, food or offers of shelter.

Among businesses, quickest to re-establish themselves were the taverns and alehouses. Some rebuilt on the old site, others moved; few closed for good. When Wren received the mandate from Parliament to reconstruct forty-nine churches, an early concern was the provision of pubs for his workmen. Visitors to St Bride's Fleet Street, should notice the Old Bell Tavern nearby: it was used by Wren's workmen. They should also take note of the church steeple; an early nineteenth-century pastrycook called Mr Rich used it as a model for his daughter's wedding cake, starting a fashion for tiered and pillared 'bride's cakes' which continues to this day. Nearby in Salisbury Court a plaque marks the site of Pepys's birthplace.

If Pepys and Evelyn differed in their attitude to taverns and alehouses, both had a real interest in food. It has been said that Evelyn was not concerned with what he ate. Certainly he seldom refers to specific dishes, but a few diary entries (especially when he travelled abroad in his youth) show that he enjoyed a good meal. In 1644, his first taste of truffles at Vienne in the south of France prompted him to enthusiasm: 'in truth an incomparable meate'. (He seems to have changed his mind in old age, for he then described them as 'rank and provocative Excrescences'.) In Venice, he ate excellent oysters 'like our Colchester . . . the first, as I remember, that in my life I ever could eat; for I had naturally an aversion to them'. Also in Venice, he dined with the captain of a British ship then in the harbour and enjoyed his 'good dinner, of English powdered [salted] beefe, and other good meate, with store of Wine'. And at Padua, he extolled the English potted venison offered him by another expatriate.

The tone of the memoirs changes once he is back in England. Probably he had too many other things on his mind to think much about food; he also became more religious and may have felt that concern with meals was frivolous. But he could still be serious on the topic. When put in charge of the welfare of Dutch prisoners of war, he was struck by their complaints that the bread they were given was too fine. Within months, he had written and published *Panificium*, or 'the several manners of making bread in France, where by general consent the best bread is eaten'.

Towards the end of his life, Evelyn published another little work with a fancy Latin name. This was *Acetaria, a Discourse of Sallets*. Its popularity and the very favourable reception which his earlier translation of a French book on gardening had received go some way to proving that there was no neglect of vegetables in Restoration England.

The pamphlet opens with a florid dedication, but after two pages Evelyn disarms our irritation by acknowledging that it may seem strange 'to usher in a Trifle with so much Magnificence, and end at last in a fine Receipt for the Dressing of a Sallet, with a handful of Pot-herbs'. However, he says, this subject is a part of Natural History, and were it in his power, he would recall the world to a much more wholesome and temperate diet than is now in fashion. There follows a run-through of vegetables and herbs in common use, describing their health-giving properties and some ways of cooking or serving them – for his 'sallets' may be eaten raw or cooked, blanched or candied. Like Gerard, he ascribes properties to vegetables in accordance with the medieval idea of bodily humours, but he is much more interested in cookery than Gerard. Asparagus must be 'speedily boiled, as not to lose the verdure and agreeable tenderness; which is done by letting the water boil before you put them in'. Only the Dutch eat raw cabbage, thought to allay fumes and prevent intoxication. 'Some accuse it of lying in the stomach, and provoking eructations.' Lettuce 'ever was, and still continues, the principal Foundation of the universal Tribe of Sallets'. It allays heat, bridles choler, extinguishes thirst, excites appetite, represses vapours, conciliates sleep and mitigates pain. It also has a beneficial effect upon morals, temperance and chastity.

Pepys had an altogether more worldly approach to food, as eager to try a new dish as to see a picture or learn a piece of music. (His own phrase was that he was 'with Child to see any strange Thing'.) His position favoured his curiosity, for he was often given little presents of epicurean delicacies. Returning from the office one day, he found a quantity of chocolate, he knew not from whom; on another occasion the gift was 'a brave Turkey carpet and a jar of olives'. Often the gift was wine.

He also enjoyed shopping for food. Once, having done his accounts and found himself in funds, he yielded to his wife's pleadings and agreed to buy her a pearl necklace. They went together in the evening to choose it; then, highly pleased with their purchase and each other, they turned aside on the way home to buy a rabbit and two little lobsters for their supper, rounding off a satisfactory day in a most delightful manner. On another occasion, they went to market at Leadenhall, 'where she and I, it being candle-light, bought meat for tomorrow, having ne'er a maid to do it; and I myself bought, while my wife was gone to another shop, a leg of beef, a good one, for sixpence, and my wife says is worth my money'.

By the second half of the seventeenth century permanent food shops were competing with the street market stalls where farmer and housewife met. This situation was not to last much longer, for in 1674 street stalls were banned within the city walls, and royal charters were granted for covered retail markets at Leadenhall,

Newgate, Billingsgate and Stocks. The city streets, rebuilt after the Fire, were no longer appropriate for the congested conglomeration of carts, stalls, shoppers, goods and animals which was becoming unmanageable even in Shakespeare's day.

For the fact was that between 1600 and 1660, London's population had jumped from 200,000 to 400,000 inhabitants. Many of these people lived in the suburbs, especially in Clerkenwell, Whitechapel, Shoreditch and Holborn. After the Fire, the suburban population grew as former City-dwellers moved to newly built homes outside the walls. To the west, in Strand, Soho and Piccadilly, land and property boomed, and the owners of great estates rapidly made themselves into speculative builders and estate agents. (Pepys himself joined the exodus in 1684 when he moved to Buckingham Street, Strand.)

In all these districts, food markets were now provided. South of Lincoln's Inn Fields, the Earl of Clare laid out one which was to become London's principal source of pork. Sir Edward Hungerford established a mixed food market not far from Hungerford Bridge, and in the same year (1680), Henry Jermyn, Earl of St Albans, opened the St James market to supply the inhabitants of his newly built St James's Square. North of the city wall, the principal market was the one set up in 1682 for the colony of Huguenot refugees who had settled in Spitalfields. (They were mostly weavers, but perhaps their most important contribution to the English lifestyle is that, according to the historian G.M. Trevelyan, they set up the first gardening societies in Britain.)

One of the most famous, as well as one of the earliest, of all London's markets is Covent Garden, established in 1671 on land originally attached to Westminster Abbey. The site, together with the neighbouring Long Acre, had been granted to the Russell family after the dissolution of the monasteries, but the garden had not been built on and was still worked by gardeners who sold the surplus produce to the public. In time, people from the villages round about also set up their stalls under Long Acre wall. Then in 1630, the great architect Inigo Jones was commissioned by the head of the Russell family, the Earl of Bedford, to lay out the area as a square with houses on two sides and a church to the west, the garden wall of Bedford House forming the remaining boundary. By the 1660s, the opening of the Theatre Royal nearby in Drury Lane had made the area populous and fashionable, and in 1671, Charles II granted a market licence to the Earl's son (later to become the first Duke of Bedford), who henceforth had control over the stallholders, their rents and their behaviour. By 1680, twenty-three stallholders were paying him annual dues, and the market had become celebrated for the quality of its produce. According to a contemporary, John Strype, it was a pleasant place:

> The south side of Covent Garden Square lieth open to Bedford Garden, where there is a small grotto of trees, most pleasant in the summer season; and on this side there is kept a market for fruits, herbs, roots and flowers every Tuesday, Thursday and Saturday; which is grown to a considerable account, and well served with choice goods, which make it much resorted to.

There, for the present, we must leave the Garden and return to Pepys.

As the Pepyses grew richer, they entertained family, friends or Samuel's colleagues. The first of their parties was given in 'my Lord's lodgings' – their own premises being too small and cramped. Hard work it was, but resulted in:

> a very fine dinner – viz. a dish of marrow bones; a leg of mutton; a loin of veal; a dish of fowl, three pullets, and two dozen of larks all in a dish; a great tart, a neat's tongue, a dish of anchovies; a dish of prawns and cheese.

All this for about eleven people. Perhaps appetites *were* larger, but we must remember also that joints and poultry were smaller than they are today.

Three years later, in January 1663, another dinner party gave even more trouble:

> My poor wife rose by five o'clock in the morning, before day, and went to market and bought fowls and many other things for dinner, with which I was highly pleased; and the chine of beef was down also before six o'clock, and my own jack, of which I was doubtfull, do carry it very well. Things being put in order, and the cook come, I went to the office, where we sat till noon and then broke up, and I home; whither by and

by comes Dr Clerke and his lady, his sister and a she-cozen, and Mr Pierce and his wife; which was all my guests. I had for them, after oysters, at first course a hash of rabbits, a lamb, and a rare chine of beef. Next a great dish of roasted fowl, cost me about 30s, and a tart; and then fruit and cheese. My dinner was noble and enough. I had my house mighty clean and neat; my room below with a good fire in it; my dining-room above, and my chamber being made a withdrawing-chamber; and my wife's a good fire also. I find my new table very proper, and will hold nine or ten people well, but eight with great room. After dinner the women to cards in my wife's chamber, and the Dr and Mr Pierce in mine, because the dining-room smokes unless I keep a good charcoal fire, which I was not then provided with. At night to supper, had a good sack posset and cold meat, and sent my guests away about ten o'clock at night, both them and myself highly pleased with our management of this day; and indeed their company was very fine, and Mrs Clerke a very witty, fine lady, though a little conceited and proud. So weary, so to bed. I believe this day's feast will cost me near £5.

The grandest dinner party of all took place on 3 January 1669. This time the guests were some of his superiors and colleagues at the Navy Office: Lord Sandwich (Pepys's cousin and patron), Lord Peterborough, Sir Charles Harbord, Lord Hinchinbroke, Lord Sandwich's son Mr Sidney, and Sir William Godolphin. By now, Pepys was too sophisticated to itemise the food. He writes only that the dinner consisted of about six or eight dishes, 'as noble as any man need to have, I think'. He was especially proud of his choice of wines, both for their variety and quality. The *Diary* exults that all had been done in the noblest manner, nor had he ever seen better, even at Court. The party was 'the best of its kind, and the fullest of honour and content to me that ever I had in my life, and shall not easily have so good again'.

Evelyn, as we saw, gives us many very specific recipes in his book on salads. From Pepys we have only one, given him by no less a person than the Duke of York, who had learnt it from the Spanish ambassador. Described by the giver as 'the best universal sauce in the world', suitable for flesh, fowl or fish, it turns out to be a disappointing compound of dry toast, parsley, vinegar, salt and pepper, beaten together in a mortar – very medieval and hardly, one would have thought, a gourmet's delight.

But Pepys is valuable for realism – less what ought to be than what is. If the mutton is underdone and has to be sent back to the kitchen, he tells us. When his wife tries out the new oven for the first time and overbakes her pies and tarts, it is recorded in the *Diary*. So too are the bad meals he gets from friends and the curious tastes of some acquaintances, like a certain Mr Andrews who preferred his meat so undercooked that 'he eats it with no pleasure unless the blood run about his chops'.

As his wealth and consequence increased, Pepys's style of living became grander. He was immensely proud of his pewter and silver plate, and the tapestry hangings of his dining room. But his taste in food seems to have altered little. The oysters he enjoyed buying by the barrel were still relatively cheap, so probably was the salmon to which he once treated a party of pretty women at an ordinary. Lobsters, asparagus, fresh oranges and chines of beef appear more frequently in entries towards the close of the *Diary*, but he still appreciated a dish of tripe and, when hungry, 'dined like a prince' on cold chicken and a glass of wine. One of his favourite snacks was 'a messe of creame' – perhaps clotted cream, or perhaps what fifty years earlier had been called a trifle (see recipes).

He was himself aware, nevertheless, that fashions in food were changing. Indeed, he and his friends discussed the matter once at a dinner party (2 September 1667). Unfortunately he records little of the conversation, beyond a Mr Ashburnham recalling that once the most popular fruit, eaten by the King and Queen as the best fruit, was the Katharine pear, 'though they knew at the time other fruits of France and our own country'.

One of the topics which may have been discussed was the disappearance of fast-days, which under the Commonwealth had once again been abolished. The fact was that the fishing industry was now in disarray; hard hit by the Dutch wars, which kept the fleets in harbour and caused their crews to be impressed at regular intervals for the Navy, it lacked men, money and organisation. Dutch competition for the catches in the North Sea and the Channel was fierce, and the Navy was unable to protect whatever fishing rights Parliament tried to impose. Under these conditions, the sporadic attempts by Charles II to revive fast-days could not succeed, but the old habits did not die out completely, for on Good

Friday 1663, Pepys took his father home with him to dinner: 'Our dinner, it being Good Friday, was only sugar-sopps and fish; the only time that we have had a Lenten dinner all this Lent.' The old man at least would have remembered the time when anything but a fast-day dinner during Lent was out of the question. But by now, the trend towards meat had become very evident. Evelyn's only reference to fish is the comparison between Venetian and Colchester oysters. We have seen that Pepys bought oysters by the barrel for his own use or as presents and also liked lobsters. A ling and herring pie, 'the best of the kind that ever I had', is the subject of one entry; the implication is that while he had had it before, it was not a common dish.

The increased demand for meat required improved farming methods. While progress was slow, experimental winter feeding of stock with turnips was beginning to give good results. A few farmers were putting whole fields under grass grown from Dutch seed so that cattle could be kept in reasonable condition on hay during the winter, but the Agricultural Revolution was still very much in its infancy, and salt beef remained the winter staple for many years to come.

Nevertheless, as in Shakespeare's time, foreigners were much struck by the quantity of meat eaten. A Frenchman, F.M. Misson, wrote of 'the middling sort of people' having a choice of ten or twelve sorts of meat from which to make their dinners. For family meals, it was usual to have two dishes – Misson gives as example a pudding and a piece of roast beef. Before roasting, the meat would have been marinaded in wine, herbs and spices. Fifty years later, one of Hogarth's most popular engravings was entitled *The Roast Beef of Old England.*

Lamb and mutton were almost as popular as beef. Most of Pepys's grand dinners included a lamb or a side of lamb as well as a leg of mutton and a chine of beef. Sometimes the mutton was roasted, sometimes boiled with herbs.

Venison was beginning, perhaps, to be less accessible to the ordinary Londoner. Once someone offered Pepys a 'damned venison pasty that stunk like the devil', and on another occasion his own cousin gave Pepys and his wife a very good dinner, 'only' – indignantly – 'the venison pasty was palpable beef, which was not handsome'. Later, when he was in the Tower awaiting trial on a ridiculous charge concocted by his enemies, he must have been slightly comforted by the thoughtfulness of his friend Evelyn: 'sending a piece of venison to Mr Pepys Secretary of the Admiralty, still a prisoner, I went and dined with him.' (Evelyn, *Diary*, 3 July 1679).

Although coal was now cheaper and private ovens more common, London cookshops were still thriving. The day the Pepyses moved from their first home in Axe Yard to the Navy Office, they worked till nightfall arranging the furniture, then Elizabeth and the servant went to buy something for supper. The quarter of lamb they brought back was badly underdone, grumbles the *Diary*, but they ate it all the same. On washdays, the cookshop was useful too, for people did their washing about once a month and made a day of it – no time to cook. This explains the entry for 8 September 1663: 'Dined at home with my wife. It being washing day we had a good pie baked of a leg of mutton.'

As in previous centuries, vegetables are not much in evidence. Pepys mentions peas, and once he took home a hundred asparagus spears with a little bit of salmon for supper. Probably he only noted down the vegetables eaten on their own. What modern diarist or letter-writer would think of mentioning the Brussels sprouts which accompanied the roast beef, or the carrots and potatoes eaten with the steak and kidney pie? It is only Evelyn's keen interest in gardening which has preserved for us the recipes for his favourite salads.

Neither Pepys nor Evelyn refers to potatoes. Whereas Irish peasants had already realised their virtues, the wealthier southern English, with a relative abundance of other food, took much longer to adopt them.

The topic of Pepys and drink has been the occasion of at least one book. What is particularly noticeable in the *Diary* is the variety of drink consumed, and historians must be grateful that he was so specific in his entries. He drank many types of ale: Margate, Northdown, Lambeth, cock, and horseradish ale are all mentioned as well as 'lamb's wool' and beer. The first three are called by the place of brewing, cock-ale has already been explained, and horseradish ale was infused with that vegetable for medicinal purposes, and supposedly very good for 'the stone'. Lamb's wool was sweetened hot ale mixed with a purée of roast apples, flavoured with nutmeg. Very occasionally, Pepys refers to beer; he always adds a comment like 'the best I ever drank', which suggests it was not an everyday drink with him. 'Mum' crops up quite often; this beer, strong and flavoured with many herbs, was first made in Germany by Christian Mumme in the fifteenth century. It later became very popular in London, where it was sold at special mum-houses – the one Pepys liked best was the Fleece in Leadenhall. Mum lost ground to ordinary beer by the end of the seventeenth century in England, a little later in Scotland. Sack was a favourite drink, as it had been with Falstaff – drunk as it came from the bottle or in the form of raspberry sack (was this sack diluted with raspberry syrup?), mulled, or used to make possets and caudles. On one occasion, he tasted a Malago sack said to be thirty years old, which he described as 'an excellent wine, like a spirit rather than wine'. (The cork had yet to be invented, from which it follows that most wines had to be drunk young.) Among red wines, tent (see previous chapter), claret and wine from Navarre and Alicante all receive favourable mention. An exciting *Diary* entry for modern lovers of French wines is the one for 10 April 1663: 'to the Royall Oak Tavern . . . and here drank a sort of French wine, called Ho Bryan, that hath a good and most particular taste that I never met with'. This is the first mention in English literature of a named claret; it puts Pepys for all time among the oenophiles, though modern Haut Brion must taste very different to the simple young wine he enjoyed so much.

It would be a mistake to rely for our knowledge of seventeenth-century London food merely on the entries in two diaries, however enthusiastic and well informed. One more of Pepys's entries, though, is too significant to be passed over without comment. On 26 August 1668, he went with his wife to a party. They had recently both had lessons from a dancing master and were pleased to find that their new skill was called upon. The dancing went on all night, pausing only for supper. But at about two in the morning, to everybody's surprise the table was again spread, 'for a noble breakfast, beyond all moderation, that put me out of countenance, so much and so good'. This is the first hint we have of the incipient rise in social standing of a meal hitherto deemed to be entirely without significance or interest.

Of mealtimes in general at this period, little can be observed beyond that, regardless of social status, the usual dinner hour in London was noon. Pepys probably breakfasted early, for he often implies, without ever actually saying it, that he has got through a great deal of work before going home or to a tavern for his dinner.

When preparing for a party, Mrs Pepys rose at five in the morning and Pepys himself at six, but another entry, on a Sunday, tells us that they 'lay abed' till nine o'clock. Of the evening meal (always called supper) there is equal uncertainty, though it may have been around six o'clock, since walks or music after supper are often mentioned.

The seventeenth century produced a great number of recipe books. Some, like *The French Cook* (1653) and *A Perfect School of Instruction for the Officers of the Mouth* (1682), are direct translations from the French. Others are genuinely English productions. Among these, Robert May's *The Accomplisht Cook* (1660) shows much influence from France, Italy and Spain, and makes greater use of vegetables than any preceding cookbook; *The Court and Kitchen of Elizabeth commonly called Joan Cromwell* (1664), originally published by Royalists after the Restoration to demonstrate the Protector's meanness and common tastes, simply reveals that his wife was a very able cook; and Sir Kenelm Digby's *Closet of the Eminently Learned Sir Kenelm Digby Knight Opened* (1669) concentrates on drinks but, as we saw in the last chapter, has some interesting ideas. A manuscript book, *The Receipt Book of Mrs Ann Blencowe AD 1694*, first published in 1925, is of particular interest because, like Elizabeth Cromwell's book, it takes account of quantities, temperatures and cooking times. To my mind this confirms that the Cromwell is a genuine household book and shows too that the professional writers, as imprecise as their medieval predecessors, were not yet aware of what their readers wanted. All the books show that the English middle class, like the French, was using its prosperity to enjoy eating and drinking in a style which hitherto had been the prerogative of the nobility. There is, as we shall see in the recipes, sophistication in the trend away from visual display towards emphasis on taste and texture. The symbolic value of food has changed: from conveying the wealth and power of the eater, it has moved to suggesting the security of his social position and his ability to enjoy the pleasures of the table without feeling guilty of gluttony.

RECIPES

AN EXCELLENT POTTAGE CALLED SKINK

When Pepys and his wife dined at his wig-maker's ordinary, they began with 'a mess of potage'. It may have been something like the following. The word 'skink', incidentally, is still used in Scotland of certain thick soups.

1 lb (500 g) boiling beef
3 cloves
½ tsp mace
6 whole peppercorns
herbs – marjoram, rosemary, thyme, winter savory, sage and parsley. If using dried herbs, ¼ tsp would be sufficient of all except the parsley, of which a little more should be used.
2–3 onions
1 marrow-bone if available
2 tbsp fine or medium oatmeal
salt
½ tsp saffron
1 slice of bread per person

Put the beef into a pot with enough water to cover it, and add the cloves, mace and pepper. Bring to the boil and skim. Then put in the herbs, onions and some salt – about 1½ teaspoons. About an hour before dinner, mix the oatmeal with a little cold water to make a thin paste, then dilute it with about a cupful of the broth and pour the mixture into the pot. Put in also the marrow-bone, if you have one. Continue to simmer for about an hour. Just before serving, add your saffron and stir it well. Remove the beef and the marrow-bone and keep warm. Dish up the soup and when it is eaten make a slice of toast for each person. Serve the beef and marrow-bone with the toast cut into triangles around it. You might serve with this a purée of turnips or carrots.

(from *The Court and Kitchen of Elizabeth commonly called Joan Cromwell*, 1664)

PEA SOUP

1 lb (500 g) shelled peas
water or chicken stock
1 leek
2 oz (60 g) streaky bacon, chopped
sweet herbs – sprigs of thyme, tarragon, marjoram
2 oz (60 g) butter
1 oz (30 g) spinach
the heart of a spring cabbage, finely sliced
about ½ a lettuce (use the outer leaves), finely sliced
about 10 leaves of sorrel, chopped, if you can get them
½ punnet cress
1 stick celery, chopped
2–3 leaves fresh mint or ¼ tsp dried mint
1 shallot or 3 spring onions
1 very small pinch ground cloves
1 pinch mace
salt and pepper
1 slice white bread per person

Put the peas in a saucepan with water to cover, add the sliced leek, bacon and the sprigs of herbs, and boil for about 20 minutes. Pass through a sieve or, better, liquidize in the food processor and then pass through a sieve. In a heavy pan, melt the butter and add all the other vegetables and herbs. Cover and cook very gently, stirring once or twice, until the celery is tender. (If they begin to dry, add a tablespoon or two of water or stock.) Add the pea purée and reheat. Season with the spices and salt. Toast the bread, or dry it in the oven, and put one slice in each soup plate, then pour the soup over.

Compare this many-flavoured soup with the one on p. 29.

(from The Court and Kitchen of Elizabeth commonly called Joan
Cromwell, 1664)

To boil Capon or Chickens with Sugar Peas

The interesting thing about this recipe is the sugar peas – another example of new foods coming to Britain. They seem to have been developed by those great gardeners the Dutch, and as late as 1651, only 13 years before this recipe was published, Nicolas de Bonnefons wrote in *Le Jardinier français*: 'There is a species which can be eaten green which is called the Dutch pea and was very rare not long ago.' They make a delicious sauce for plain boiled chicken.

1 chicken with its giblets
1 onion stuck with 2 cloves
1 large carrot, sliced
2 sticks celery
1 bunch herbs – parsley, thyme, marjoram, a bay leaf (or use dried herbs to taste)
salt and pepper
for the sauce
½ lb (250 g) sugar peas
1 oz (30 g) butter
1 tbsp good salad oil (but not olive oil – its flavour would swamp the other ingredients)
2 egg yolks
1 cup sherry or dry white wine
1 small pinch mace
salt and pepper

Get the best chicken you can find and put it in a heavy pot with the giblets, vegetables, herbs and seasonings. Half fill the pot with water, bring to the boil, cover and cook gently for 1–1½ hours, turning the chicken from time to time. About half an hour before serving, rinse the peas in cold water. In another heavy pan put the butter and the salad oil. When the butter has melted, add the peas, cover the pan and let them sweat over low heat for a few minutes. Then add about 2 tbsp water, the mace, salt and pepper, and cook, covered, over very gentle heat for 20–30 minutes. Put your chicken on a warm dish. Take the peas off the heat. Beat the egg yolks with the wine, pour this mixture over the peas and stir, return to low heat for a few minutes, stirring carefully, then pour this sauce over the chicken and serve.

(from Robert May, *The Accomplisht Cook*, 2nd edn, 1664)

A PLAIN BUT GOOD SPANISH OGLIA

Both Pepys and Evelyn enjoyed an 'Oglia' or 'Oleo' – what is now called in Spain an *olla podrida*. It is usually made for a large company – the recipe given here is adapted from one calling for a rump of beef, a loin of mutton, the fleshy part of a leg of veal and 'a capon or two, or three great tame Pigeons'. This adaptation should feed 6–8 people.

1 lb (500 g) shoulder steak
6 oz (175 g) streaky bacon, cut in one piece, and diced
1 pig's trotter
8–10 oz (225–275 g) dried chickpeas, soaked at least 24 hours and then simmered for 2 hours
water or stock – about 1½ pts (850 ml)
4 lamb chops, trimmed of fat
3 chicken joints
1 pigeon
3 onions
2 leeks, sliced
2 carrots, sliced
½ white cabbage, sliced
2 'ends' from a loaf of bread
a bunch of sweet herbs – lots of parsley, some thyme, tarragon, bay leaf, rosemary
¼ tsp ground cloves
¼ tsp nutmeg
1 tsp saffron
salt and pepper

Put the shoulder steak, bacon, pig's trotter, bread and chickpeas into a heavy casserole with water or stock to cover. Bring to a slow boil, skim, and simmer for about 1 hour. Then stir well and add the lamb, chicken, pigeon and onions. Check that the broth still covers the meat and simmer for a further half-hour. Then add the rest of the vegetables and the herbs. Take out a cupful of the broth, put the spices with some salt and pepper into it, mix well and return to the pot, stirring it in. Simmer for a further 30 minutes. Serve in deep plates, making sure everyone gets a piece of each kind of meat.

(from *The Closet of the Eminently Learned Sir Kenelm Digby Knight Opened*, 1669)

To Dobe a Rump of Beef

At the ordinary, Pepys and his wife followed the potage with pigeons 'à la esterve'; these were probably cooked with very little liquid in a pot with a tight-fitting lid, like the Scots dish stoved chicken, but I have not been able to find a recipe. However, they also ate 'boeuf-à-la-mode', the first reference I have seen to this dish. It was cooked in a very similar way to the following recipe.

2–3 lb (1–1½ kg) rump steak in one piece
2 slices streaky bacon
1 tbsp cider vinegar
3 oz (60 g) butter
1 pt (600 ml) full-bodied red wine
½ tsp allspice
2 onions, each stuck with one clove
1 bunch herbs – parsley, thyme and marjoram
½ head of celery
1 lb (500 g) carrots
2 parsnips or turnips
4 small potatoes
4 artichoke hearts (optional)
¼ lb (125 g) mushrooms
1 tbsp flour
1 lemon, cut into quarters

Dip the pieces of bacon in vinegar, then use them to lard your beef. Melt half the butter in a heavy pan and brown the beef in it, then pour over the wine 'and sharpen it with vinegar to your taste' (you may prefer not to do this). Add the onions, allspice and herbs, with 1 carrot, 1 parsnip or turnip, and 1 stick of celery, all diced. Cover it and let it cook for 3 or 4 hours over low heat. Then make a 'Ragoo' – the word is used here in its original sense of a savoury sauce. Dice the rest of the vegetables and boil them gently until they are tender. Melt the rest of the butter in a pan and stir in the flour, then slowly add some of the vegetable stock, say half a cup. When this is well incorporated, add some of the broth from the meat, and then put in the cooked vegetables. Mrs Blencowe suggests adding also one cooked sweetbread and little quenelles of minced meat. Put your beef onto the serving dish and pour the 'Ragoo' around. Garnish with quarters of lemon.

(from *The Receipt Book of Mrs Ann Blencowe AD 1694*, 1925)

OLIVES OF BEEF STEWED OR ROAST

Again, a foreign recipe, and very similar to modern beef olives, but note that they are still to be served on sippets with a sharp sauce, harking back to earlier tastes.

1 lb (500 g) rump steak, cut into thin slices
3 slices streaky bacon
herbs – parsley, marjoram, a sprig of thyme
2 shallots
yolks of 2 hard-boiled eggs
4 oz (125 g) gooseberries, gently stewed in a little water
a little grated nutmeg
salt and pepper
3 tbsp oil
2 tbsp red wine
sippets of bread
slices of orange or lemon, or green grapes, to garnish

Cut the meat into neat slices about 15 cm by 10 cm. Lay a piece of bacon on each slice. Season them with salt, pepper and nutmeg. Chop the onions, herbs and egg yolks, and mix in enough gooseberries (about 1 tablespoon) to make the stuffing moist. Lay a spoonful of stuffing on each slice of meat, roll up, and secure with toothpicks or by winding thread round them. (If you use thread, don't forget to remove it before serving.) Or you could, as the original recipe suggests, wrap each 'olive' in a thin skin of suet. Heat the oil in a heavy pan and brown the meat on all sides, then add the wine and an equal quantity of water and cook, covered, for about 2 hours. Serve on the sippets of bread, surrounded by the gravy and garnished with fruit.

(from Robert May, *The Accomplisht Cook*, 1664)

JOHN EVELYN'S IDEAS FOR ARTICHOKES

The Heads being slit in quarters first eaten raw, with oil, a little Vinegar, salt and Pepper, gratefully recommend a Glass of Wine . . . whilst tender small, fried in fresh Butter crisp with Parsley [they] become a most delicate and excellent Restorative.

The Bottoms are also baked in Pies, with Marrow, Dates, and other rich Ingredients.

In Italy they sometimes broil them, and as the scaly leaves open, baste them with fresh and sweet Oyl; but with Care extraordinary, for if a Drop fall upon the Coals, all is marr'd; that Hazard escaped, then eat them with the Juice of Orange and Sugar.

(John Evelyn, *Acetaria*, 1699)

THE COMPOSITION OF A SALAD

In the Composure of a Sallet, every Plant should come in to bear its part, without being over-powered by some Herb of a stronger Taste, so as to endanger the native Sapor and Vertue of the rest; but fall into their Places, like the Notes in Music, in which there should be nothing harsh or grating; altho' admitting some discords (to distinguish and illustrate the rest) striking in the more sprightly, and sometimes gentler Notes, reconcile all Dissonancies, and melt them into an agreeable Composition.

Evelyn goes on to recommend:

**Oil, very clean, not high-colour'd nor yellow, but with an Eye rather of a pallid Olive Green
the best Wine Vinegar
Salt of the brightest Bay-gray salt
Mustard of the best Tewkesbury or of the soundest and weightiest Yorkshire seed
Pepper not bruised to too small a dust
Orange and lemon peel
the yolks of fresh and new-laid Eggs, boil'd moderately hard, to be mingled and mashed with Mustard, Oil and vinegar, and part to cut into quarters, and eat with herbs**

a knife of silver and by no means of steel, which all acids are apt to corrode
a saladière of porcelain or of Holland-Delft ware.

To dress Parsnips

3–4 large parsnips
about ½–¾ pt (275–425 ml) milk

Peel the parsnips and slice them, then put them in a small heavy saucepan with enough milk to cover them. Bring to the boil and cook gently without a lid, taking care the milk does not boil over, until the parsnips are tender. Then take out the parsnips and sieve or process them to a purée. Put them in a greased double boiler, and add a little of the milk they cooked in. The purée should absorb it, so continue adding milk little by little until the parsnips will take no more. This should take about half an hour. 'Eat them so, without Sugar or Butter; for they will have a natural sweetness, that is beyond sugar, and will be Unctuous, so as not to need Butter.'

(from *The Closet of the Eminently Learned Sir Kenelm Digby Knight Opened*, 1669)

The following two recipes are both from Sir Kenelm Digby and attempt to show what Pepys meant by 'a good dish of cream'.

A good dish of Cream

2 pts (1.1 l) double cream
1 stick cinnamon
½ tsp grated nutmeg
2 oz (60 g) sugar
whites of 4 eggs

Set aside half a cup of cream. Boil the rest gently with the spices and sugar for about half an hour. Beat the egg whites until stiff, then add the reserved cream and beat a little more. Pour this mixture into the boiling cream and let it just come to the boil again. Then pour it into a muslin bag and leave to drain for several hours. Finally, put into a bowl with a little orange-flower water or rosewater, and eat with slices of brown bread.

An excellent Spanish Cream

2 qts (2.2 l) double cream
2 oz (60 g) sugar

Take 2 quarts (you must not exceed this proportion in one vessel) perfectly Sweet cream, that hath not been jogged with carriage; and in a Posnet [porringer] set it upon a clear lighted Charcoal fire, not too hot. When it beginneth to boil, cast into it a piece of double refined hard Sugar about as much as two Walnuts, and with a spoon stir the Cream all one way. After two or three rounds, you will perceive a thick Cream rise at the top. Scum it off with your spoon, and lay it in another dish. And always stir it the same way, and More Cream will rise; which as it doth rise, you put into this dish, one lare [layer] upon an other. And thus almost all the Cream will turn into this thick Cream, to within 2–3 spoonfuls. If you would have it sweeter, you may strew some Sugar upon the top of it. You must be careful not to have the heat too much; for then it will turn to oyl; as also if the Cream had been carried. If you would have it warm, set the dish you lay it in, upon a Chafing-dish of Coals.

Chapter 4

SAMUEL JOHNSON

I look upon it that he who does not mind his belly
will hardly mind anything else.

Samuel Johnson

Initially one dislikes him. He was a man who hated disagreement, crushing ideas to which he objected and dismissing opinions at variance with his own. Often pompous and dictatorial, he was seldom careful of the feelings of others and sometimes intolerably rude. He was also ugly, ungainly, greedy, careless of personal hygiene and appearance, and suffered from a nervous tic as well as from obsessive compulsions. At first encounter, Dr Samuel Johnson has few attractive qualities.

This first impression, however, is misleading and unfair. Johnson was one of the English language's major stylists and its first great lexicographer, but as we read his life, other attributes begin to impress: integrity and passion for truth, generosity, real kindness to those in distress, deep religious feeling, humility, good sense and wit. His neuroses excite our pity. In the end, like so many of his contemporaries, we are won over by the charm, intelligence and vulnerability of this man who became one of London's most celebrated inhabitants.

He was born in Lichfield in 1709, the son of a bookseller. A sickly baby, of whom his aunt declared she 'would not have picked up such a poor creature in the street', he was taken at the age of two and a half to London by his mother, who believed like many people that the touch of the reigning monarch could cure scrofula. The expedition failed in its object, but as the boy grew, his health improved, although both sight and hearing remained defective all his life. It was his mental abilities which were soon seen to be remarkable. Thanks to a phenomenal memory and quickness of understanding, by the age of sixteen, although by his own account indolent, he was an excellent Latinist and widely read. His conversation was intelligent and witty, and despite his unprepossessing appearance and manners, he became a favourite companion of the educated men who lived locally. In time, a small bequest allowed his mother to enrol him at Pembroke College, Oxford.

The tutors soon recognised his gifts, but after only thirteen months, lack of money forced him to return home. Not surprisingly, depression ensued, and he acquired neuroses which were never to leave him. He believed he had a hereditary tendency to madness, and this induced in him acute terror accompanied by a permanent sense of guilt. The kind of psychological paralysis he suffered would now be recognised as a symptom of clinical depression, but he ascribed his inability to work to laziness and later found in it further cause for guilt and self-hatred.

In 1731, after his father's death and a short unhappy spell as assistant master in a grammar school, he went on a six-month visit to a friend in Birmingham, where he tried his hand at journalism and made new friends. Among them were Henry Porter and his wife, who, recognising his ability at their first meeting, told her daughter: 'That is the most sensible man I ever met in my life.' Her admiration was reciprocated, and some ten months after Henry Porter's death, the couple married, Johnson at twenty-five being almost half the age of his wife.

Elizabeth Porter was later described as a short, fat, coarse woman, fond of make-up and gaudy clothes, something of a dipsomaniac. But in her portrait, bright brown eyes return the spectator's gaze from a face of pleasing plumpness. The corners of the mouth turn upwards with a hint of amusement, the broad brow and the long but well-shaped nose give an impression of shrewdness and some breeding. Certainly Johnson adored his 'Tetty', and although their seventeen years together were difficult and often unhappy, he always treated her tenderly, and mourned her sincerely when she died.

The newly-weds' first action was to set up a school, but with such little success that after eighteen months Johnson abandoned the attempt and in the company of one of his few pupils, David Garrick (later to become a famous actor), but without Tetty, went to try his luck in London.

The two years of poverty which followed were the worst that he had ever known. He lived by hack work for small publishers, sometimes sleeping rough and often going without food, though a friend from Lichfield days gave him generous support. 'Harry Hervey,' he said once, 'was a vicious man; but he was very kind to me. If you call a dog Hervey, I shall love him.' From this unhappy time, he retained all his life the behaviour of deprivation and humiliation: slovenliness, gluttony, bad temper and an abnormal sensitivity to insults.

Though his original writings were acclaimed, they made him no money, but in 1747 he was approached to write a *Dictionary of the English Language*. This, when it appeared after eight years' work, was greeted with universal praise, but recognition had come too late to give him real pleasure. Tetty was by now dead, and he could not share his new fame with her, who had early given him rational approval as well as love. Nor was he any richer, having long ago spent the advance of 1,500 guineas on lodging and medical care for her. To keep afloat, he wrote a series of weekly essays, *The Rambler*, which proved popular and was followed by another no less eagerly read, *The Idler*. His novel, *Rasselas*, was written in a week to pay his mother's funeral expenses.

In 1760, a government sympathetic to the arts came to power, and two years later Johnson was offered a pension of £300 a year. He hesitated, for he had defined the word as 'generally understood to mean pay given to a state hireling for treason to his country'. 'It is not given you for anything you are to do, but for what you have done,' he was told, so he accepted. No longer was he forced to drudge. His wants were modest: what he liked best was to talk, what he hated most was going to bed. Now he could sleep late into the morning, visit friends, go with them to pub or tavern or private house, and return home late at night to drink tea with one of his dependants, the blind Mrs Williams. There would be a little money for travel, and for the rest he would be able to continue sheltering and feeding a houseful of impecunious people as well as supporting various indigent relatives, while giving way to his 'indolence'.

He was surrounded now by friends and admirers, although so uncertain was his temper that many called him 'the Bear'. In his intimate circle were David Garrick, the painter Sir Joshua Reynolds, the playwright Oliver Goldsmith and the politician Edmund Burke, besides the man who was to become his most famous biographer, James Boswell. (Mrs Boswell, resenting his influence over her husband, said she had often seen a bear led by a man, but never before a man led by a bear; Goldsmith, more indulgent, declared, 'He has nothing of the bear but his skin.')

There were also the Thrales. Henry Thrale, a wealthy brewer, was amiable and tolerant. His wife Hester was vivacious, intelligent and feminine, with a great capacity for sympathy and enormous patience. Both enjoyed entertaining, and they provided a good table at their house in Southwark and their country estate at Streatham. Johnson made a note in his diary for 1782 of one of the dinners at Streatham:

> a roast leg of lamb with spinach chopped fine, the stuffing of flour with raisins, a sirloin of beef and a turkey poult; and after the first course figs, grapes not very ripe owing to the bad season, with peaches – hard ones.

But this was an informal meal; an Irishman who went to dinner recorded three courses,

> first course soups at head and foot removed by fish and a saddle of mutton – second course a fowl they called Galena at head, and a capon (larger than some of our Irish turkeys) at foot; third course four different sorts of ices, viz., pineapple, grape, raspberry and a fourth; in each remove I think there were fourteen dishes. The two first courses were served in massy plate.

The Thrales soon became Johnson's intimate friends. To them he admitted his battle with depression, and during one of his worst bouts, they persuaded him to accompany them to Streatham, where he stayed for three months. It was a timely rescue. In an environment where all his material wants were provided as a matter of course, where the atmosphere was one of generous indulgence and tolerant acceptance, he felt secure. Mrs Thrale particularly was as sensitive a friend as he could wish. Each time he visited Streatham, she spoilt him, sitting quietly with him and making tea or talking, or sometimes praying, till the small hours of each morning, despite the fact that she was often pregnant, and weary from helping her husband campaign for a seat in Parliament. She was always ready to listen, and her own gaiety responded when Johnson was in amusing mood, so that sometimes the house was full of laughter.

For nearly twenty years, Streatham was sanctuary for Johnson, but by the time of Henry Thrale's death in 1781, the relationship had for various reasons become less intimate. Johnson himself was now far from well. On 17 June 1783, a stroke temporarily suppressed his ability to speak (it is characteristic of him that he immediately composed a prayer in Latin to see if his intellect had been affected). One of his first letters when he began to recover was to Mrs Thrale:

> I am sitting down in no cheerful solitude to write a narrative which would once have affected you with tenderness and sorrow, but which you will perhaps pass over now with the careless glance of frigid indifference . . . I have loved you with virtuous affection, I have honoured you with sincere esteem. Let not all our endearment be forgotten, but let me have in this great distress your pity and your prayers.

Mrs Thrale replied kindly, offered to visit him, but did not invite him to join her in Bath. A few months later, she broke the news of her marriage to Gabriel Piozzi, an Italian opera singer. Johnson's reaction is typical of the worst side of his nature: in a violently abusive and brutal letter, he accused her of abandoning her children and her religion, of folly and wickedness. Later he was ashamed of his outburst. In his last letter to her, he expressed a wish to 'breathe out one sigh more of tenderness . . . whatever I can contribute to your happiness, I am very ready to repay for that kindness which soothed twenty years of a life radically wretched . . . the tears stand in my eyes'.

Whatever his mental wretchedness had been in the past, his physical suffering was now very great. Asthma and dropsy gave him no ease: he could not sleep and was often in great pain. But he lost the fear of death which had so troubled the greater part of his life. When his doctor told him he was dying, he refused to take further medication, even his opiates, 'for I have prayed that I may render up my soul to God unclouded'. He died in the evening of 13 December 1784.

Few English writers have had so strong a sense of place as Samuel Johnson. None has expressed so often, and with such fervour, love of his adopted city. Perhaps the most famous of all his remarks is his reply to Boswell's anxiety that the 'exquisite zest' he relished on his occasional visits from Scotland might disappear were he to live in London. 'Why, Sir, you find no man, at all intellectual, who is willing to leave London. No, Sir, when a man is tired of London, he is tired of life; for there is in London all that life can afford.' Once, when he and Boswell had taken a boat to Greenwich and were strolling in the magnificent park, he said to Boswell, 'Is not this very fine?'

'Yes, Sir, but not equal to Fleet Street.'

'You are right, Sir.'

(It is fair to add that some years later Boswell, exaggerating as usual, declared that to his mind Fleet Street was more delightful than Tempe. He was brought neatly but kindly down to earth. 'Ay, Sir, but let it be compared with Mull.')

Why Johnson loved London so much is not difficult to understand. It was at last truly England's capital city, a focus for financial, intellectual and fashionable life. Parliament's greater powers since the 1688 Revolution had tempted numbers of able men into politics; the naval reforms of Pepys and his colleagues had wrested from the Dutch the control of the oceans and of world trade. Power was moving from the aristocracy to the middle classes, and art, literature, politics and business throve in the newly prosperous climate of England's biggest city. It was this atmosphere of activity, intellectual and social, which Johnson appreciated. He thought that a man stored his mind better in London than anywhere else, and also that 'no place cured a man's vanity or arrogance so well as London; for . . . he was sure to find in the metropolis many his equals, and some his superiors'. Yet it was most of all as a lonely man, uncertain of his own worth and dependent on the reassuring presence of others, that he valued London:

Sir, if you wish to have a just notion of the magnitude of this city, you must not be satisfied with seeing its great streets and squares, but must survey the innumerable little lanes and courts. It is not in the showy evolutions of buildings, but in the multiplicity of human habitations, which are crowded together, that the wonderful immensity of London consists . . . the intellectual man is struck with it as comprehending the whole of human life in all its variety, the contemplation of which is inexhaustible.

Next to the pleasures of London, friendship and good conversation, Johnson put those of eating and drinking, particularly the former. 'Some people,' he said once, 'have a foolish way of not minding, or pretending not to mind, what they eat. For my part, I mind my belly very studiously, and very carefully; for I look upon it that he who does not mind his belly will hardly mind anything else.'

'When at table,' wrote Boswell:

he was totally absorbed in the business of the moment; his looks seemed riveted to his plate; nor would he, unless when in very high company, say one word, or even pay the least attention to what was said by others, till he had satisfied his appetite; which was so fierce, and indulged with such intenseness, that while in the act of eating, the veins of his forehead swelled, and generally a strong perspiration was visible . . . it must be owned that Johnson, though he could be rigidly *abstemious*, was not a *temperate* man either in eating or drinking. He could refrain, but he could not use moderately.

If invited to dinner, he expected that special pains would be taken with the meal. Sometimes he was disappointed: coming from a friend's house one day, he said sadly, 'A good dinner enough to be sure, but it was not a dinner to *ask* a man to.' But on another occasion, when he had dined with a neighbour whose old housekeeper had taken special pains, he exclaimed: 'Sir, we could not have had a better dinner had there been a Synod of cooks.' Boswell's was not a complete portrait, for Johnson set more store by the company than the food. From a friend of long standing he once received a message: 'Sir, Dr Taylor sends his compliments to you, and begs you will dine with him to-morrow. He has got a hare.' 'My compliments,' was the reply, 'and I'll dine with him – hare or rabbit.'

Nevertheless, Boswell tells us that he 'boasted of the niceness of his palate'. He claimed that he could write:

> a better book of cookery than has ever yet been written; it should be a book upon philosophical principles . . . I would tell what is the best butcher's meat, the best beef, the best pieces; how to choose young fowls; the proper seasons of different vegetables; and then how to roast, and boil, and compound . . . you shall see what a book of cookery I shall make.

'That would be Hercules with the distaff indeed,' remarked a lady who was present.

'No, Madam,' Johnson replied. 'Women can spin very well; but they cannot make a good book of cookery.'

The book which prompted these remarks was the most celebrated cookbook of the eighteenth century, *The Art of Cookery made plain and easy*, 'by a Lady', first published in 1747. By the time (1778) Johnson rejected the idea that it was by a woman, because it was too good; condemned the author for his/her imperfect knowledge of chemistry; and claimed he could do better, the book had gone into several editions and the author's identity was known, although her name did not appear on the title page until after her death. While Mrs Hannah Glasse relied quite heavily for her recipes on other authors (of both sexes) she was innovative in transcribing these recipes (and expressing her own) in clear terms which could be readily understood. 'If I have not wrote in the high, polite Stile,' she wrote, 'I hope I shall be forgiven; for my Intention is to instruct the lower Sort, and therefore must treat them in their own way.' Almost all previous cookbooks had been aimed at the employer who spent much of her time in kitchen, pantry or stillroom directing her maids and doing the more interesting parts of the job; but by now a green baize door, metaphorically if not physically, separated mistress and servant in many households, as Mrs Glasse recognised. She must also have been aware of the many middle-class women in newly affluent families whose education was perhaps not up to 'the high, polite Stile'. *The Art of Cookery* is also famous for its attack on French extravagance and the foolishness of those who employ French cooks. 'So much is the blind Folly of this Age, that they would rather be impos'd on by a French Booby, than give Encouragement to a good English cook.' Some of her own recipes were very expensive, and one, for Essence of Ham, is virtually identical with a French recipe strongly condemned on a previous page, so perhaps her outburst simply echoed the patriotic British feeling of the age.

As the century progressed, many more cookbooks, increasingly written by women, were published. Elizabeth Raffald's *The Experienced English Housekeeper* (1769) went into thirteen legitimate editions. Its title was no misnomer; before opening a confectioner's shop in Manchester and also setting up an employment agency, she had worked as a housekeeper. The preface to the first edition shows that she had also studied Hannah Glasse:

> I am not afraid of being called extravagant, if my reader does not think that I have erred on the frugal hand . . . though I have given some of my dishes French names, as they are known only by those names, yet they will not be found very expensive . . . but as plain as the nature of the dish will admit of.

And although all the receipts 'are truly written from my own experience', the publishers took the precaution, in a new edition of 1789, of stating that she had 'inserted some celebrated Receipts by other Modern Authors'. Unlike *The Art of Cookery*, her book had a well-constructed index, and the recipes were put into categories – meat, fish, game, and so on, as we do today.

A third published book must be mentioned, as directly relevant to London. This is *The London Art of Cookery*, by John Farley, which first appeared in 1783. Farley was cook at the London Tavern, purpose-built in the grand manner in 1767 after a fire had left a convenient gap site in Bishopsgate Street Within. Due surely to Farley's cooking as much as to its luxurious appointments (one entire cellar was taken up with a tank for live turtles; the others were filled with thousands of bottles of wine to all tastes), the Tavern quickly became popular and famous, a meeting-place for radical politicians (the Supporters of the Bill of Rights and the Revolution Society), as well as rather less contentious groups like the directors of the East India Company, who held dinners there until 1834. In later centuries, it was well known to Dickens and his friends, but it became the Bank of

Scotland in 1876. About one-third of Farley's recipes are plagiarised; but since the book presumably represents the dishes which were actually cooked at the Tavern, plagiarism is perhaps the wrong term. Farley developed Mrs Glasse's approach, spelling out his instructions in detail. 'Take particular care that your cloth be clean, and remember to dip it in boiling water . . . when it be [cooked] enough . . . take off the basin and cloth very carefully, light puddings being apt to break.' But *The London Art of Cookery*'s most innovative features come at the beginning and end, with advice on 'marketing', i.e. shopping (just as Johnson would have wished) and an appendix on culinary poisons, especially those resulting from the use of copper vessels and lead-glazed pottery. In this, Farley was ahead of his time; it was a topic which was to command more attention in the following century.

Recipe books by professionals are unsatisfactory to the historian, since they often contain new rather than current recipes. To see what *was* eaten, it is best to look at personal manuscript collections. The discovery of Margaretta Acworth's receipt book in the Public Record Office and the publication, by Alice and Frank Prochaska, of an edited collection of the recipes (*Margaretta Acworth's Georgian Cookery Book*, London, 1987) brings us much closer to what was probably served to Johnson and his friends when they dined with, for example, the Thrales. The Acworths (he was a government official) lived in a large house in Great Smith Street, fashionably near the country villages of Chelsea and Kensington, but close enough to St James's Park, Covent Garden and Whitehall to feel themselves near the centre of government and artistic society. The receipt book contains a number of recipes written in by Margaretta's mother, so it is an excellent witness to fashionable London gastronomy from about 1720 to the 1790s. A few recipes are transcriptions from published work, but neither Mrs Glasse nor Mrs Raffald are sources, and there is a predictably old-fashioned air to the collection. Almonds are still a major ingredient in soups and for thickening; cock's-combs (absent from Raffald and Farley) appear frequently in sauces, forcemeats and 'ragoos'; a turkey pie has a duck placed inside a boned turkey before the whole is covered with a pastry crust; young pigeons with the heads on are served 'ye little bills peeping out of ye [scallop] shell'. (Mrs Raffald, it is true, gives a recipe for 'transmogrified pigeons' which puts the birds into hollowed-out pieces of cucumber, a bunch of barberries in each little bill.) An artichoke pie is definitely medieval in its use of cinnamon, nutmeg, sugar and rosewater, especially if compared with Farley's recipe, in which the artichokes, mixed with truffles, morels and hard-boiled egg yolks, are given a savoury flavouring of mace, peppercorns and salt. Nothing more clearly demonstrates that, gastronomically, this was an age in transition; even in London, even in fashionable society, households clung to the old way of doing things, and we may guess that Johnson, who had been brought up in a small provincial town, enjoyed the old dishes more than the new.

If we are unsure about what he ate, we have clear information about what he drank. By the time Boswell met him, he was almost teetotal, and the advantages of sobriety were a frequent topic of his conversation. He had no objection to people drinking in moderation, but of this he felt himself incapable. After many years of abstinence he declared:

> I did not leave off wine because I could not bear [be affected by] it. I have drunk three bottles of port without being the worse for it . . . it is so much better for a man to be sure that he is never to be intoxicated, never to lose the power over himself. I shall not begin to drink wine till I grow old and want it.

A few months later, he admitted that he had often drunk wine when alone, 'to get rid of myself, to send myself away'. For other drinkers he had a word of advice: 'Claret is the liquor for boys; port for men; but he who aspires to be a hero,' he added with a smile, 'must drink brandy.'

Claret was in fact slightly less popular and considerably more expensive in England than it had been in Pepys's time. The reason was political. In 1703, the Methuen Treaty with Portugal gave preference in the matter of import duties to Portuguese wines, in exchange for similar consideration by the Portuguese of ships of dried and salted fish. Not only were French wines henceforth very much more expensive, but in the light of current attitudes to France, to drink them was thought to be unpatriotic. (In Scotland, which still had strong ties with France, the reverse was true.) Some Spanish and Italian wines, and a few Rhenish ones, were coming into Britain, but now it was port which appealed most to the English palate. Nevertheless, a surprising amount of smuggled claret, and more importantly – since punch was a favourite eighteenth-century drink – cognac, was on the market.

If Johnson abstained from wine, he had what amounted to an addiction to tea. In the previous century, coffee and chocolate had taken London by storm, but now tea was *the* fashionable drink. Twining's tea shop in the Strand is the oldest shop in London still owned by its founding family and on its original site, having been established in 1706. Both Christopher Wren and Queen Anne are said to have bought their tea here. The heavy import tax levied by successive governments did nothing to dampen the craze; it simply suggested to smugglers a new commodity for their attention. In 1784, it was estimated that of the thirteen million pounds of tea consumed, only five and a half million had come into the country legitimately. It was the Twining of the day who advised the Prime Minister, William Pitt the Younger, to bring down the duty on tea to a tenth of its existing level. That put an end to the smuggling but increased consumption, so that the lower tax actually raised more money. Tea's quick rise to popularity surprised most people and alarmed the reactionaries, who believed ale and beer to be the only proper beverages for Englishmen. By the end of the century, even the families of agricultural labourers drank large quantities of tea, causing serious misgivings among the upper classes. It has to be said that there was a sound nutritional basis for their anxiety. 'Whether this exotic is more palatable or more nutritious than home-raised barley converted into broth,' wrote Sir Frederic Eden in *The State of the Poor* (1797), 'I leave to Medical Gentlemen to determine.' He was, of course, correct. But there were others who argued that tea was bad for the morals no less than the digestion, brushing aside the fact that most tea was drunk by the upper and middle classes, who seemed not to be suffering in either their virtue (apart from connivance at smuggling) or their health.

One such critic was Jonas Hanway, who wrote in his *Essay on Tea* dated 1757: 'It is the curse of this nation, that the laborer and mechanic will ape the lord.' He went on:

> Were they the sons of tea-sippers, who won the fields of Cressy and Agincourt, or dyed the Danube's streams with Gallic blood? What will be the end of such effeminate customs extended to those persons who must get their bread by the labours of the field! . . . Nay, your servants' servants,

down to the very beggars, will not be satisfied unless they consume the produce of the remote country of China . . . When will this evil stop? Your very chambermaids have lost their bloom, I suppose by sipping tea.

Johnson, who drank tea by the pint, could not let this pass. Describing himself as 'a hardened and shameless tea-drinker, who has for many years diluted his meals with only the infusion of this fascinating plant; whose kettle has scarcely time to cool; who with tea amuses the evening, with tea solaces the midnights, with tea welcomes the morning', he wrote a spirited defence of his beloved tipple. Modern medical opinion might ascribe his insomnia and perhaps some other troubles at least in part to his addiction, but he believed that he 'never felt the least inconvenience from it'.

Unabashed by controversy, tea-drinkers continued to enjoy the fragrant leaf. By mid-century, they could choose from a number of different varieties, of which the most famous perhaps was Bohea, whose name became a poetic synonym for tea. Others, like Souchon, Pekoe and Gunpowder are still with us. A variety called Twankay may be responsible for the naming of one of pantomime's most celebrated characters.

The first London tea shop for ladies was opened in 1717 by that astute merchant, Thomas Twining. Excluded as they were from coffee-houses, women were delighted with it, but a few years later it was supplanted by a new craze, tea gardens. At Vauxhall or Ranelagh, Marylebone or White Conduit House, anyone could join the great and the rich, the happy and the fair as they strolled among pavilions, rotundas, grottoes, cascades and Chinese, Moorish or Greek temples; there were concerts and fireworks, masked balls and routs, acrobatic displays and balloon ascents; the refreshments offered included tea, chocolate, punch, orange-brandy and arrack. Later still, it was the Old Chelsea Bun House, Pimlico Road, which drew huge crowds every Sunday until it was destroyed by fire in 1839. They came not only to eat the delicious spicy buns and drink tea, but also to gape at the museum of freaks set up by the enterprising owners and to watch their King and Queen (George III and Charlotte) indulge in the same innocent pleasures. Such places continued to be immensely popular, especially with the younger set, well into the next century. But in the home, tea-drinking became a typically feminine and domestic activity, whose ritual, with the aid of tea-table, tin-lined lockable caddy made of the finest woods, specially designed cups imported from China, and beautiful silverware, commended it particularly to women of leisure, providing a fashionable and charming occasion for social contact. A German visitor to London, Sophie von La Roche, was invited to a tea-party at Windsor by a lady-in-waiting to the Queen (another guest was Fanny Burney, author of the novel *Evelina*). Enthusiast that Sophie was for everything English, she found the event much to her taste:

> Here was a picture . . . of a first-class English tea-party. The tone was intimate and refined: the hostess busies herself delightfully and just enough to allow of grace and deftness. While Madame La Fite prepared tea, the ladies continued their fancywork, sewing bands of fine muslin. While we sipped at our tea, pretty and practical discussions took place.

Throughout most of the country coffee-houses retained their importance. Lord Macaulay, whose (incomplete) five-volume *History of England* ends with a vivid picture of the age of William and Mary, wrote, 'the coffee-house was the Londoner's home, and . . . those who wished to find a gentleman commonly asked, not whether he lived in Fleet Street or Chancery Lane, but whether he frequented the Grecian or the Rainbow'. There were over 2,000 to choose from. A Swiss traveller wrote to his family:

> If you would know our manner of Living 'tis thus: we rise by Nine, and those that frequent great Men's Levees find Entertainment at them till Eleven, or, as in Holland, go to Tea Tables. About Twelve the Beau Monde assembles in several Coffee or Chocolate Houses; the best of which are the Cocoa-Tree and White's Chocolate Houses, St James's, the Smyrna, Mrs Rochford's and the British Coffee-houses, all these so near one another that in less than an Hour you see the Company of them all . . . At Two we generally go to Dinner: Ordinaries are not so common here as Abroad, yet the French have set up two or three pretty good ones, for the Conveniency of Foreigners, in Suffolk Street, where one is tolerably well served; but the general way here is to make a party at the Coffee-house to go and dine at the Tavern, where

we sit till six that we go to the Play, except that you are invited to the Table of some great Man, which Strangers are always courted to and nobly entertain'd.

Coffee-houses were sometimes called 'Penny Universities'; one of their chief functions was as changing-houses for news. Not surprisingly, this role was gradually extended, and we find Steele launching the first issue of *The Tatler* with 'Accounts of Gallantry, Pleasure, and Entertainment . . . under the article of White's Chocolate House', poetry under that of Will's Coffee-house, and foreign and domestic news from St James's Coffee-house. But the most famous of all the coffee-houses was Lloyd's of Lombard Street, frequented largely by businessmen. Here commodities were auctioned 'by the candle': bidding began on the lighting of a candle one inch high, and the successful bidder was the man who made his bid just before the candle burnt out. Pepys had attended such an auction, of wine, but even ships were sold in this way. Lloyd's was from the beginning a haunt of underwriters and insurers of ships' cargoes; when the first Lloyd's List was issued, giving exchange rates and prices and the latest shipping news, its future career was assured.

Johnson had his favourite coffee-houses, but he preferred taverns. 'There is no private house,' he told Boswell, 'in which people can enjoy themselves as well as in a capital tavern.' He and Boswell frequently dined at the Mitre, Johnson taking care always to order 'a chicken, a sweetbread, or any other little nice thing' to be sent up, ready-dressed, to his blind friend Mrs Williams. The convivial tavern atmosphere and the fact that many had rooms available for private parties made them ideal meeting-places for the clubs which proliferated during this period, and led to the downfall of coffee-houses. Johnson himself was responsible for founding three clubs, the first of which usually met on Tuesday evenings at the King's Head in Ivy Lane for conversation and beefsteak. On one occasion the club went instead at Johnson's invitation to supper in the Turk's Head in Gerrard Street, Soho, to celebrate the publication of a first novel by a friend. He had ordered a magnificent apple pie stuck with bay leaves, and after an invocation to the Muses, the authoress's brow was ceremonially encircled with a laurel wreath made by the Doctor's own genial, clumsy fingers. The night passed in pleasant conversation and harmless mirth and no doubt wine was drunk as well as tea and coffee. Johnson drank only lemonade, but about five in the morning his face was seen to shine 'with meridian splendour'. The waiters grew sleepy, but still the party continued, dispersing finally at nearly eight o'clock in the morning.

The Turk's Head was the venue for Johnson's second club, the Literary, which he and Joshua Reynolds founded in 1764. Goldsmith and Edmund Burke were other distinguished members, and they all dined together once a fortnight during parliamentary sessions. Finally, a year before he died, the old Ivy Lane club was reanimated in the Essex Head Club. Johnson himself wrote out the rules; members dined twice a week at the Essex Head and once in Johnson's house. Penalty for non-attendance was twopence. Boswell was in Scotland at this time, but Johnson insisted on his being elected a member. 'Boswell,' he explained, 'is a very clubbable man.'

There was a vast difference between Pepys's London and Johnson's. For Pepys, London was still the City. For Johnson, it centred on Fleet Street and the Strand. After the Fire, the City had been rebuilt in brick and stone. Streets had been widened, frontages straightened, Wren's new churches charmed the eye. But the population was expanding, and moving west and east. Defoe estimated 'London' to have a circumference of thirty-six miles 'and how much further it may spread God knows'. Horace Walpole described rows of houses 'shooting out every day like a polypus'. In the West End, private owners were building elegant squares and streets on their family estates; developments like Mayfair, Grosvenor Square and Bloomsbury were the result. Here lived the fashionable world of the wealthy and aristocratic. Areas round the Strand and Fleet Street now accommodated a more mixed population. Butchers and journalists, painters and tallow chandlers, grocers and leatherworkers rubbed shoulders with the nobility and gentry. But in the backstreets and narrow alleys, a slum population harboured crime, malnutrition and disease.

As the centre of a growing Empire, London needed vast numbers of workers, from unskilled labourers able to service the port and the docks to merchants and businessmen. But it was also becoming the country's most important manufacturing centre, famous for specific trades like silk-weaving, clock-making and coach-building. These were manned very largely by newcomers: many had moved in from the country as the latest wave of agrarian reforms hit rural employment. Many others, like the Huguenots and Jews, had come from abroad. It was they who were responsible for the eastward and northern expansion which populated Spitalfields and swallowed up villages like Clerkenwell, Shoreditch, and Deptford south of the river.

It would be wrong to put the entire blame for the poverty of the backstreets on industrial development. Poverty had always existed, and evaded legislation. It was now aggravated by a totally new factor: the introduction of cheap spirits. Beer and ale, the Englishman's birthright, could only be sold on licensed premises. Spirits carried no such restriction. Among the imports from Holland introduced after the end of the Anglo–Dutch wars came gin, which until 1736 carried a duty of only twopence a gallon. As if this were not cheap enough, people began to make home-made spirits from a variety of dubious ingredients and sold that cheaper still. It is reckoned that for every man, woman and child in London two pints of gin were drunk per week in the middle of the century, and over 9,000 children per year died from drinking spirits – often given to infants to keep them from crying. The effect on the poor was devastating, and Hogarth's terrible engraving *Gin Lane* hardly exaggerates what might be seen in a London slum any day. Three houses in Gin Lane stand trim and prosperous amid a huddle of broken-down dwellings: those of Gripe the pawnbroker, Kilman the distiller and an unnamed undertaker. Outside the pawnbroker's, people crowd to offer him their possessions; a poor wretch sits gnawing a bone, and a half-naked woman lies in a stupor on the steps, her infant falling from her arms into the street below. Over the gin-shop is an advertisement: 'Drunk for a penny, dead drunk for twopence, clean straw for nothing'. In the background, the undertaker prepares a body for burial, while outside the distiller's a fight is going on. Through the broken wall of a tumbledown building can be seen a suicide's corpse hanging from a beam. To point the moral, Hogarth printed a companion engraving, *Beer Street*, depicting neat bright houses, cheerful people and prosperous businesses.

The Gin Act of 1736, although it raised the duty, was too weak to be effective. The tax could be avoided by selling gin as medicine, in the guise of gripe- or colic-water, and spirits became one of the smugglers' most desirable wares. But successive governments continued at intervals to increase the duty, and great efforts were made to eradicate smuggling, so that by the end of the century less gin was being drunk. By then, however, other factors were creating a new wave of urban deprivation.

All this goes some way to explain the paradoxical nature of eighteenth-century London, in which great wealth and total deprivation could be found side by side; polite society was confronted by barbaric crime and brutal squalor, and the flowering of the arts and literature coexisted with industrial conditions of appalling inhumanity.

Nevertheless, when it came to food, the paradoxes are less evident; for the first half of the century, a reasonable diet was both available and cheap. Even poor people could afford meat, a fact which, as before, amazed foreigners. The agricultural reforms begun in the previous century were slowly having their effect. In 1710, cattle and sheep taken to Smithfield weighed less than half what was normal by the end of the century, and it was still common practice for all except breeding stock to be slaughtered and salted down in the autumn. The ideas of Jethro Tull and Lord Townsend ('Turnip' Townsend) on the winter feeding of cattle did not begin to circulate until about 1730, and their fellow farmers needed to be convinced that the abolition of the strip system and the enclosure of fields would improve both their beasts and their profits. In time, however, farmers like Lord Coke in Norfolk turned much of their land over to turnips, potatoes and grass, and were thus able to keep cattle in good condition over the winter. By the 1770s, gentleman farmers were also working to improve breeding stock; particular strides had been made in pig-breeding, crossing the native animals with imported Chinese pigs of greater size.

The last years of the eighteenth century saw significant changes in the type of meat being eaten. There were four main meat markets in London:

> Shall the large Mutton smoke upon your Boards?
> Such *Newgate's* copious Market best affords;
> Woulds't thou with mighty Beef augment thy Meal?
> Seek *Leadenhall*; *Saint James's* sends thee Veal.
> (Anon., quoted in John Ashton, *Social Life in the Reign of Queen Anne*, London 1882)

(Clare market, unmentioned, was outside the City, south of Lincoln's Inn Fields, and specialised in pork.) By the 1780s, well-to-do Londoners had access to fresh beef, mutton and pork for the greater part of the year. Foreign opinion of British meat varied a great deal. A Frenchman who visited London in 1771 thought it inferior to what he could buy in Paris, but Sophie von La Roche was impressed. Walking near Green Park, she hit upon some of the streets in which the butchers were housed and was delighted to find:

> the meat so fine and shops so deliciously clean; all the goods were spread on snow-white cloths, and cloths of similar whiteness were stretched out behind the large hunks of meat hanging up; no blood anywhere, no dirt; the shop-walls and doors were all spruce, balance and weights highly polished.

Sophie corroborates remarks about the quantity of meat eaten, and offers an explanation:

> A completely English repast suggested the reason why such large dishes are to be seen in silver, pewter, china and crockery shops; to wit, because a quarter of a calf, half a lamb and monstrous pieces of other meats are dished up, and everyone receives almost an entire fish. But since England knows nothing of separate cooking for servants, who partake of all the courses sampled by the masters, the latter having first choice and the servants what remains – hence the large dishes and portions.

Sophie's first English supper was eaten at an inn at Ingatestone. It consisted of thinly sliced pieces of beef and veal, beaten, sprinkled with breadcrumbs and grilled, served with fine big potatoes with salt butter. To drink, there was 'delicious beer and a good Bordeaux wine'. But Sophie was a confessed Anglophile. One of her compatriots, Herr Lichtenberg, disliked the 'rost-beef' because it was underdone, and presumably had the same complaint about English soups. He said that he thought the English cooked their soup in their stomachs.

Another Frenchman, Henri Misson de Valberg, also observed the wealthy middle-class Londoner at table. The usual dinner consisted of two substantial dishes – perhaps a pudding and a piece of roast beef, or boiled meat 'besiege[d] with five or six Heaps of Cabbage, Carrots, Turnips, or some other Herbs or Roots, well pepper'd and salted and swimming in Butter'. Fowls, pigs, ox tripes, tongues, rabbits and pigeons might all be treated in the same way. If boiled meat was served, 'there is sometimes one of the Company that will have the Broth; this is a kind of Soup, with a little Oatmeal in it, and some Leaves of Thyme or Sage, or other such small Herbs. They bring up this in as many Porringers as there are People that desire it; those that please, crumble a little Bread in it, and this makes a kind of Potage.' Misson's remarks on puddings also deserve to be quoted:

> The Pudding is a Dish very difficult to be describ'd because of the several Sorts there are of it; Flower, Milk, Eggs, Butter, Sugar, Suet, Marrow, Raisins, etc. etc. are the most common ingredients of a pudding. They bake them in an Oven, they boil them with Meat, they make them fifty several Ways: *Blessed be he that invented the pudding*, for it is a Manna that hits the Palates of all Sorts of People; a Manna better than that of the Wilderness, because the People are never weary of it . . . 'To come in Pudding Time' is as much as to say, to come in the most lucky moment in the World.

Clearly there have taken place, by this time, considerable divergences of gastronomic culture. Misson's tone is almost that of an explorer among aborigines. Yet the food he is describing, apart from the melted butter sauce and the puddings, is not far different from contemporary provincial bourgeois fare in his own country. The real reason for his surprise is that the Englishman who invited him to dine came from London and from the class of the Thrales and the Acworths, not from the lower end of the scale. His French equivalent would undoubtedly have considered such a meal old-fashioned, for in France by this time, the food of the *haute bourgeoisie* aimed to emulate, within financial limitations, that of the aristocracy. The systematic, modular approach to cooking was now well established, so that dishes containing one or perhaps a few main ingredients were prepared using some more or less standard combination of preparations such as stocks, purées, concentrated sauces known as coulis, and stuffings. Sauces were light and smooth, but made from costly ingredients, and expensive in terms of kitchen equipment and labour. It was all very sophisticated, and only those Londoners who had French cooks – the Duke of Newcastle and his chef Monsieur de St Clouet, who trained the owner of the White

Hart Inn at Lewes, William Verral, is an example – were aware of the growing difference in national styles.

But London was essentially a middle-class city, and the traditional dislike of foreigners reinforced a distrust of the nobility. The roast beef of Old England – a fictitious entity, as David Hume observed – became a symbol of John Bull and his no-nonsense values. Writers like Hannah Glasse, who decried the extravagance of French recipes, had to fall back for the most part on simplified versions of the old 'frigasceys', 'ragoos' and 'hashes' if they wished to avoid modern French influence.

It was the presentation of dishes, and the ingredients, which altered in England, rather than the general approach to cooking as in France. For example, the game laws had been reformulated in the middle of the seventeenth century; now, although Londoners could still buy game, it had become rarer and more expensive. Wild duck, pheasant and partridge cost about the same as farm poultry, but were difficult to find. However, as late as 1770, you could still get female blackbirds and thrushes for the table, because a demand for the males as caged songbirds encouraged indiscriminate trapping. Pigeons were popular, but otherwise farm poultry was replacing wildfowl. From the Home Counties, guinea fowl, hens, geese and turkeys were driven to London on foot; Aylesbury ducks were already famous. The turkeys waddling clumsily and noisily along must have looked amusing, equipped as they were with little leather boots to save their feet; the more independent geese, refusing boots, had their feet protected with a coat of tar covered with grit – hence the old saying 'like shoeing a goose' to describe any impossible scheme. Less amusing was the treatment meted out to the poor birds when they reached the city: they were put into coops to fatten and, according to Smollett, were sewn up by the gut, a process which might increase their weight but subjected them to a fever which often putrefied the flesh.

If the Agricultural Revolution was altering meat-eating, there were also developments in the fishing industry. Early in the seventeenth century someone had invented wells for fishing boats – tanks containing seawater in which the fish could be brought back to port alive. Later, a well-vessel was devised, with a tank which ran from wall to wall across the hull, with perforated sides through which seawater could circulate. Another innovation was the use of ice, following the observations of a director of the East India Company who had visited China and had seen fish packed in snow. Visitors to London sometimes sent home a present of fish packed in this way, and Scotch salmon, long exported to London in its pickled form, could now be dispatched fresh.

Wells filled with fresh water, not salt, also made possible a new luxury which became, like the medieval roast swan or porpoise, a symbol of wealth, power and status. This was the West Indian green turtle. Surely more impressive even than the cost of its transport were its portly shape and ponderous movements; the powerful people whose tables it graced must have believed, if subconsciously, in sympathetic magic. A large turtle could provide an entire course for a banquet. In *The Experienced English Housekeeper*, Elizabeth Raffald set out the yield from a turtle weighing 100 lb: a top dish made from the thick part of the fins, a bottom dish from the flesh next to the top shell, a centre dish of soup from the head, heart and lights (lungs), a first corner dish from the chicken, or flesh next to the bottom shell, a second from the small fins, a third from the guts stuffed with 'the fishy part', and a fourth from the drained head, heart and lights, now garnished with the fried liver and slices of lemon. Somewhat surprisingly, in view of the enormous amount of work this must have given several cooks, the turtle was only to be killed the night before.

Shellfish were still plentiful. Sophie von La Roche had never tasted oysters, but seeing a load which had just arrived at Billingsgate and the people eagerly buying and carrying them off while others ate them on the spot, she was persuaded to try them and entered an inn:

> The cubicles were neat, the tables were laid with white cloths, and there were delightful wicker-chairs to sit in. A fisher-woman with a basket of oysters, a youngster with lemons and a small basket containing bread, plates and knives followed immediately after us . . . I liked them very much.

Oysters were also a favourite ingredient of made dishes. Sometimes they only added interest to a sauce, but often they were used to stuff poultry or a leg of mutton; or they could be wrapped in slices of rump steak and baked in a pie. Lobsters too were a popular delicacy now that they could be brought alive into London, and like oysters were used in all sorts of ways. So were shrimps; potted shrimps and potted lobster were fashionable dishes at tables like the Thrales'.

Not all fish arrived fresh and sweet. Defoe, in the early part of the century, speaks of stinking fish brought from the east coast by road, and Smollett also wrote of the effect of hot weather on fish that came a long distance. Among varieties, mackerel and cod were popular, as were eels and whiting, and lampreys seem to have made a minor comeback. *The Experienced English Housekeeper* (1789 edition) gives four recipes for lamprey.

Sophie's mention of lemons with oysters is interesting because it is the first reference I have been able to find to this combination. By now, lemons and sweet oranges were being imported regularly in large quantities. Their juice replaced verjuice in older recipes and was an important ingredient of the thinner sauces now served with meat and fish. They were also much valued as a garnish, and orange-flower water vied with rosewater both as cosmetic and as flavouring for cakes and biscuits. When limes were imported from the West Indies, they quickly became an important constituent of that most popular eighteenth-century drink, punch.

As we saw in an earlier chapter, scurvy was a common complaint at the end of the winter. Now, with England's power so dependent on an efficient Navy, medical science was much concerned with finding a treatment. Wild theories were put forward and strange experiments devised, but it was gradually observed that fresh vegetables and the juice of some acid fruits could solve the problem. Not until the last years of the century were citrus fruits fixed on as the best method of combating scurvy at sea, but before then the general value of fresh raw fruit was recognised, and the old medieval prejudice against it finally disappeared. Increased demand led to yet more market gardens being set up around London; Lambeth on the south bank of the river was soon matched by the area on the north bank from Chelsea to Westminster, and by 1800 it was estimated that at the little village of Ealing, much further west, there were 250 market gardens. The rich alluvial soil in these areas was made richer by horse-dung from the city and 'night-soil' brought down in barges. Battersea was famous for its asparagus, other areas for strawberries, mulberries, figs (under glass?) and cherries. All night, the roads round London were alive with carts bringing fresh country produce to the markets, and at dawn the Thames too was crowded with heavily loaded barges from the market gardens. Steele, writing in *The Spectator* in 1712, described the cheerful bustle on the river:

When we first put off from shore, we soon fell in with a fleet of gardeners bound for the several market-ports of London; and it was the pleasantest scene imaginable to see the cheerfulness with which those industrious people plied their way to a certain sale of their goods. The banks on each side are as well peopled, and beautified with agreeable plantations, as any spot on the earth; but the Thames itself, loaded with the product of each shore, added very much to the landscape . . . Nothing remarkable happened in our voyage; but I landed with ten sail of apricot boats at Strand-bridge, after having put in at Nine Elms, and taken in melons, consigned by Mr Cuffe of that place, to Sarah Sewell and company, at their stall in Covent Garden. We arrived at Strand-bridge at six of the clock, and were unloading, when the hackney-coachmen of the foregoing night took their leave of each other . . . Chimney-sweepers passed by us as we made up to the market, and some raillery happened between one of the fruit-wenches and those black men, about the Devil and Eve, with allusion to their several professions. I could not believe any place more entertaining than Covent Garden, where I strolled from one fruit-shop to another, with crowds of agreeable young women around me who were purchasing fruit for their respective families.

This pleasing picture has, alas, to be contrasted with Smollett's account in *The Expedition of Humphry Clinker* (1771):

It was but yesterday that I saw a dirty barrow-bunter in the street, cleaning her dusty fruit with her own spittle; and who knows but some fine lady of St. James's parish might admit into her delicate mouth those very cherries which had been rolled and moistened between the filthy, and perhaps ulcerated, chops of a St. Giles's huckster?

A remark by a Frenchman writing in 1772 shows that even then pollution from coal fires caused serious problems:

All [vegetables] that grow in the country about London, cabbage, radishes, and spinnage, being impregnated with the smoke of sea-coal, which fills the atmosphere of that town, have a very disagreeable taste . . . I ate nothing good of this sort in London, but some asparagus.

Londoners, of course, hardly noticed the soot, or if they did, perhaps imagined vegetables always came like that. As Sir Jack Drummond wrote in *The Englishman's Food* (London, 1939), it was indeed a sign of changing habits when Thames watermen could taunt a boatload of Lambeth gardeners with being 'You . . . who can't afford Butter to your Cabbage, or Bacon to your Sprouts'.

Dairy products are a special feature of eighteenth-century food, with butter constituting a kind of universal sauce for everything from shellfish to steamed pudding. Although it was no longer possible to walk out of London to buy milk, cream and butter, dairy farms still existed within the city. A Board of Agriculture report in 1794 estimated that 8,500 milking cows were being kept in the East End, Islington, Paddington, Westminster, Lambeth, and the outer suburbs. In St James's Park, a favourite haunt of Londoners, one could buy a glass of milk produced by one of the cows grazing placidly nearby. (This facility continued to exist until the building of the Admiralty Arch in 1905, when the two old ladies who represented the last remnant of the tradition were moved, with their cows, to a stall nearer the lake. They continued to sell milk at a penny a cup for another fifteen years.) In Chelsea, Hoxton and Islington, there were green fields to be bought or rented for summer grazing. Demand for milk was high: in 1727, a dairywoman told an enquirer that she sold 'twice as many gallons in a week as she has customers'. Because of this, it became customary for dairies to adulterate their milk, making use of 'the cow with the iron tail', that is, the local water pump. Towards the end of the century, the amount of grazing land diminished, and animals were often poorly nourished and kept in filthy, cramped conditions. In *The Expedition of Humphry Clinker*, Smollett had plenty of uncomplimentary things to say about London's milk:

> But the milk itself should not pass unanalysed, the produce of faded cabbage-leaves and sour draff, lowered with hot water, frothed with bruised snails; carried through the streets in open pails, exposed to foul rinsings discharged from doors and windows, spittle, snot, and tobacco quids, from foot-passengers, overflowing from mud carts, spatterings from

coach wheels, dirt and trash chucked into it by roguish boys for the joke's sake; the spewings of infants, who have slabbered in the tin-measure, which is thrown back in that condition among the milk, for the benefit of the next customer; and, finally, the vermin that drops from the rags of the nasty drab that vends this precious mixture, under the respectable denomination of milkmaid.

Despite this unappetising description, 'fresh' London milk sold for a higher price than the country product, chiefly because the latter, by the time it had been transported in unrefrigerated churns along bumpy roads, was often unpleasantly sour. The milk most in favour was that milked by the dairywoman on demand as she drove her cow through the streets. Undefiled and unadulterated, it was understandably sought after.

Adulteration of food, especially bread, was beginning to be an emotive issue. White bread made from pure wheat had always been regarded as superior to any other; it was the food of the nobility, and more pleasant in taste and texture than the coarse bread of mixed grain eaten by the poor. The whiter the flour, the better it was liked. As early as 1616, a grocer noted that 'the poor would not buy barley or rye, either alone or even if mixed with two-thirds wheat'.

From 1715 to 1755, farmers increasingly went over to wheat, and a succession of good harvests brought the price of flour tumbling. By the time a series of bad seasons resulted in severe shortages, Londoners in particular were used to white wheaten bread and complained vociferously when the bakers supplemented their meagre allowance of wheat flour with that made from other cereals, or, as in the old days, bean- and peasemeal. In the worst famine years, Parliament sponsored a 'standard' loaf, stamped on the side with a large 'S' and containing a higher proportion of bran, but it was ill received.

Not unnaturally, the bakers tried to respond to public demand. They mixed a compound of alum and salt (known diplomatically as 'stuff') with the flour. This increased the size and improved the texture and colour of the loaves, but it did not satisfy public demand for long, or rather – as commonly happens with new developments in the manufacture of food – it split demand into two camps. While the masses might appreciate the whiter bread, a movement arose against adulteration. It began with the publication in 1757 of an anonymous pamphlet entitled *Poison Detected: or Frightful Truths: and alarming to the British Metropolis*. Alarming they were: the writer described alum, correctly, as a very powerful astringent and styptic, 'occasioning heat and costiveness', and went on to claim that bakers added lime, chalk and – most horrifying – ground bones from the charnel houses to their flour. Shortly afterwards, another writer hinted at the use of white lead, a deadly poison.

In response, the bakers sponsored defensive pamphlets. A chemist, H. Jackson, in an *Essay on Bread*, did not deny the use of alum, but pointed out that the other ingredients mentioned would actually reduce the size and impair the texture of bread, so that it was hardly likely that bakers would use them. But the seed had been sown. In such affairs, popular novels carry more weight among the reading public than any number of pamphlets, and Smollett, picking up the issue, made it part of his *Humphry Clinker* diatribe:

> The bread I eat in London is a deleterious paste, mixed up with chalk, alum, and bone-ashes; insipid to the taste and destructive to the constitution. The good people are not ignorant of this adulteration; but they prefer it to wholesome bread, because it is whiter than the meal of corn. Thus they sacrifice their taste and their health, and the lives of their tender infants, to a most absurd gratification of a misjudging eye; and the miller or the baker, is obliged to poison them and their families, in order to live by his profession.

The controversies continued well into the next century, and have been renewed in recent times. They did not, however, prevent the appearance, about 1760, of a brand-new dish for which bread of some sort was absolutely indispensable. It is pleasing to note that its inventor was none other than a descendant of Pepys's cousin, patron and friend, Lord Edward Montagu, first Earl of Sandwich. As the story goes, the fourth Earl one evening waved away friends who urged him to leave the gaming table and go to dinner; let them bring him, he begged, something he could eat while playing – anything would do, even pieces of meat between slices of bread and butter. The sandwich had been invented. You will observe that it is the trencher all over again, only now there are two, and they are thinner and, being buttered, no longer absorb the gravy.

We may conclude remarks on the bread of Johnson's day with a word about toast. Its origins are obscure, but a traveller in 1617 wrote that 'all within the sound of Bow Bells are in reproch called cochnies, and eaters of buttered tostes' – so we know at least that there was an early and specific connection between Londoners and toast, though it must surely have been eaten in other parts of the country. Popular medieval snacks had been enriched toast made from grilled bread soaked in wine and recrisped, or spread thick with a spiced and sweetened paste – compare the cinnamon toast which used to be so popular in the United States. However, by the eighteenth century, savoury spreads were in vogue: scrambled or buttered eggs, ham, anchovy paste, or cheese melted with a little beer or wine – again, variations on the medieval trencher. There was also a fashion, which continued into the nineteenth century, for 'toast and water', supposed to have therapeutic properties, especially for people with weak bowels. Bread was thinly toasted until extremely brown and hard, but not black. The slice was then put into a jug of cold water and left for at least an hour. When the liquid was 'of a fine brown colour', it was poured off and drunk.

The hour at which toast really came into its own was five o'clock in the afternoon, when the fashionable world observed the new ritual of afternoon tea. Bread and butter, cut thin as poppy leaves, was admired by visiting foreigners; but it was toast made by the fire and spread with melting butter, served heaped in dishes to accompany tea in thin china cups, which was declared 'incomparably good'.

RECIPES

SOUPE À-LA-REINE

This soup and the following were the two most fashionable soups of the eighteenth century. Even the philosopher David Hume boasted of his ability to make Soupe à-la-Reine, which is supposed to have been served at the court of Marguerite of Valois, Queen of France from 1589 to 1610.

1 knuckle of veal
2 lb (1 kg) boiling beef
3 large onions
1 large carrot
1 head celery
1 parsnip
1 leek
3 sprigs fresh thyme or 1 tsp dried thyme
5 fl oz (150 ml) single cream
5 slices of white bread, decrusted
¼ lb (125 g) ground almonds
yolks of 3 hard-boiled eggs
salt and pepper

Put the veal and beef in a large pot with water to cover. When it boils skim it well, then put in the vegetables and the thyme, add about 1 tbsp salt and a good grind of pepper, and simmer gently for 2–3 hours. Strain it and let it stand for an hour, then skim off as much fat as possible and gently, so as not to disturb the sediment which should have settled, pour it into a clean pan. In a smaller pan, boil half the cream; put three of the slices of bread in a bowl and pour the boiling cream over them. When they are well soaked, beat them to a mash with a wooden spoon and add the almonds and egg yolks. Beat all together, with a further tablespoon of cream. Then heat up the broth, pour some into the almond mixture, beating well, and either process or sieve the mixture very finely. Add the remaining cream and return to the pan, and while it reheats, cube the remaining slices of bread and fry them in butter to make croutons. Serve very hot.

(from Raffald, *The Experienced English Housekeeper*, 1789 edition)

WHITE SOUP

1 knuckle of veal
1 boiling chicken
¼ lb (125 g) lean bacon, in one piece
¼ lb (125 g) rice
1 large onion
½ head celery
1 bouquet garni
salt and peppercorns
5 fl oz (150 ml) single cream
yolk of one egg
¼ lb (125 g) ground almonds

Put the veal, bacon and chicken in a large pot with the rice, vegetables, herbs and a few peppercorns, and water to cover. Bring slowly to the boil, skim and simmer for about 2 hours, skimming occasionally. Strain the broth and leave in a cool place overnight. Take off the fat. Set the broth to reheat. Meanwhile, put the almonds in a bowl and beat them with a little broth, the cream and the yolk of egg. While you beat the almond mixture, pour in a ladleful of hot broth, then return all to the pan and instantly lower the heat. Taste to check the seasoning, bring the soup *almost* to the boil and serve.

(from Raffald, *The Experienced English Housekeeper*, 1789)

TO CAVEACH FISH

'To caveach' is not a verb in common use, even in cookery books. It seems to have been a short-term method of preserving cooked fish. I have chosen this recipe because of its fascinating resemblance to a dish given in *Cooking the Greek Way* by Anne Theoharous (London, 1979). Mrs Theoharous's father, who lived in New York for many years, called his version 'Fish Savoy'. Mrs Raffald's recipe is very similar and tastes just as delicious; what, if any, is the historical connection between the two I have not discovered.

4 pieces filleted firm fish – haddock, whiting, sole or trout
salt and pepper

2–3 tbsp flour
¾ cup olive or other good oil
¾ cup wine vinegar
1–2 cloves garlic
¼ tsp ground mace
6–7 black peppercorns
1 onion, chopped

Season the fish with pepper and salt, leave it for an hour, dry it with kitchen paper, flour the fillets well on both sides and fry them in 2–3 tbsp of the oil. Remove the fish from the pan and add to the pan the rest of the oil, the vinegar, crushed garlic, mace and pepper, and boil up once, scraping the bottom of the pan. Allow this liquor to get quite cold. In a suitable dish put a layer of chopped onion, then the fish all in one layer, then more onion if any remains. Pour over the marinade and put in the fridge. Leave for at least 3 days, turning once or twice. (Mrs Raffald says it will keep 3 or 4 months, well stoppered, but one would not wish to test this assertion.) Eat cold with salads.

(from Raffald, *The Experienced English Housekeeper*, 1789)

BUTTERED CRABS

1 lb (500 g) fresh or frozen crabmeat
3 tbsp red wine
1 tbsp vinegar
½ tsp nutmeg
½ tsp salt
1 tsp anchovy essence, or 2 anchovy fillets
1 egg yolk
4 oz (125 g) butter
toast, lemon and parsley to garnish

Beat all the ingredients together well or blend them in a food processor. Heat them gently in a saucepan, stirring occasionally. Pile the mixture into crab or scallop shells or some other suitable small dishes, and serve with triangles of toast, garnished with thin slices of lemon and a sprig of parsley.

(Margaretta Acworth, by kind permission of Frank and Alice Prochaska)

CHICKEN FRICASSEE

Another name for this particular fricassee is 'pulled chicken' – for obvious reasons.

1 boiling chicken
1 large onion
1 clove
1 large carrot
2 sticks celery
1 bunch sweet herbs or bouquet garni
5 oz (150 g) single cream
2 tbsp chopped parsley
1 oz (30 g) butter
1 tbsp flour
salt and pepper
1 tbsp white wine (optional)

Put the chicken into a pot with the vegetables (stick the clove into the onion), the herbs, salt and water to cover. Bring to the boil, skim, and simmer for 35–40 minutes. Take the chicken from the pot and, while it is still warm, skin it and take off all the white flesh over a bowl so that the juice which runs out is saved. The pieces of chicken should be 'as broad as your finger, and half as long'. Melt the butter in a heavy pan and stir in the flour. Then add the juice from the chicken and, gradually, 3–4 tablespoons of the water the chicken was cooked in. Put in the pieces of 'pulled' chicken and gradually stir in the cream over low heat. Allow to bubble for a few minutes while you keep stirring. If the sauce is very thick add more broth or some white wine. Check for seasoning, then put into a warmed dish, sprinkle with parsley and serve.

(from Farley, *The London Art of Cookery*, 1783)

BEEF TREMBLONQUE [TREMBLANT]

3–4 lb (1½–1¾ kg) piece of brisket beef
1 tbsp allspice berries
2 turnips
2 onions
1 carrot
salt
for the sauce
1 oz (30 g) butter
2 tbsp flour
¾ pt (425 ml) strong beef stock
1 tsp mushroom ketchup
1 tsp gravy browning (optional)
1 glass white wine
2 carrots, chopped small
2 turnips, chopped small
pickles to garnish

Put the meat, allspice and vegetables into a pan with water to cover. Bring to the boil, skim and add 3 tsp salt. Simmer for 3–4 hours. About an hour before serving, prepare the sauce. Melt the butter in a heavy pan, stir in the flour and cook for a minute or two. Then gradually add the beef stock (you may make this by taking liquid from the boiling meat and adding a stock cube, provided enough is left to keep the meat cooking). Next stir in the ketchup and browning (both typical of the period, but you can dispense with the browning if you wish), the wine and the vegetables. Bring to a simmer and cook until the vegetables are tender. Check the sauce for seasoning, put the beef in a warm dish, and pour the sauce over it. Garnish with pickles of any sort.

(from Glasse, *The Art of Cookery made plain and easy*, 1747)

Roast Saddle of Mutton

A very popular and very delicious dish for 6–8 people.

6–8 lb (2½ –3½ kg) saddle of mutton or lamb (Ask the butcher not to take the skin off entirely, but to separate it from the meat without tearing it, so that you can put the flavourings underneath it.)
4 oz (125 g) lean cooked ham, chopped
2 truffles (optional)
2 morels (get dried ones from a delicatessen store, then soak and chop them)
6–8 spring onions, chopped
3 tbsp chopped parsley
2 sprigs thyme or 1 tsp dried thyme
1 bay leaf
2 tbsp chopped mixed herbs – marjoram, rosemary, savory or other
1 tsp ground allspice
2 tsp salt
a good grind of black peppercorns
1 oz (30 g) butter
2 oz (60 g) fresh breadcrumbs
1 tbsp flour
1 glass white wine

Heat the oven to 375°F/175°C/Gas Mark 5. Mix the chopped ham, truffles and chopped mushrooms, chopped spring onions and herbs with the spices and salt. Spread this mixture over the meat under the skin. Replace the skin neatly and cover the meat with a well-buttered piece of greaseproof paper tied on with string. Put into the oven and after 20 minutes, reduce the heat to 325°F/150°C/Gas Mark 3. Allow a total time of 20–25 minutes per lb plus 20 minutes. 20 minutes before the meat is cooked remove the paper and strew the breadcrumbs over the meat. Twenty minutes later put the meat into a clean warm dish and keep it warm. It should be left for about 15 minutes to ensure even distribution of the juices. Meanwhile, pour off most of the fat from the roasting pan, stir in the flour and then the wine, season with salt and pepper, cook for a few minutes and pour into a gravy boat.

(from Farley, *The London Art of Cookery*, 1783)

JUGGED HARE

A very old and popular method of cooking game was to 'jug' it in a deep stoneware jug with a close-fitting lid, set to cook in a saucepan of boiling water. We can achieve almost the same effect using a heavy casserole in the oven.

1 hare (including the blood and the liver)
1 tsp vinegar
1 tsp salt
several good grinds of black peppercorns
¼ tsp ground mace
¼ tsp ground nutmeg
3 tbsp flour
oil for frying
1 onion
a bunch of sweet herbs or a bouquet garni
about 1 pt (575 ml) beef or chicken stock
1 glass red wine
1 anchovy fillet
cayenne pepper

Set the oven at 325°F/150°C/Gas Mark 3. Joint the hare neatly. Set aside the liver for the forcemeat balls (see next recipe) and put the blood in a bowl with the vinegar to keep it from curdling. Mix the flour with the salt, pepper, mace and nutmeg, and dredge the joints. Heat the oil in a frying pan and fry the meat until light brown, then transfer it to a casserole with the onion and herbs and pour over the boiling stock. Put it into the oven and cook for about three hours. Meanwhile, prepare forcemeat balls. When the meat is cooked, transfer it to a serving dish and keep warm. Strain the cooking liquor into a pan and add the wine, anchovy and a little cayenne pepper. Bring this to the boil and put a little into the blood, stirring well. Return this mixture to the pan and heat through, but do not allow to boil or it will curdle. Garnish the meat with the forcemeat balls, and pour the gravy over or serve it separately.

(from Raffald, *The Experienced English Housekeeper*, 1789)

FORCEMEAT BALLS

2 oz (60 g) bacon
2 tsp grated lemon rind
hare liver
4 oz (125 g) shredded suet
1 tbsp chopped parsley
1 tbsp mixed sweet herbs (or 1 tsp dried herbs)
a little grated nutmeg
6 oz (175 g) fresh breadcrumbs
salt and pepper
1 egg, beaten

Boil some water in a small saucepan and put in the hare's liver.
Allow to cook for five minutes and set aside. Chop the bacon and
mix with the lemon rind, suet and herbs. Mash the liver and add it
to the mixture with the breadcrumbs and other seasonings, and mix
well, then put in the egg. The mixture should be fairly firm but not
dry. Shape it into balls and fry in butter, or bake them in butter or
lard in the oven for half an hour, turning them once or twice.

(from Raffald, *The Experienced English Housekeeper*, 1789)

ONION PIE

This makes a pleasant lunch or supper dish, or individual pies can
be made as a starter.

1½ lb (750 g) shortcrust pastry
2 medium potatoes
2 medium onions
2 Cox's Orange Pippin or russet apples
2 oz (60 g) butter
½ tsp ground mace
a little freshly grated nutmeg
a few grinds of black peppercorns
1 tsp salt
4 hard-boiled eggs

Set the oven to 350°F/175°C/Gas Mark 4. Peel and slice thinly the potatoes, onions and apples. Slice the eggs. Line a 9-inch pie dish with half the pastry. Beat half the butter with a wooden spoon until it is slightly soft, then spread it on the pastry in the dish. Mix together the spices, salt and pepper. Sprinkle a little of this mixture over the pastry, then arrange the onions, potatoes, apples and eggs in alternate layers, sprinkling a little spice mixture over each layer. Cut the remaining butter into small pieces and lay them on the top then put in 4 tablespoons water. Cover with the rest of the pastry and bake for an hour or until the potatoes are tender.

(from Glasse, *The Art of Cookery made plain and easy*, 1747)

CUCUMBERS WITH EGGS

This is a good little dish for a light meal. Without the poached eggs, it makes an excellent accompaniment for baked salmon or trout, or the roast saddle of mutton above. The liquidity of the sauce must be watched – it should be neither thick nor watery, but smooth and unctuous. Much depends on the juiciness of the cucumbers.

2 cucumbers
1 onion stuck with 1 clove
4 slices back bacon
2 oz (60 g) butter
1 tbsp flour
2 tbsp strong stock or 1 tbsp soy sauce and 1 tbsp water
5 eggs
2 tbsp thick cream
a few drops lemon juice

Peel the cucumbers and cut them into small dice, then blanch them for 2 minutes in boiling water. Take them out of the water and put them in a heavy pan with the bacon, butter and onion. Cover the pan and cook over very low heat for about a quarter of an hour, shaking occasionally. Put the flour in a cup and mix it with the stock or soy sauce and water until there are no lumps. Blend in some of the liquid from the pan, and then return all to the pan and cook over low heat for a few minutes, stirring gently. Take one of the eggs and, having separated off the white, beat the yolk with the cream and set aside. Poach the remaining four eggs. Stir the cream/egg-yolk mixture into the cucumbers, make sure it is hot but do not allow to boil, squeeze in a very little lemon juice, and then put the whole into a heated serving dish. Make four little dents and put the poached eggs in them.

(from Raffald, *The Experienced English Housekeeper*, 1789)

GOOSEBERRY CREAM

In the original recipe, spinach juice is called for and would have been made by pounding a handful of raw spinach in a mortar and then pressing the pulp through a hair sieve. I have substituted food colouring because it is so much easier.

**1 lb (500 g) gooseberries
3 eggs
½ oz (15 g) butter
4–6 oz (125–175 g) sugar
green food colouring
1 tbsp orange-flower water or white wine**

Cook the gooseberries in about 2 tbsp water, covered, over low heat until they are soft. Drain off about half a cup of the liquid and put the pulp through a sieve. Measure the purée – you should have about a pint – and the proportion of eggs to purée is three to a pint. Beat the eggs well and add them to the gooseberries with enough sugar to sweeten, and the butter. Put over a very low heat and stir gently until the mixture thickens. The eggs will curdle if you allow it to boil. Remove from the heat, and when it is almost cold add the colouring and the orange-flower water or wine. Serve in glass dishes with sponge fingers.

(from Glasse, *The Art of Cookery made plain and easy*, 1747)

SNOW AND CREAM

When I was a child, we sometimes had this dessert, which we called Floating Islands. Just before eating we were allowed to sprinkle it with chocolate vermicelli or hundreds-and-thousands, a touch of which I am sure John Farley would have approved. Mrs Raffald gives an alternative version, which she calls Apple Floating Islands, in which the pulp of baked apples is well beaten with sugar and then added to the beaten whites of egg, the whole not cooked at all but gently laid in spoonfuls on the custard.

1 pt (600 ml) whole milk or equal quantities milk and cream
4 eggs
2 oz (60 g) and 1tbsp vanilla-flavoured sugar
¼ tsp cinnamon (optional)
1 tbsp orange-flower water
1 tsp rosewater

Separate the eggs and beat the whites until very stiff, then beat in gradually 1 tbsp sugar. Fold in the rosewater. In a wide saucepan or deep frying pan, bring the milk or milk and cream to a slow boil and then, using a large serving spoon, drop in the egg white in neat spoonfuls. Poach them for 1–2 minutes, then remove them and put them carefully in a wide glass dish. Remove the milk/cream from the heat and stir in the sugar until dissolved, and the cinnamon, if liked. Beat the egg yolks with the orange-flower water (this helps to prevent the cream from separating). When the milk is cool, pour it gently into the egg yolks, beating as you do so, and then return to the heat. Stir it carefully in one direction only until it thickens and is almost, but not quite, boiling. Then gently pour it into the dish with the 'islands', which will rise as you do so. Garnish just before serving.

(from Farley, *The London Art of Cookery*, 1783)

APPLE DUMPLINGS

This traditional dish, in danger of being forgotten, is too good to sink into oblivion. The original recipe calls for the dumplings to be boiled in a cloth, but baking is easier and just as good.

8 oz (250 g) flour
1 egg yolk
4 oz (125 g) butter, or butter and lard
a pinch of salt
4 good eating apples
4 tsp marmalade, or raisins, or sugar and cinnamon

Set the oven at 400°F/200°C/Gas Mark 6. Make the pastry with the flour, fat, egg yolk, salt and a little water, and put it to rest while you peel and core the apples. Divide the pastry into four equal portions, and roll each piece out thinly. Lay each apple on a piece of pastry and cut out the pastry to come a little more than halfway up the apple. Fill the hollow inside the apple with marmalade or your other chosen filling. Fold the pastry up round the apple and cut another piece to go over the top and come down to overlap the bottom piece. Use a little cold water on the tip of your finger to stick the two pieces together. Bake about 35–40 minutes. Serve with melted butter or cream.

(from Raffald, *The Experienced English Housekeeper*, 1789)

WIGS

Most eighteenth-century cookbooks give recipes for wigs, although they date back to at least 300 years earlier. I am grateful to Alice and Frank Prochaska for permission to use their version of Margaretta Acworth's wigs, which are much spicier and more interesting than Mrs Raffald's, from whom John Farley copied his.

about 12 oz (375 g) wheatmeal flour
4 oz (125 g) strong white bread flour
1 tsp dried yeast
8 fl oz (250 ml) water
¼ tsp sugar
5 oz (150 g) butter or margarine
1 tsp each salt, ground mace, ginger, nutmeg and cloves
1 tbsp caraway seeds
1 tbsp more of sugar
2 eggs
8 fl oz (250 ml) milk

Sift the flours together into a mixing bowl and leave it to stand in a warm place while you dissolve the yeast in the water, which you have heated to blood heat (98.6°F/37°C) with the quarter teaspoon of sugar. Cut the butter or margarine into small pieces and rub it into the flour as you would for pastry, until the mixture is the consistency of fine breadcrumbs. Mix the other dry ingredients including the caraway seeds and extra sugar into the flour. Whisk the eggs, warm the milk to blood heat and when the yeast is frothy mix all the liquid ingredients together and stir them into the flour mixture. Knead the dough until it is soft, adding a little more warm milk or a little extra flour as necessary to make it smooth and malleable. Cover the bowl with a cloth and leave it in a warm place to rise for 30 minutes. Shape the dough into two round, flat buns, score them into wedges with a sharp knife, and bake on floured baking trays at 400°F/200°C/Gas Mark 6, for about 30 minutes.

Chapter 5

CHARLES DICKENS

It was a nice little dinner – seemed to me then, a
very Lord Mayor's Feast – and it acquired
additional relish from being eaten under those
independent circumstances, with no old people
by, and with London all around us.

Great Expectations, Chapter 22

Dickens was just seven years older than Queen Victoria, and
beginning to make his name, when she came to the throne in
1837 at the age of eighteen. He had already published *Sketches by Boz*
and had just embarked on the book which first brought him an
adoring public, *The Pickwick Papers*. He was thus contemporary with
the Victorian age, of which his books may be taken as a fair
representation.

He was born in Portsmouth on 7 February 1812, the son of an
improvident dreamer who worked as a clerk in the Navy Office.
When Charles was ten years old, his parents moved to Camden
Town in London where, crammed into a small depressing house in
Bayham Street with six children, a maid and a lodger, they struggled

with mounting debts. One of their first economies was to take Charles away from school – an act for which he never forgave them.

At first, he used his free time to read the books which remained to the family from a happier period; when the day came that the books had to be sold, he spent many hours exploring the streets of London. An impressionable and sensitive child, he retained and later put to good use the images of poverty, squalor and deprivation he saw on his wanderings.

His freedom was short-lived. Two days after his twelfth birthday, he was sent out to work: twelve hours a day in Warren's boot-blacking factory at Hungerford Stairs, below the Strand. Had he come from a working-class background it would have been nothing unusual, but for young Charles the experience was profoundly disturbing. He who had always been decently dressed, spoke educated English, knew some Latin and had a passion for learning suddenly became, in his own words, 'a poor little drudge, penetrated with grief and humiliation', without a word of sympathy from anyone. Worse still, his father was soon afterwards committed to the Marshalsea prison in Southwark for debt. While most of the family moved into the prison, Charles went into lodgings in Lant Street, Southwark, in the back attic of a house now demolished. It was then that he acquired his intimate knowledge of the backstreets and slums of the district, used to such good effect in *Little Dorrit*; the slums have gone, but Lant Street still exists and Dickens is commemorated in the names of new streets such as Copperfield Street (west of Southwark Bridge Road) and Little Dorrit Court and Pickwick Street (between Southwark Bridge Road and the Borough High Street).

Luckily, within a few months, a small legacy helped John Dickens pay his debts. He was released, and eventually Charles was enrolled in a new school in Hampstead Road. Thus ended the blacking factory episode; five months of unremitted nightmare, too painful ever to speak of save once in adult life, to a close friend. Twenty-five years later, not even Dickens' family guessed that the wine warehouse episode in *David Copperfield* was founded on the author's own experiences.

Within three years, improvidence had again put the family into difficulties. This time, Charles was apprenticed as office boy in a legal firm. Bored, he taught himself shorthand and when he had mastered it, set up as a freelance reporter of court cases. Bored again, he was delighted to be asked to take down the debates in the House of Commons. Here he excelled and by the age of eighteen was entrusted with the most difficult debates and was earning well, for he was able to sell his parliamentary reports to several papers.

But his ambitions went beyond reporting. In 1833, a newspaper accepted his first sketch of London life and he was asked for more. Soon, *Sketches by Boz* appeared every week in the *Morning Chronicle* and led to a commission to write twenty comic episodes to be published in instalments. The result was *The Pickwick Papers*, which began its career in March 1836. Once the character of Sam Weller had been introduced, it took the reading public by storm. People queued for each new issue and copies were passed from hand to hand so that the whole nation seemed spellbound by the doings of the Pickwick Club. Charles Dickens had become a household name.

Marriage to Kate Hogarth, the daughter of a publisher, meant a move from his bachelor quarters at Furnivals Inn, Holborn (now demolished), to a more fashionable address. No. 48 Doughty Street is now Dickens House and a museum, and although the family lived there for only two years, it was there that *The Pickwick Papers* was finished, *Oliver Twist* and *Nicholas Nickleby* written, and *Barnaby Rudge* begun. Marriage also brought children and domestic happiness, marred by the sudden death of a beloved sister-in-law who lived with the family. After an initial depression, Dickens seems to have found in grief a source of creativity. Over the next few years, novels, stories and sketches poured from his hand. His success was enormous and his energy prodigious. Several times a week, he walked twenty miles or more through the streets of London or in the country around Broadstairs, where the family often went for a short holiday. The topography of all his novels was carefully researched on these walks, with the result that while actual buildings can rarely be identified, streets often can, and districts are always accurately depicted. So much has changed in the last fifty years that it would be wrong to expect now to find much remaining of the London Dickens knew, but in the early years of the twentieth century, a favourite pastime of Dickens-lovers was identifying locations described in the novels. The Red Lion pub in Whitehall, for example, has been rebuilt since Dickens' day; it was at another bar that he stood, a timid twelve-year-old, asking for a glass of 'your best – your *very best* Genuine Stunning'. But although the building is not the same, the site's connection with the author of *David Copperfield* has not been forgotten, and a bust of Dickens sits above the second window. Sad to say, the Old Curiosity Shop in Portsmouth Street near Lincoln's Inn Fields, while undoubtedly the oldest surviving shop in London, has a very dubious claim to being the original of the story.

In 1842, Dickens went for the first time, with Kate and a friend, to the United States. Until he made a speech in Boston criticising the lack of an American law on copyright (through which he himself had lost thousands of pounds), the tour was a great success. By July, the Dickenses were back in London, to a new house (now demolished) in Devonshire Terrace; the rest of the year was spent writing up the American experiences and planning *Martin Chuzzlewit*, which came out the following year in instalments. Christmas 1843 saw the publication of *A Christmas Carol*.

The Chimes and *Dombey and Son* were written under more stress than usual. Five children and a lavish standard of living (all his life he loved to be surrounded by friends and to put on splendid parties) put a heavy strain on his earnings, and his marriage was not going well. He found Kate clumsy and dull, unable to keep up with his quick mind and changeable spirit. She, frightened and depressed by his brilliance, thought him demanding and selfish. Once again, stress encouraged creativity, and in February 1849, he began *David Copperfield*, arguably his finest novel, neatly interweaving autobiography and fiction. Because he put in it so much of his own childhood, he later said that he could never approach it with absolute composure, 'it had such perfect possession of me when I wrote it'. Its success was immediate and phenomenal.

Meanwhile, he was editing a popular weekly miscellany, *Household Words*, and cajoling his prominent friends to appear in or attend lavish amateur theatricals which he delighted in producing. Profits from benefit performances went to help impoverished writers and artists.

Tavistock House, Tavistock Square (now the home of the British Medical Association), was his last London home. Here he wrote *Bleak House*, which, despite grim scenes and often savage satire of England's legal system, sold particularly well. 'I have never had so many readers,' he wrote delightedly. It was followed by *Hard Times* and then by *Little Dorrit*, in which he attacked another topic he knew at first hand, imprisonment for debt.

Through his theatricals, Dickens had met a charming eighteen-year-old actress, Ellen Ternan. A separation from his wife followed.

Rumour, scandal and speculation were inevitable, and Dickens exhausted himself issuing explicit statements, counter-accusations and denials. He also began to work harder than ever, for he now had to support his wife, his family, his mistress and his mistress's family. *A Tale of Two Cities* was followed by *Great Expectations*, which ranks with *David Copperfield* as his finest work.

He had also (in 1859) begun to give public readings from his novels, which he enjoyed, for he had the ability to move an audience to tears or laughter as he wished. His health, however, was beginning to fail. He suffered from gout and his heart was not good. His children were causing him distress and worry. Altogether, life was becoming unpleasant and difficult, and even his writing was slowing down. He did not begin *Our Mutual Friend* until 1864, three years after finishing *Great Expectations*. It was his last complete work.

His readings, attracting enormous crowds, were by now being given in the United States as well as at home. The murder of Nancy in Oliver Twist was one of his most accomplished performances and although audiences reacted with near-hysteria, it was always in demand. Each reading totally exhausted him. At length, in March 1870, he took the advice of his doctors, his friends and his manager, and gave up the readings.

A new novel, *The Mystery of Edwin Drood*, was in production, each fresh instalment from Gad's Hill (the large house near Rochester to which he had moved) creating a new sales record. But he was obviously very unwell. At dinner on 8 June, he fell when trying to rise from the table. Next day, he died in the presence of his sister-in-law Georgina Hogarth, Ellen Ternan and several of his children.

Although almost one hundred years separate the death of Johnson from that of Dickens, only twenty-eight years passed between Johnson's death and Dickens' birth. The London of 1812, however, was already very different from that of 1784, and as the nineteenth century advanced and change accelerated, the gap between the Georgian city and the Victorian grew wider even than that between Chaucer's city and Shakespeare's. In all its most commonplace aspects, London life altered almost out of recognition, and London food altered with it.

The cause was the Industrial Revolution; we have a first-hand account of many of its effects in George Dodd's *The Food of London*, written in 1856. Dodd studied every aspect of the capital's food supply, from production techniques to marketing – motivated, he tells us, by remarks in an American book called *The Attaché, or Sam Slick in England*, which had appeared in 1843–4. Sam Slick had no good opinion of London food:

> Veal, to be good, must look like anythin' else than veal; you mustn't know it when you see it, or it's vulgar. Mutton must be incog. too. Beef must have a mask on. Anythin' that looks solid, take a spoon to; anythin' that looks light, cut with a knife. If a thing looks like fish, you may take your oath it is flesh; and if it seems rael flesh, it's only disguised, for it's sure to be fish. Nothin' must be nateral; nater is out of fashion here. This is a manufacturin' country; everythin' is done by machinery; and that that ain't must be made to look like it.

Dodd aimed to get the facts about food in its natural state, as it came into London. His book's strength does not lie in statistics; as he points out, it was very difficult to assess how much of what came in was actually consumed in the city. The interest lies in the picture of a culture in mid-development. Through Dodd's eyes we can see, for example, how the discovery of steam power transformed London diet. Fast transport facilities did not just mean fresher goods. 'Double the speed,' as Dodd explained, 'and you increase four-fold the area of country from whence provisions can be sent in a given time to London.' The first railway line, from London Bridge to Deptford, opened in 1836. Next came long-distance lines to the North, the Midlands and the West Country, each company building its own stations. To the nineteenth century, these epitomised the ideals and advances of the age, as monasteries and cathedrals had done 600 years earlier, and this was also true of the railhead markets to which many were linked, for Londoners were as proud of the city's trading status as they had ever been. The London and North East Railway Company set up King's Cross potato market in 1865, 15 years after the opening of the station itself. Within a year, it was handling 85,000 tons of potatoes daily, from Lincolnshire, Yorkshire, Cambridgeshire and Scotland. King's Cross was also the railhead for fish from Scotland and the North-east, and a depot for rhubarb, green peas and celery from East Anglia. In like manner, the Great Midland Railway Company built Somers Town market, which handled vegetables, next to St Pancras Station.

Steam power also revolutionised sea transport, and quite quickly the value of linking steamships and railway lines was recognised. For example, when lucrative oyster beds were discovered between the English coast and the Channel Islands, fast steamers brought the molluscs to Brighton within a few hours; within a few more, courtesy of the Brighton Railway Company, they were in Billingsgate. No one foresaw that steam power would thus contribute to a complete reversal of gastronomic mores. 'It's a wery remarkable circumstance, sir,' Sam Weller had said to Mr Pickwick in 1836, 'that poverty and oysters always seem to go together . . . Blessed if I don't think that ven a man's wery poor he rushes out of his lodgings, and eats oysters in reg'lar desperation.' But less than twenty years later, it was observed that oysters were scarcer (which made the newly discovered beds even more valuable), and by the end of the century, poor people would have been hard put to it to find the money for even a single oyster.

As with oysters, so with other fish. Lobsters netted off the Brittany or Irish coasts were fattened near Southampton, then brought by screw-steamer direct to London. In this way, a cargo of 20,000 lobsters could reach Billingsgate without damage; a good salesman could sell 15,000 lobsters in a morning, so great was the demand from private houses, restaurants and clubs. In *Dombey and Son*, even the servants, on the occasion of Mr Dombey's marriage to Edith Skewton, breakfast on champagne, roast fowl and lobster salad. But only the more fragile fish came all the way by boat; more commonly the fishermen put their catch ashore at a port such as Yarmouth or Lowestoft, where it was packed into hampers and loaded onto an overnight train for the 5 a.m. market at Billingsgate. By the 1850s, nearly half the fish for London travelled up by rail, and Billingsgate had become one of the sights recommended for both Londoners and tourists. A writer for the *Quarterly Review* described some of its stock-in-trade: gigantic Scotch or Irish salmon, delicate red mullet from Cornwall, opalescent smelts brought in by Dutch boats, pyramids of lobsters, 'a moving mass of spiteful claws and restless feelers, savage at their late abduction from some Norwegian fjord', great heaps of pink shrimps, huge white-bellied turbot, and from our own waters the humbler plaice and dabs, all forming a mingled scene of strange shapes and vivid colours.

If steam power brought larger quantities of fresher food more quickly into London, that was not its only function. In effect, it changed marketing. The meat trade is a prime example. It had long been felt that to have a live meat market at Smithfield threatened public hygiene; moreover, at certain seasons, traffic in the narrow streets of central London became completely clogged by the mass movement of 30,000 or so animals and their drovers. The advent of the railways allowed a new live meat market to be built at North Islington and opened officially in 1855 by Prince Albert. Newgate Shambles were demolished and resurrected as Paternoster Square. Smithfield was closed, rebuilt, and reopened for the sale of dead meat only in 1868. Country-killed meat could now reach London by rail in a matter of hours. The effect on the city's health may be imagined, once the underground abattoirs, whose stink rose to the crowded streets and whose detritus trickled dangerously through rotting wooden sewers to the Thames, were abolished.

Fruit and vegetable supplies too were transformed by faster transport; items which a few years before had been difficult to get became almost commonplace. Others were much cheaper. Luxuries poured in. In the huge, specially built warehouses in Botolph and Pudding lanes, floor upon floor was piled and heaped and blocked up with chests, boxes, sacks, baskets and parcels of grapes, chestnuts, pineapples, walnuts, hazelnuts and citrus fruits.

Covent Garden remained the principal fruit and vegetable market, despite its distance from railhead depots. The inadequate and ramshackle sheds of previous centuries had been replaced by a custom-built hall, with a central section for the shops selling choice fruit and flowers. Here, horsepower and human backs still had their part to play. In one of the *Sketches by Boz*, Dickens describes how the streets leading to the Garden, faintly tinged with the light of the rising sun, gradually resumed their daytime animation:

> Market-carts roll slowly along: the sleepy waggoner impatiently urging on his tired horses, or vainly endeavouring to awaken the boy, who, luxuriously stretched on the top of the fruit-baskets, forgets, in happy oblivion, his long-cherished curiosity to behold the wonders of London . . . little deal tables, with the ordinary preparations for a street breakfast, make their appearance . . . Numbers of men and women (principally the latter), carrying upon their heads heavy baskets of fruit, toil down the park side of Piccadilly, on their way to Covent Garden, and, following each other in rapid

succession, form a long straggling line from thence to the turn of the road at Knightsbridge . . . Covent Garden market, and the avenues leading to it, are thronged with carts of all sorts, sizes, and descriptions, from the heavy lumbering waggon, with its four stout horses, to the jingling costermonger's cart, with its consumptive donkey.

According to Dodd, during the strawberry season the fruit-pickers in the fields of Isleworth, Brentford, Ealing, Hammersmith, Fulham and Mortlake loaded their punnets into baskets weighing from thirty to forty pounds and with these on their heads, travelled at a smooth trot, keeping up a pace of about five miles an hour, all the way to the market. The erect posture adopted by the girls to keep the baskets steady made them much admired.

Fifty or so years later, the 'milk train' would become for Londoners the very symbol of early-morning activity, but initially milk supplies were little affected by the coming of the railway. After some public outcry in the eighteenth century, the most unhygienic practices were phasing out; dairymen now made a selling point of the hygiene and purity of their product. The number of street cows was falling anyway (though one was still being milked on street corners in Stepney in 1900). In 1829, a pamphlet lambasting unventilated cowhouses and neglected animals was published by William Harley, who achieved royal patronage for his own business. With native entrepreneurial skill (he came from Glasgow), he made a feature of his well-appointed dairy, charging visitors a shilling a head to watch the cows being milked. Quality was what the wealthy middle-class families wanted, and astute dairy firms responded by buying healthy cows with a high milk yield and keeping them in sweet and clean conditions. Often the cows were fed on mash from the breweries. Sometimes breweries themselves set up model herds, as Whitbread's did in Battersea. Waste vegetables from Covent Garden and Spitalfields Market were also used as cattle food, and in summer, the dairymen, many of them small Welsh farmers who had been forced off the land, could still take up the grazing rights on old common lands such as Hackney Marshes, Wanstead Flats, Clapham Common and Victoria Park. Even after railway transport became commonplace, the 'freshness' of London milk gave it the edge over country milk. It was also much in demand in the East End, where Jewish immigrant families wanted to be sure their food was kosher.

Paradoxically, the Age of Steam was also the great age of sail, and until late in the nineteenth century, sailing clippers kept control of trade with the East. One of the most celebrated was the *Cutty Sark*, a beautiful ship made of iron, teak and rock-elm. Fast and easily handled, she was commissioned for the China tea trade in 1869 – ironically the year the Suez Canal was opened. Her fastest voyage to England, in 1871, took just 107 days; but the Canal tolled a death knell for the tea-clippers, and 6 years later, she was transferred to the Australia wool trade.

However, at the time of Dodd's book, a splendid mix of steam and sail crowded the Thames docks. Baron Dupin, one of the French commissioners attending the Great Exhibition of 1851, was amazed at the throng of vessels . . .

> . . . arrayed like an army of giants in transversal ranks, succeeding each other almost without interval for a league in length, and leaving in the middle of the crowded mass a space animated with vessels, either steamers or under sail, which are going to or coming from all quarters of the globe!

Probably most of these vessels carried food of one sort or another. Since 1815, the whole world had been ransacked for the Englishman's table, and the cargoes of the ships Baron Dupin saw might well have included live turtles from the West Indies, chutneys and curry spices from India, hams from Portugal and Westphalia, reindeer tongues from Lapland, olives from France, Italy or Spain, and cheeses from Italy and Switzerland.

It was at this time that the great London grocers made their names and fortunes. Fortnum & Mason, it is true, had already been filling Londoners' larders with delicacies for over one hundred years. In 1707, Mr Mason was a grocer, and Mr Fortnum, his lodger, a royal footman whose special daily duty it was to put new candles into the State rooms. By selling the used candles to the ladies of the Household, Fortnum soon made enough money to go into partnership with his landlord; thus one of London's most famous stores was born. The Court connection brought invaluable custom. By the end of the eighteenth century, Fortnum & Mason were established as purveyors of food to all England's aristocracy. In the nineteenth century, they sold not only groceries but what we now call delicatessen: boned portions of poultry and game in aspic jelly decorated with lobsters and prawns; potted meats; hard-boiled eggs in forcemeat; eggs in brandy-soaked cake with whipped cream; mince pies, savoury patties, and fruits fresh and dried. They were au fait with what was required by an officer on the Peninsular campaign or an administrator in some lonely outpost of Empire. They packed hampers for explorers and tuck-boxes for hungry schoolboys; they sent, at the command of Queen Victoria, 250 lbs of Concentrated Beef Tea to Florence Nightingale in the Crimea; and Dickens, after going to the Derby, declared:

> If I were on the turf, and had a horse to enter for the Derby, I would call that horse Fortnum & Mason, convinced that with that name he would beat the field. Public opinion would bring him in somehow. Look where I will – in some connexion with the carriages – made fast upon the top, or occupying the box, or peeping out of a window – I see Fortnum & Mason. And now, Heavens! All the hampers fly wide open and the green Downs burst into a blossom of lobster-salad!
>
> (*Household Words*, 1851)

Rather different was the development of Harrods. Charles Henry Harrod, a tea merchant, took over a small grocery business in what is now the Brompton Road in 1849. Eleven years later, the shop passed to his son, Charles Digby, a forceful young man determined to expand his business. As a result, by 1867, the shop not only had a new front but was selling patent medicines, perfumery and stationery as well as food. In time, a two-storey extension was built in the back garden, the adjoining shops on either side were bought in, and by 1883, 'Harrod's Stores' was selling a wide range of goods. A severe fire just before Christmas of that year was a setback to trade; but Charles Digby Harrod was not one to be beaten by a mere fire. On the following day he sent out a letter to all customers:

> Madam,
> I greatly regret to inform you, that in consequence of the above premises being burnt down, your order will be delayed in the execution a day or two. I hope, in the course of Tuesday or Wednesday next, to be able to forward it.
> In the meantime may I ask for your kind indulgence.

Your obedient servant,

C.D. Harrod

He was as good as his word; the Christmas trade that year beat all previous records, and the new premises opened in 1884 were bigger and carried a wider range of goods than ever before. By 1894, Harrods was a true department store, with food but one of its many lines.

Different again in conception was the Army & Navy Stores, incorporated as a co-operative society in 1871. The basic idea was to supply shareholders, subscribers and their friends with articles of the highest quality at lower prices than those current in other places. The name makes clear the limitations on membership; in some ways it was as much a club as a shop, and as a co-operative society, it could do much more than any department store. The customer was looked after, if he wished, at every stage of life from infancy to death. The Stores could provide his clothes, medicaments, sporting equipment, house, furniture, coal, food, books, carriage or motor car and at the end, the headstone over his grave. The savings, even on food, were substantial: where crystallised apricots, for instance, cost three shillings in the West End, they cost two shillings at the Stores. It is clear from the catalogues that the highest standards were always aimed at. As a result, the Stores achieved an unusual, and sometimes disconcerting, level of customer loyalty. Almost within living memory is the lady who would only eat Army & Navy bread; every day one loaf was delivered to her – in Brighton.

But amid all the prosperity, while the shops expanded and the warehouses bulged with exotic and delicious comestibles, all was not well with the food trade. The increase in London's population was putting huge strains on the suppliers, and the public was becoming more demanding if less discriminating. Adding to this the factor of human greed, it is easy to understand that food adulteration, which had troubled not a few thoughtful people in the previous century, became a major issue between 1820 and the 1870s.

The matter caught the public eye in 1820, with the appearance of *A Treatise on the Adulterations of Food, and Culinary Poisons*. Its author, Frederick Accum, had come from Germany to work as a pharmacist in London in 1793, quickly establishing his reputation as an experimental chemist and teacher with a particular interest in the composition of foods. By the time he published his treatise, his credentials were impeccable: he was a member of the Royal Irish Academy, Fellow of the Linnean Society, Member of the Royal Academy of Sciences and Member of the Royal Society of Arts of Berlin. His material contained many already published reports from various sources, including the law courts; but by assembling these within a framework of opinion and preceding it all with a fervent plea to Government to enforce laws protecting the consumer, he was striking new ground. Even so, his work might have passed unremarked by the general public but for two things: first, on the dramatic title page was an engraving of an urn wreathed with snakes and surmounted by a grinning skull, with a quotation from the Book of Kings, 'There is Death in the Pot'; second, wherever possible in his text, he actually named London manufacturers and shopkeepers convicted of malicious adulteration. The range of food covered in his book included bread, beer, wine, spiritous liquors, tea, coffee, cream, confectionery, vinegar, mustard, pepper, cheese, olive oil and pickles. Not all the adulterations were deliberate and not all were harmful. Nevertheless, the facts were sensational enough – together with the knowledge that the perpetrators in most cases were still practising their trade – to arouse public terror and indignation. Accum's book sold out in a month and ran through four editions in two years.

Some of the most dangerous deceptions involved the use of lead and copper. Fraudulent wine merchants used lead to clarify spoiled white wine, and red lead was added to inferior cayenne pepper and anchovy sauce. There could be inadvertent contamination too, as where lead shot was used to clean old wine bottles, or Spanish olive oil had been stored by its producers in lead cisterns, or vermilion mixed with red lead had been substituted for anatto to colour Gloucester cheese. As for copper, Accum quoted another scientist:

> Our food receives its quantity of poison in the kitchen by the use of copper pans and dishes. The brewer mingles poison in our beer, by boiling it in copper vessels. The sugar-baker employs copper pans; the pastry-cook bakes our tarts in copper moulds, the confectioner uses copper vessels; the oilman boils his pickles in copper or brass vessels, and verdigrise [sic] is plentifully formed by the action of the vinegar on the metal.

Many London brewers were also deceiving the public, breaking the law by using *Cocculus indicus*, a poisonous drug, as a substitute for malt and hops, and to prevent secondary fermentation in bottled beer. Less perilous but still sometimes harmful to health were illicit substances used to flavour inferior liquor – quassia, coriander, capsicum, ginger and grains of paradise. Alum was often added 'to give a smack of age'. As if these disclosures were not bad enough, Accum went on to publish lists of names: of breweries and brewers' druggists holding illegal ingredients, of druggists and grocers convicted of selling illegal ingredients to brewers, and of publicans convicted of adulterating their wares. Quite naturally, the trade was in an uproar.

Not even there did Accum stop. Transgressors in other fields were also named and their crimes spelled out. Bakers who made their flour go further by adding to it alum and boiled potatoes; grocers who manufactured counterfeit tea leaves from sloe, ash and elder leaves, drying them on copper sheets and actually adding verdigris to produce the right colour; others who ground up beans, peas and grains of sand, mixing it all with a little real coffee to sell under the name of British coffee: all were listed. Accum quoted a grocer's advice to a friend: 'Never, my good fellow, purchase from a grocer any thing which passes through his mill.'

It was not to be expected that the accused would remain passive. Unable to contest the evidence of the courts and the laboratory, they sought to disgrace him on personal grounds, persuading the Royal Institution to bring a trumped-up charge of theft against him because he had apparently cut blank flyleaves from books in the library. Although a magistrate dismissed the case as trivial, another charge, of mutilating the books, was pressed. The smear campaign mounted against him unnerved Accum, and he did not appear when the case came to trial, preferring to forfeit his bail. Soon afterwards, he left Britain and never returned.

But all the efforts of his enemies could not prevent the seed he had planted from growing. It is true that malpractice was hardly less rife in London in the 1850s, when Dodd was writing *The Food of London*, than it had been in 1820. But the matter was only dormant, waiting for a new initiative. It came when the medical journal *The Lancet* decided to take action. In a series of articles no less widely read than Accum's *Treatise* had been, over a period of four years, writers systematically exposed the brick-dust in the chocolate, the vitriol in the beer, the chalk in the milk. As a result, the first Food and Drugs Act came into being in 1860. Ineffective though it was, its very existence demonstrated that Government recognised some responsibility and it was replaced in 1872 by an amended version with far wider scope and powers.

Accum was but one of many thousands of foreigners who wished to settle in Britain. Throughout the century, their number swelled, for London had long been a refuge for the displaced and homeless. Earlier had come successive waves of Huguenots, then émigrés fleeing the French Revolution. Now, in addition to Jewish refugees from Eastern Europe and Russia, two of the largest groups were Irishmen and Italians forced from their homes by famine. The Italians became street vendors or musicians, or worked as waiters. Most of the Irish laboured on the roads or railways whose construction was tearing up whole districts of the city and replacing old slums with new ones.

That Dickens, in *Dombey and Son*, saw the railway as a beneficent agent of slum-clearance is hardly surprising. In *Sketches by Boz*, written just one year before the Queen's accession, he had grimly spelt out the conditions under which some of her future subjects lived. In the area between Tottenham Court Road and Drury Lane, roughly where New Oxford Street is now, lay the district known as 'The Rookery':

> Wretched houses with broken windows patched with rags and paper: every room let out to a different family, and in many instances to two or even three – fruit and 'sweet-stuff' manufacturers in the cellars, barbers and red-herring vendors in the front parlours, cobblers in the back; a bird-fancier on the first floor, three families on the second, starvation in the attics, Irishmen in the passage, a 'musician' in the front kitchen, and a char-woman and five hungry children in the back one – filth everywhere – a gutter before the houses and a drain behind – clothes drying and slops emptying from the windows; girls of fourteen or fifteen, with matted hair, walking about barefoot, and in white greatcoats, almost their only covering; boys of all ages, in coats of all sizes and no coats at all; men and women, in every variety of scanty and dirty apparel, lounging, scolding, drinking, smoking, squabbling, fighting, and swearing.

Such descriptions of the poorest parts of London can be found in most of his books. What he did not properly realise was that those displaced by the railways, too poor to move to the pleasant new suburbs being built on the outskirts of the city, went to some other part of inner London and turned *that* into a slum. Land enclosure and agricultural reform were still forcing people off the land and into the towns; the return of soldiers at the end of the Napoleonic Wars added to the numbers looking for work; and the early stages of industrialisation were creating violent fluctuations of employment. Napoleon had jibed that England was a nation of shopkeepers, and London more than ever was Europe's warehouse. But in the unsettled post-war period, there were times when some markets were closed to British goods, or when the supply of raw materials failed. Then especially, the urban poor suffered, as thousands of able-bodied men, women and children struggled to find work, food and shelter. To make matters worse, during the war years, home-grown wheat had risen in price, bringing prosperity to the farmers but making bread very dear. After Waterloo, with foreign wheat once again available, prices fell sharply, and a protectionist Parliament (composed largely of farming landlords) passed the unpopular Corn Laws preventing the import of cheap foreign wheat. From earliest times, bread had been a staple food, especially for the working class. Now some could no longer afford it; like the Irish, they turned to potatoes. Engels, in his *Condition of the Working Class in England* (1844) gives us precise information about the diet of the poor:

> The better-paid workers, especially those in whose families every member is able to earn something, have good food as long as this state of things lasts; meat daily, and bacon and cheese for supper. Where wages are less, meat is used only two or three times a week, and the proportion of bread and potatoes increases. Descending gradually, we find the animal food reduced to a small piece of bacon cut up with the potatoes; lower still, even this disappears, and there remains only bread, cheese, porridge and potatoes, until, on the lowest round of the ladder, among the Irish, potatoes form the sole food.

The weekly wage needed by a London workman to support a wife and five children was estimated at thirty shillings. Deducting money for rent, fuel, candles and laundry necessaries (soap, blue for whitening the clothes, starch and soda), what remained hardly bought luxuries: a little meat, a little bacon, some herrings; sixpence went on green or root vegetables, and one shilling and sixpence on eighteen pounds of potatoes. The major item of food was twelve loaves of bread. Besides these, one and a half pounds of butter, three pounds of sugar and a little tea and coffee comprised the family's purchases.

Such people would be among Engels' better-paid workers. Their life was precarious and vulnerable should they be visited by illness or death. The survey from which this is taken also cited a widow with four children whose income came from charing and brush-making. Paying three shillings a week rent and earning a maximum of five shillings and eight pence, she was forced to buy provisions daily according to what she had in hand; in one week the family bought potatoes for two and a half pence, bacon for two pence, tea and sugar for two pence, and one loaf. In addition, it received five loaves from the parish.

This family was on the verge of destitution, but many others were even worse off. Mayhew's *London Labour and the London Poor*, published in 1862, shocked its readers with 'a picture of London life so wonderful, so awful, so piteous and pathetic, so exciting and terrible' – to quote *Punch* – 'that readers of romances own they never read anything like to it'. But Mayhew was not romancing. Stories like that of the little watercress-seller, eight years old, who before dawn every day bought and bunched her wares with frozen fingers at Farringdon Market, then trudged the streets until all was sold, were not exceptional. This child got her breakfast – two slices of bread and butter and a cup of tea – after her work was done. She had no dinner, and tea was the same as breakfast. Her mother had the same, and, she thought, was very good to her – 'she don't often beat me.' Two sisters aged fifteen and eleven had kept themselves since the death of their mother when the eldest was eight. They sold flowers which they bought at Covent Garden, and sometimes oranges. They lived on bread and tea, and an occasional fresh herring. Sometimes they had to use their stock-money to buy bread, and then their landlady lent them a shilling to get the next day's flowers.

Society was not altogether unheeding; the fact that surveys were being made, and that Dickens and Mayhew were setting down their indignation for all to read, is evidence of that. Throughout the century, the condition of the poor was a continuing, if unresolved, topic for debate in both Houses. Outside Parliament too, wealthy people took up the subject. Some confined their interest to castigating the improvidence of the working classes and their reprehensible liking for alcohol, strong tea and sugar. Others advocated teaching them how to make cheap, nourishing soups – forgetting that, had they fuel to cook with, they might work it out for themselves. There was also much private charity.

Recipe books from the first half of the nineteenth century frequently include advice on feeding the poor. The following, from *The New London Cookery, adapted to the use of Private Families*, by S.W. (1836) is representative:

> Nothing should be thrown away. The boiling of meat, however salt, might, with the addition of vegetables, bones, and bits of meat collected from the plates, with rice, barley, oatmeal, or grits that have been boiled, &c., stewed for a length of time, be the means of affording nourishment for the poor families who have neither the fuel nor time to dress it for themselves.
>
> Fish bones, heads, and fins, all afford great nourishment. After the fish is served, let part of the liquor be put by; the bones, head, &c., bits collected from the plates, as likewise any gravy that may be left. Boiled together it makes a very nice broth, with the addition of a little rice flour rubbed smooth, and seasoned with pepper, salt, and an onion. When strained it is a great improvement to meat soups, particularly for the sick.
>
> The fat should never be taken from anything, as it affords nourishment, and the poor prefer it.

S.W.'s recipes are not ungenerous – a 'baked soup' contains a pound of meat, with vegetables, rice and split peas, while 'A good wholesome Pudding' is made of rice, milk, sugar or treacle, and dripping. 'Brewis' was a rather less generous dish, and certainly less nutritious:

> Cut a thick upper crust of bread, and put it into the pot where salt beef is boiling, and nearly ready; it will attract some of the fat; and, when swelled out, will be very palatable to those who seldom taste meat.

Another writer, Mrs Rundell (whose very popular *New System of Domestic Cookery* S.W. largely plagiarised), calculated that if ten wealthy London families each made ten gallons of soup daily, forty poor families could by this means be fed at minimum cost. In cities, this kind of charity was sometimes practised on a larger scale with the setting-up of soup kitchens. No wonder that, as Sir Jack Drummond remarked in *The Englishman's Food*, there is to this day an association in the English mind between soup and pauperism.

S.W. and Mrs Rundell wrote for the middle classes, and both were scornful of their own generation. 'There was a time when ladies knew nothing *beyond* their own family concerns; but in the present day there are many who know nothing *about* them,' lamented S.W. 'Generally speaking,' wrote Mrs Rundell, 'there is a universal distaste among the educated classes of the female community of England to the details of housekeeping.' The literature of the century bears this out, with Mrs Bennet in *Pride and Prejudice* (1813) expressing indignation when Mr Collins asks her 'to which of his fair cousins the excellence of [the dinner's] cookery was owing'. Mrs Bennet 'assured him with some asperity that they were very well able to keep a good cook, and that her daughters had nothing to do in the kitchen'. Both S.W. and Mrs Rundell stress the importance of thrift and living within one's income, which could only be achieved by a thorough knowledge of domestic affairs.

It is at this moment that we see the gap – smaller in past centuries, a mere crack – begin to widen between the cookery of France and that of England. Some observers have thought that the rise of Puritanism caused the first split in gastronomic values; others believe that the move off the land into the cities was to blame, because it distanced the consumer from the producer. Probably both trends, and Francophobia besides, caused Britain to take her own culinary path. Perhaps also the Napoleonic Wars, which enriched some but ruined many, brought home to ordinary people just how vulnerable economically an island can be. It is certainly noticeable that many Victorian recipe books stress thrift and economy with very little regard to quality. A seventeenth-century French writer had informed his readers that 'Messieurs your husbands will exert themselves in vain to amass wealth if you do not spent it prudently'; the message, it appears, crossed the Channel, where it found a more enthusiastic audience than in its place of origin.

In pre-Revolutionary France, court cookery had become ever

more lavish and more complex, a concentrated search for subtle flavourings and delicate textures at whatever cost. The food of the wealthy middle class had a similarly sensual approach in its emphasis on the quality and freshness of ingredients, although the sauces were less recherché and extravagant. Surprisingly perhaps, the Revolution and the Napoleonic Wars did not destroy French gastronomy, although many cooks from aristocratic houses emigrated to Britain, bringing their methods with them. It is only fair to say that their approach did influence cooking in those great English houses where patriotism was less important than 'minding one's belly'. Coming from an environment of refined extravagance, their recipes were, and were intended to be, expensive. The new English employers, as Barbara Ketcham Wheaton says (*Savouring the Past*, 1983), were often more interested in the prestige connected with employing an expensive French cook than in understanding that cook's food, so that French methods and aims remained obscure. We have seen Mrs Hannah Glasse's Francophobia at work in the previous chapter, but even she 'borrowed' some recipes word for word from the French. Inevitably, there was a backlash in public opinion, with curious results. While simplicity and thrift led the list of virtues among those who thought of themselves as true, honest John Bulls, the same people acquired a muddled notion that food at dinner parties, banquets and in restaurants must be complicated to be worth paying for. The combination of these two ideas led to the worst possible kind of cooking, in which thrift is exercised in the preparation of complicated dishes made from cheap ingredients.

But it would be wrong to think that all middle-class Victorian food was of this type. Much was both lavish and delicious, and the worst that can be said is that it is caught in a time warp, still relying on heavy sauces and high seasoning for its effect. The Victorians were deeply interested in food, as anyone can see who reads Dickens carefully. *The Pickwick Papers* is probably the work which has most references to food, but in all the novels meals are meticulously detailed, sometimes with gusto, sometimes almost tenderly. Among so many, it is impossible to make rational choice, but here are three fine examples:

> 'I think, young woman,' said Mrs Gamp to the assistant
> chambermaid, in a tone expressive of weakness, 'that I could
> pick a little bit of pickled salmon, with a nice little sprig of

fennel, and a sprinkling of white pepper. I takes new bread, my dear, with just a little pat of fresh butter, and a mossel of cheese. In case there should be such a thing as a cowcumber in the 'ouse, will you be so kind as bring it, for I'm rather partial to 'em, and they does a world of good in a sick room. If they draws the Brighton Old Tipper here, I takes *that* ale at night, my love; it bein' considered wakeful by the doctors.'

(*Martin Chuzzlewit*, Chapter 25)

Mrs Crupp said, 'Don't say that; oysters was in, why not them?' So *that* was settled. Mrs Crupp then said that what she would recommend would be this. A pair of hot roast fowls – from the pastry-cook's; a dish of stewed beef, with vegetables – from the pastry-cook's; two little corner things, as a raised pie and a dish of kidneys – from the pastry-cook's; a tart, and (if I liked) a shape of jelly – from the pastry-cook's. This, Mrs Crupp said, would leave her at full liberty to concentrate her mind on the potatoes, and to serve up the cheese and celery as she could wish to see it done.

(*David Copperfield*, Chapter 24)

'May the present moment,' said Dick, sticking his fork into a large carbuncular potato, 'be the worst of our lives! I like this plan of sending 'em with the peel on; there's a charm in drawing a potato from its native element (if I may so express it) to which the rich and powerful are strangers.'

(*The Old Curiosity Shop*, Chapter 8)

For further Dickensian menus we may turn not to his own writings, but to a short book published in 1865, with an unusually straightforward title. The author of *What shall we have for Dinner?*, Lady Maria Clutterbuck, reflecting in her preface on 'a surplusage of cold mutton or a redundancy of chops . . . making the Club more attractive than the Home, and rendering "business in the city" of more frequent occurrence than it used to be' in the homes of her acquaintance, has produced Bills of Fare for varying numbers of diners, from two or three to twenty persons, with a short appendix of recipes. All, she tells us, met with the approval of 'the late Sir Jonas Clutterbuck' – a somewhat poignant statement in the eyes of a twentieth-century reader, for Lady Maria Clutterbuck was none other than Kate Dickens, and the book was published but two years before her separation from her husband.

What relation the menus bore to the Dickens' diet, one can only conjecture, but they make interesting reading. Those designed for two or three persons are economical and of domestic character. A first course of fish or soup is usually followed by meat and two veg, after which comes a pudding or a savoury, or sometimes both. Mutton is the predominant meat, most often roasted but sometimes minced, occasionally in a haricot, and sometimes also served cold. Only once is it reheated in a hash – disappointing to those who know Dickens' letter to a five-year-old reader of *Nicholas Nickleby*:

> Nicholas had his roast lamb as you said he was to, but he could not eat it all, and says if you do not mind his doing so he should like to have the rest hashed tomorrow with some greens, which he is very fond of, and so am I.

It is this first section which gives most insight into middle-class domestic diet of the period, and undoubtedly it contains some oddities. What an extraordinary fondness the 'Clutterbucks' had for mashed potatoes! There are fewer steamed puddings than one might expect; in their place we find sweet omelettes, tarts, cheesecakes and apple fritters, and this, we know, reflects Dickens' taste. But what is one to make of the raspberry jam sandwiches? To modern eyes, too, many of the savouries seem rather extraordinary: no less than thirteen meals in this section end with macaroni after the pudding. Strewed cheese and bloaters also come up frequently. On the whole, though, meals are appetising and well balanced, for example:

Pickled Salmon
Stewed rump steak French beans Potatoes
Rice and Apples
Toasted Cheese Radishes and Spring Onions
Broiled Salmon Shrimp Sauce
Roast Fillet of Beef, stuffed Cauliflower
Potatoes
Baked Bread-and-Butter Pudding
Cheese Water Cresses

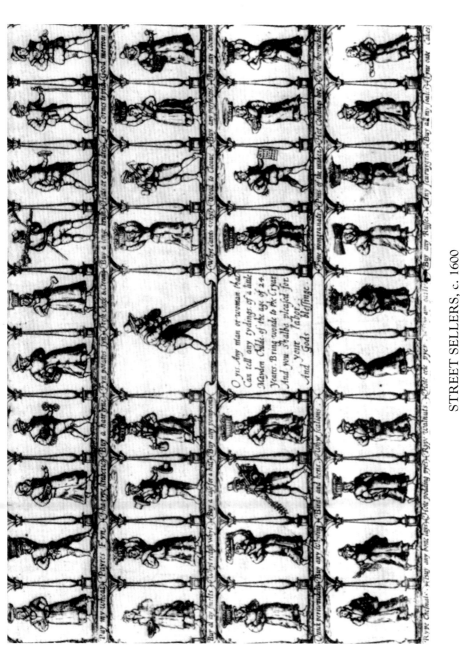

STREET SELLERS, c. 1600

Late in the sixteenth century, prints showing itinerant traders in different European cities became very popular. This is one of the earliest extant series of *Cries of London*. (© Copyright the Trustees of the British Museum)

Top: A LONDON WATER-CARRIER
The *album amicorum* was an early form of autograph book, whose
owner requested friends or famous artists to illustrate it. The blind
water-carrier with his little dog seems to have been a favourite subject.
(By kind permission of Edinburgh University Library)

Above: FISH ALL ALIVE-O!
Some fishwives kept live fish in a tub of water, to be killed and gutted
only when selected by the customer. (By kind permission of B.T. Batsford)

Opposite page: THE LONDON OF PEPYS AND EVELYN
Map by John Oliver, c. 1680.
(By kind permission of the Guildhall Library, London)

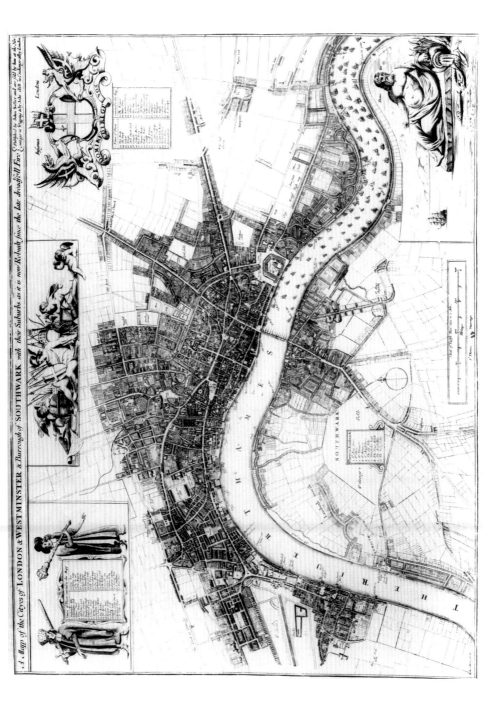

A Mapp of the Cityes of LONDON & WESTMINSTER & Burrough of SOUTHWARK with their Suburbs as it is now Re-built since the late dreadfull Fire

Right: PREPARING A
SEVENTEENTH-
CENTURY DINNER
PARTY
From the title page of *The
Gentlewoman's Delight in
Cookery*. (By courtesy of the
Pepys Library, Magdalene
College, Cambridge)

Below: A LITERARY
PARTY AT SIR JOSHUA
REYNOLDS' HOUSE.
Johnson is the second
figure from the left and
Boswell is sitting behind
him. (Reproduced by
courtesy of the Trustees of
the Dr. Johnson's House
Trust)

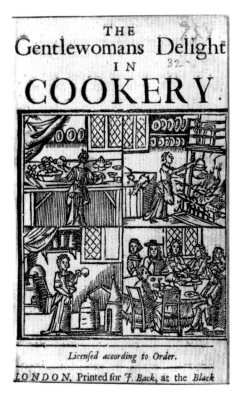

THE
Gentlewomans Delight
IN 32
COOKERY.

Licenfed according to Order.

LONDON, Printed for *J. Back*, at the *Black*

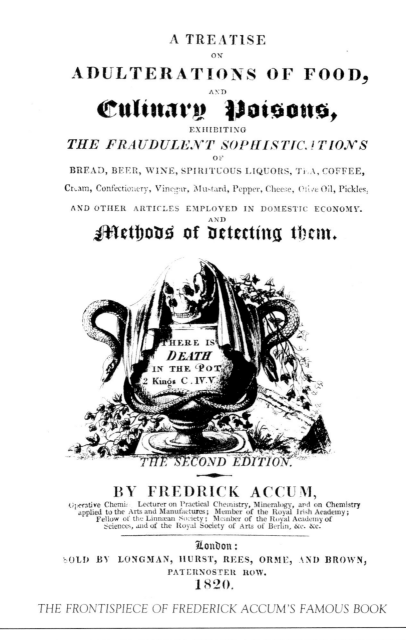

A TREATISE

ON

ADULTERATIONS OF FOOD,

AND

Culinary Poisons,

EXHIBITING

THE FRAUDULENT SOPHISTICATIONS

OF

BREAD, BEER, WINE, SPIRITUOUS LIQUORS, TEA, COFFEE,

Cream, Confectionery, Vinegar, Mustard, Pepper, Cheese, Olive Oil, Pickles,

AND OTHER ARTICLES EMPLOYED IN DOMESTIC ECONOMY.

AND

Methods of Detecting them.

THERE IS
DEATH
IN THE POT
2 Kings C . IV. V.

THE SECOND EDITION.

BY FREDRICK ACCUM,

Operative Chemist Lecturer on Practical Chemistry, Mineralogy, and on Chemistry
applied to the Arts and Manufactures; Member of the Royal Irish Academy;
Fellow of the Linnæan Society; Member of the Royal Academy of
Sciences, and of the Royal Society of Arts of Berlin, &c. &c.

London:

SOLD BY LONGMAN, HURST, REES, ORME, AND BROWN,
PATERNOSTER ROW.

1820.

THE FRONTISPIECE OF FREDERICK ACCUM'S FAMOUS BOOK

THE FRONTISPIECE OF FREDERICK ACCUM'S FAMOUS BOOK

Above: ALEXIS SOYER SHOWING VISITORS ROUND THE KITCHENS OF THE REFORM CLUB (By kind permission of the Directors of the Reform Club)

Far Left: BILLINGSGATE FISH PORTERS, 1920, BY FRANK BRANGWYN.
The strain of balancing the heavy boxes clearly shows on the men's faces. (By courtesy of the Museum of London)

Left: FISH ALL ALIVE-O! (TWENTIETH CENTURY STYLE)
Robert Cooke in the kitchen of his eel-and-pie shop, Broadway Market, 1989. (Photograph by Andy Faulds)

RULES: THE DICKENS ROOM AND THE RESTAURANT'S EXTERIOR. (both © Gary Alexander/Rules)

used the pseudonym Meg Dods; the Macaroni served as a savoury turns out to be, as one had feared, macaroni cheese. But there is also a delicious-sounding Queen's Pudding made from eggs and cream, and a very medieval Mayonnaise: 'A cold roast fowl divided into quarters, young lettuce cut in quarters and placed on the dish with salad dressing, eggs boiled hard and cut in quarters, placed round the dish as a garnish; capers and anchovies are sometimes added.'

Lady Clutterbuck's thoughtful menus are let down by conservative and somewhat uneven recipes. No such criticism can be levelled at what is probably the best Victorian cookbook, Miss Eliza Acton's *Modern Cookery for Private Families*, published in 1845.

Modern Cookery set new standards of clarity, explicitness and, above all, expression of personal opinion. The author had tried out all the recipes herself and was therefore qualified to make such remarks as, 'Some cooks pound with the bread and chickens the yolks of three or four hard-boiled eggs, but these improve neither the colour nor the flavour of the *potage*', or, 'This is the best *practical* application that we can give of Baron Liebig's instructions.' She also gave reasons for her methods: writing that fish should always be baked at a mild degree of heat, she explained: 'This penetrates the flesh gradually, and converts it into wholesome succulent food; whereas, a *hot oven* evaporates all the juices rapidly, and renders the fish hard and dry.' The book has a refreshing personal quality lacking in most of its predecessors (John Farley must be excepted), together with a careful attention to detail which inspires confidence. This is not to say that its recipes are without the defects of their period. Seven kinds of melted butter sauce give support to Voltaire's dictum that 'the English have forty-two religions but only two sauces'; nor would anyone nowadays boil cabbage for an hour or more. Miss Acton believed that the custom of serving vegetables crisp, 'which means, in reality, only half-boiled', made them unwholesome and indigestible, but she went on to advise that 'they should not be allowed to remain in the water after they are quite done, or both their nutritive properties and their flavour will be lost'. The time she recommends for most vegetables is five to ten minutes longer than we might allow – eighteen to twenty minutes for seakale, twenty to twenty-five minutes for asparagus, fifteen to twenty minutes for green peas, twenty to twenty-five minutes for cauliflowers. But she appreciates that vegetables, treated with care and imagination, contribute as much to the character of a meal as any main dish.

As a young girl, Eliza Acton had spent at least a year in France. Some of her recipes are explicitly French, many had a distinctly French aura about them – by which I mean that they demonstrate intelligent respect for the nature of the ingredients and a clear notion of what the end result should be. *Modern Cookery* ends with a section on foreign cookery, including Jewish, Italian, Spanish and Indian dishes. It is worth reading and its recipes can be used today.

Sixteen years after its publication, Miss Acton's star was eclipsed by another. In 1861, the most famous of all English cookery books appeared. It was called *The Book of Household Management* and its author was a young woman of twenty-three, Mrs Isabella Beeton. Reading one of the early editions, one can understand its success. If it was true, as S.W. and Mrs Rundell claimed, that modern young ladies knew nothing of domestic arrangement, no better book than this could have been devised for them; it contained wise and reassuring counsel on every conceivable topic, from getting up in the morning to entertaining guests during the half-hour before dinner is served. There were sections on how to engage servants and manage them, and how to look after children. There were instructions for simple bookkeeping and medical advice. And above all, there was an enormous cookery section, containing over 3,000 recipes, with short excursions into natural history and attractive coloured plates. All the recipes were arranged in the same way, with a list of the ingredients, a method, an estimated cost, the number of people the dish would serve and the time of year when it would be seasonable. Truly could Mrs Beeton claim that she had 'striven . . . to make my work something more than a Cookery Book', and one can only stand amazed that it cost her no more than 'four years' incessant labour'.

The recipes themselves are difficult to evaluate, since a great number are lifted from other writers, including Miss Acton, often without acknowledgement. Their most striking characteristic is a perfect, impersonal clarity, so that any inexperienced housewife with a literate cook could expect to produce a reasonable dinner. It was for this that Mrs Beeton became famous. When she died of puerperal fever at the age of twenty-nine, her husband, an astute publisher whose influence on her original work may have been greater than is usually supposed, continued to put out abridged versions and new editions. After he was ruined by a bank crash, the book went to another firm and was reissued many times, but later editions bear little resemblance to the original.

One of the reasons Mrs Beeton had given for writing her book was that 'Men are now so well served out of doors, – at their clubs, well-ordered taverns, and dining-houses, – that in order to compete with the attractions of these places, a mistress must be thoroughly acquainted with the theory and practice of cookery'. It is Lady Clutterbuck's sentiment over again. The topic of clubs will be taken up in the next chapter, but taverns and chop-houses figure so prominently in Dickens' novels that they must be looked at now.

The dinner which Pip and Herbert Pocket ate 'with no old people by, and with London all around us' had been furnished from the coffee-house. We are not told much about it, save that there was bread, cheese and a boiled fowl with the inevitable melted butter sauce. Nevertheless, it is a far cry from White's, Lloyds and Pasqua Rosee; the great age of coffee-houses was over, and those which continued were forced to provide food as well as drink in order to survive. The practice had begun early, as we know from Boswell's *Diary* for 1763: 'At night, Mr Johnson and I supped in a private room at the Turk's Head Coffee-House, in the Strand; "I encourage this house," said he, " for the mistress of it is a good civil woman, and has not much business."'

By the beginning of the nineteenth century, the transformation was well under way. It is recorded of the sculptor Benjamin Haydon and the painter David Wilkie, for example, that they often enjoyed 'a small dinner at a small cost' at Old Slaughter's Coffee-house, founded in 1692 but now renamed The Old Slaughter Chop-house.

Though Johnson and Wilkie ate on the premises, Pip's meal was carried out. Throughout Dickens' novels, people bring in cooked food to eat in their lodgings; it is spoken of so frequently and in such detail that it clearly continued to be a regular and important part of London life. The lawyer's clerk Wemmick, in *Great Expectations*, offers Pip cold roast fowl 'from the cook's shop. I think it's tender, because the master of the shop was a Juryman in some cases of ours the other day, and we let him down easy. I reminded him of it when I bought the fowl.' Mr Pumblechook also entertains Pip to 'a chicken had round from the Boar . . . a tongue had round from the Boar . . . one or two little things had round from the Boar, that I hope you may not despise'. In *Oliver Twist*, Fagin and the Artful Dodger, visiting Sikes on his sickbed, bring in a rabbit pie, which, with spirits and tobacco, goes far to restore the invalid. And David Copperfield is able to entertain Steerforth and his friends to a three-course meal procured entirely from the pastrycook's.

At the lowest end of the scale, the street stalls described by Mayhew sold anything from roast chestnuts to boiled whelks. A particular London speciality was eels, sold either hot in the form of 'eel-and-mash' (eels with mashed potatoes) or jellied. They were usually imported live from Holland, though they had once been fished from the Thames, as the name of Eel Pie Island (not far from Richmond) indicates. Near Billingsgate, they were cooked in large white enamel basins before ending up on stalls in the streets of the East End, which had such special fondness for them that it was said its babies were weaned on jellied eels.

Clearly, even without cooking facilities of one's own, there was no need to eat badly if one had the money. Hard it is to imagine a twentieth-century writer describing modern takeaways with the gusto brought to the topic by Dickens.

Usually the premises of chop-houses, taverns and dining-houses were unpretentious; their food, however, could be very good, and some became quite famous. One such was the George and Vulture, to which Mr Pickwick, in the course of a convivial evening, 'severally and confidentially invited somewhere about five-and-forty people to dine with him . . . the very first time that they came to London'. It still exists and has hardly changed from Dickens' time. Another still enjoyed by today's Londoners is Rules, which, founded in 1798, claims to be the oldest restaurant in London. The Cheshire Cheese, just off Fleet Street, was known to Goldsmith and Johnson before it was frequented by Thackeray and Dickens. Its popular pudding, brought in at 6.30 p.m. precisely on alternate evenings through the winter, contained a glorious mixture of larks, kidneys, oysters and steak, surmounted by a surging billow of pastry. So satisfying was it that the management felt safe in offering second helpings free of charge, but a desperately hungry man could round off the meal with a pint of beer and some stewed cheese (i.e. melted cheese served with mustard and two triangles of toast).

One chop-house, Simpson's-in-the-Strand, began its career in 1818 as a venue for chess players; indeed it was the first place to adopt as standard pieces the rook, pawn and knight now common to chess sets worldwide. But its reputation was soon to rest chiefly on the quality of its grilled meat, said to be the best in London.

Another well-known establishment was the Cock, Temple Bar, of which the *Epicure's Almanac* recorded in 1815 that it had 'the best porter in London, fine poached eggs and other light things'. Tennyson added to its fame with his jolly poem 'Will Waterproof's Lyrical Monologue' (*English Idylls and Other Poems*), addressed to the 'plump head-waiter at the Cock', an eye-opener to anyone who knows Tennyson only in sober or romantic mood. The Cock was pulled down in 1887, and the business transferred to 22 Fleet Street, but the signboard of the original tavern survives.

During much of the century, people with a partiality for fish would take a boat at Tower Steps and travel to Greenwich. The *Morning Post* for 10 September 1835, for example, recorded that 'Yesterday the Cabinet Ministers went down the river in the ordnance barges to Lovegrove's West India Dock Tavern, Blackwall, to partake of their annual fish dinner. Covers were laid for 35 gentlemen.' Perhaps their menu was like that offered a few years later by another tavern, the Ship: two soups, one of salmon and one of flounder; lobster rissoles and fried slips; whiting pudding and stewed eels; crab omelette and salmon cutlets à l'Indienne; plain fried whitebait; devilled whitebait; coffee and liqueurs. Or at the Union Tavern (now renamed the Cutty Sark) they might have had a dinner like that described in *Our Mutual Friend*:

> What a dinner! Specimens of all the fishes that swim in the sea, surely had swum their way to it, and if samples of the fishes of divers colours that made a speech in the Arabian Nights . . . and then jumped out of the frying-pan, were not to be recognised, it was only because they had all become of one hue by being cooked in batter among the whitebait. And the dishes being seasoned with Bliss – an article which they are sometimes out of, at Greenwich – were of perfect flavour, and the golden drinks had been bottled in the golden age and hoarding up their sparkles ever since.

In this survey of Victorian London at table, one topic remains for discussion. 'It must . . . be obvious, that the health and comfort of families, and the conveniences of domestic life, are materially affected by the supply of good and wholesome water.' The quotation is from Accum. Since the construction of the New River, no further attempts had been made to provide clean sweet water for cooking and drinking. Not only had the population vastly increased, but sewage systems were beginning to break down, with the result that wells and springs were being contaminated. Yet Accum believed that 'the water of the river Thames, taken up at London at low water mark, is very soft, and good; and after rest, it contains but a very small portion of any thing that could prove pernicious or impede any manufacture'. He had observed that when a cask of Thames water was opened after being kept a month or two, 'the water is so black and offensive as hardly to be borne'. But once it had deposited its black slimy mud it became 'as clear as crystal, and remarkably sweet and palatable'. He thought that those impurities his experiments could detect had 'no perceptible influence on the salubrious quality of a mass of water so immense, and constantly kept in motion by the tides'.

Accum's opinion was not shared by everybody. He could not see far beyond lead poisoning, and the harmful effects of water kept in leaden reservoirs or passed through lead pipes or pumps seems to have concerned him to the exclusion of any other danger. But the poor sanitary conditions in the slums clearly contributed much to the bad health of the people, and soon it was suspected that cholera might actually be water-borne. At least 5,000 people died of the disease in 1832, but no effective measures were taken. However, in 1848, with the threat of another epidemic looming, a Metropolitan Commission of Sewers was created. At its head was Edwin Chadwick, a scientist and something of a visionary, who wanted all sewage and water services in London to come under a single authority instead of being in the hands of private companies indifferent to the public welfare. That this was so is clear from a moving letter published in *The Times* of 5 July 1849. The simple, ill-spelled message expressed the isolation felt by the fifty-four signatories:

> We are, Sur, as it may be, livin in a Wilderniss, so far as the rest of London knows anything of us, or as the rich and great people care about. We live in muck and filthe. We aint got no privez, no dust-bins, no drains, no water splies, and no drain or suer in the whole place. The Suer Company, in Greek Street, Soho Square, all great, rich and powerfool men, take no notice watsomedever of our conplaints. The Stench of a Gully-hole is disgustin. We al of us suffur, and numbers are ill, and if the colera comes Lord help us.

Nevertheless, as had happened with Accum, private interests were angered by Chadwick's ardent desire for reform. At this stage, the connection between cholera and drinking water was still unproved, and when the disease materialised in 1849 his first, and fatal, step was to flush out the capital's sewers into the Thames. As all the water companies and private individuals save those who had access to the New River were still taking their water from this source, the devastation caused is hardly surprising. With 14,000 dead, Chadwick was immediately sacked. But by 1850, he was able to present a *Report on the Supply of Water to the Metropolis* in which a single Water Board was suggested, which would collect water from Richmond, Farnham and Bagshot Heath, filter and aerate it, and supply it to all households in London at an inclusive charge of 2d. a week. Needless to say, his proposals were blocked and obscured; and not until 1903 was the Metropolitan Water Board founded, with licence to carry out the reforms put forward fifty years earlier. It is pleasing to be able to say that Chadwick did eventually receive recognition of his work, with a knighthood at the age of ninety.

RECIPES

ASPARAGUS SOUP

This recipe and the others from the same source need no gloss. Apart from the insertion of metric quantities, they are quoted directly, just as laid out in the original.

½ lb (250 g) of split peas
1 teacupful of gravy
4 young onions
1 lettuce cut small
¾ head of celery
½ lb (250 g) of asparagus cut small
½ pt (275 ml) of cream
3 quarts (3.3 l) of water
Colour the soup with spinach juice

Mode. – Boil the peas, and rub them through a sieve; add the gravy, and then stew by themselves the celery, onions, lettuce, and asparagus, with the water. After this, stew all together, and add the colouring and cream, and serve.

Time. – Peas 1½ hours, vegetables 1 hour; altogether 4 hours. Average cost – 1s. per quart.

(Mrs Beeton, *The Book of Household Management*, new edition, 1869)

EEL PIE

1 lb (500 g) of eels
a little chopped parsley
1 shallot
grated nutmeg
pepper and salt to taste
the juice of ½ a lemon
small quantity of forcemeat
¾ pt (450 ml) béchamel
puff-paste

Mode. – Skin and wash the eels, cut them into pieces 2 inches long, and line the bottom of the pie-dish with forcemeat. Put in the eels, and sprinkle them with the parsley, shallots, nutmeg, seasoning, and lemon-juice, and cover with puff-paste. Bake for 1 hour, or rather more; make the béchamel hot, and pour it into the pie.

Time. – Rather more than 1 hour. Average cost. – 1s. 3.d
Seasonable from August to March.

(Mrs Beeton, *The Book of Household Management*, new edition, 1869)

MELTED BUTTER

This is not what it sounds. It was *the* sauce in both eighteenth- and nineteenth-century cooking. There are several variants using the same ingredients in different proportions, according to whether it was to be eaten with a rich dish or light, delicate or dry meat or fish. Here is an easy recipe:

1½ oz (45 g) butter
1 large tsp flour

a pinch of salt
¾ pt (450 ml) water or milk

Put into a basin a large teaspoonful of flour, and a little salt, then mix with them very gradually and very smoothly a quarter of a pint of cold water; turn these into a small clean saucepan, and shake or stir them constantly over a clear fire until they have boiled a couple of minutes, then add an ounce and a half of butter cut small, keep the sauce stirred until this is entirely dissolved, give the whole a minute's boil, and serve it quickly.

(Eliza Acton, *Modern Cookery for Private Families*, 1845)

SHRIMP SAUCE FOR BROILED SALMON

When shrimps and salmon were both less expensive, this was a very popular dish. It has a very festive, summery look but may be made with frozen shrimps provided they are the best quality.

½ lb (250 g) shrimps
½ pt (300 ml) melted butter (see above)
essence of anchovies
¾ tsp mace
tiny pinch of cayenne

The fish for this sauce should be very fresh. Shell quickly one pint of shrimps and mix them with half a pint of melted butter, to which a few drops of essence of anchovies and a little mace and cayenne have been added. As soon as the shrimps are heated through, dish, and serve the sauce, which ought not to boil after they are put in. Many persons add a few spoonsful of rich cream to all shell-fish sauces.

(Eliza Acton, *Modern Cookery for Private Families*, 1845)

SCOTCH MINCED COLLOPS

2 lb (1 kg) beef fillet, minced
1 tbsp flour
½ pt (300 ml) good beef stock or gravy
2 tbsp mushroom ketchup
2 tbsp Hervey's sauce (obtainable from good grocers)
fried croutons

Take two pounds of the fillet of beef, chopped very fine, put it in a stew-pan, and add to it pepper and salt and a little flour, add a little good gravy, with a little ketchup and Hervey's sauce, and let it stew for twenty minutes over a low fire: serve up very hot, garnished with fried sippets of bread.

(Lady Maria Clutterbuck, *What shall we have for Dinner?*, 1865)

STEWED RUMP STEAK

The author of this recipe, 'Tabitha Tickletooth', was a writer of one-act plays and farces called Charles Selby. He may well have known Dickens and had a hand in the latter's own dramatic entertainments. The only copy I have seen of his recipe book, *The Dinner Question*, was bound in with Lady Clutterbuck's, and since she suggests stewed rump steak as a main dish, it seems appropriate to give Selby's recipe.

2 lb (1 kg) rump steak, cut into slices about 1½ inches thick
2 tbsp butter
1 small carrot
1 small onion
1 stick celery
½ lb (250 g) pickling onions
12 peppercorns
1 tbsp mushroom ketchup
pinch cayenne pepper
1 glass port or claret
1 tbsp flour

Peel the pickling onions and put them into a small saucepan with water just to cover. Cook gently for about one hour. Beat the steaks with a flat wooden bat or the back of a wooden spoon. Heat the butter and brown the meat and chopped vegetables, pour in the liquid from the onions (keep them for garnish) and add the peppercorns. Cover and simmer gently for an hour and a half; skim off the fat, and put the meat in another pan in a warm place. Strain the gravy and vegetables through a fine sieve into a small saucepan, add the ketchup, the cayenne pepper, and the wine. Mix the flour with a little cold water in a cup and then add some of the gravy. Stir until there are no lumps, and pour back into the gravy. Stir over low heat until it has thickened. Pour it over the meat, and simmer for two or three minutes.

(Tabitha Tickletooth, *The Dinner Question*, 1860)

A COMMON HASH OF COLD BEEF OR MUTTON

This simple recipe makes a good dish if carefully followed. It demonstrates, alas, where English cooking could go so badly wrong, because in careless hands the end result might be very nasty indeed. Compare the recipe with that of the Elizabethan cook John Murrell on p. 59.

about 1 lb (500 g) cold roast meat
1 onion
1 carrot
1 bunch thyme and parsley
4 cloves
a few peppercorns
salt
1½ pts (850 ml) water or beef stock
1 level dsp cornflour or arrowroot

Take the meat from the bones, slice it small, trim off the brown edges, and stew down the trimmings with the bones well broken, an onion, a bunch of thyme and parsley, a carrot cut into thick slices, a few peppercorns, four cloves, some salt, and a pint and a half [850 ml] of water. When this is reduced to little more than three-quarters of a pint [425 ml], strain it, clear it from the fat, thicken it with a large dessertspoonful of rice flour, or rather less of arrowroot, add salt and pepper if needed, boil the whole for a few minutes, then lay in the meat and heat it well. Boiled potatoes are sometimes sliced hot into a very common hash.

Obs. – The cook should be reminded that if the meat in a hash or mince be allowed to boil, it will immediately become hard, and can then only be rendered eatable by very *long stewing*, which is by no means desirable for meat which is already sufficiently cooked.

(Eliza Acton, *Modern Cookery for Private Families*, 1845)

LEG OF MUTTON WITH OYSTERS

This recipe, harking right back to the previous century, shows how taste in domestic households straddles old and new ideas. Six or eight mussels could be substituted for the oysters, but remember to remove the black stringy membrane which encircles each mussel, because it is tough.

3–4 oysters or 6–8 mussels, cooked
3–4 lb (1½–2 kg) leg of lamb
1 bunch parsley
1 small onion, minced or chopped
sweet herbs – tarragon, marjoram, thyme, rosemary
yolks of 2 hard-boiled eggs

Parboil some fine well-fed oysters, take off the beards and horny parts, put to them some parsley, minced onions, and sweet herbs boiled and chopped fine, and the yolks of two or three hard-boiled eggs; mix all together, and make five or six holes in the fleshy part of a leg of mutton, and put in the mixture, and dress it in either of the following ways: tie it up in a cloth and let it boil gently two and a half or three hours according to the size, or braise it, and serve it with a pungent brown sauce.

(Lady Maria Clutterbuck, *What shall we have for Dinner?*, 1865)

KALECANNON

Victorian recipe books always insist on carrots being boiled for at least an hour, although the timings for other vegetables are not very different from modern ones. Were the carrots a different variety? The green vegetables may be interchanged at will, since a colourful effect is aimed at here.

3–4 carrots
6–7 stalks broccoli, or 1 small spring cabbage, or
  1 lb (500 g) spinach
3–4 turnips
3–4 potatoes
½ oz (15 g) butter
pepper and salt

Boil three or four carrots *tender*, some nice young greens, a few turnips, a few potatoes; cut off the *outsides* of the carrots and chop them up *very fine*, also chop the greens, mash the turnips and potatoes, then place it in a melon shape to form the stripes of colours, filling up the interior of the mould with all the vegetables chopped up together with pepper and salt. Butter the mould, and boil half-an-hour.

(Lady Maria Clutterbuck, *What shall we have for Dinner?*, 1865)

BLACK CAPS

I give the recipe as it stands. When one reflects that the cook had to do all that chopping, grating, washing and picking by hand, it is amazing that she still had an hour in which to boil the pudding. As John Farley would say, remember to flour the cloth before putting the pudding in it, and tie it up securely. Note the absence of sugar in this recipe. The black caps should be eaten with a very sweet sauce, or with honey or golden syrup.

3 eggs
2 oz (60 g) flour
½ tsp grated nutmeg
1 oz (30 g) candied lemon-peel
¼ tsp powdered ginger
6 oz (175 g) suet
6 oz (175 g) currants

Put the beaten-up yolks and whites of three eggs into a basin with two ounces of flour, half a teaspoon of grated nutmeg, an ounce of candied lemon-peel, chopped in small pieces, and a quarter of a teaspoon of grated ginger, mix well with a wooden spoon to a smooth batter, then add six ounces of beef suet chopped fine, and six ounces of well washed and picked currants. Boil in a cloth an hour, or in small cups (tied in a cloth) three-quarters of an hour. Serve with melted butter, flavoured with white wine or a little rum.

(Tabitha Tickletooth, *The Dinner Question*, 1860)

The Welcome Guest's Own Pudding

Who could resist such a title? All the ingredients are easy to obtain except the ratafias, but you can find these in a good delicatessen. The pudding is a bit of trouble – perhaps that accounts for the title. Use a two-pint basin with tight-fitting lid and stand it on an upturned saucer in the pan when boiling it.

4 oz (125 g) fresh fine white breadcrumbs
4 oz (125 g) dry breadcrumbs
½ pt (300 ml) single cream or full-cream milk
4 oz (125 g) grated suet
pinch salt
3 oz (90 g) ratafia biscuits
3 oz (90 g) candied peel
rind of 1 large or 2 small lemons, grated
4 eggs
4 oz (125 g) caster sugar
for the sauce
¼ pt (150 ml) water
rind of half a lemon, grated or cut into thin strips
1½ oz (45 g) granulated sugar
1 tsp cornflour
½ glass brandy or liqueur

Pour, quite boiling, on four ounces of fine bread crumbs, an exact half-pint of new milk, or of thin cream; lay a plate over the basin and let them remain until cold; then stir to them four ounces of dry crumbs of bread, four of very finely minced beef-kidney suet, a small pinch of salt, three ounces of coarsely crushed ratifias [*sic*], three ounces of candied citron and orange-rind sliced thin, and the grated rind of one large or two small lemons. Clear, and whisk four large eggs well, throw to them by degrees four ounces of pounded sugar, and continue to whisk them until it is dissolved, and they are very light; stir them to, and beat them well up with the other ingredients; pour the mixture into a thickly buttered mould or basin which will contain nearly a quart, and which it should fill to within half an inch of the brim; lay first a buttered paper, then a well-floured pudding-cloth over the top, tie them up tightly and very securely round, gather up and fasten the corners of the cloth, and boil the pudding for two hours at the utmost. Let it stand for a minute or two before it is dished, and serve it with simple wine sauce, or with that which follows . . . Boil very gently, for about ten minutes, a full quarter of a pint of water, with the very thin rind of half a fresh lemon, and an ounce and a half of lump sugar; then take out the lemon peel, and stir in a small teaspoon of arrowroot [cornflour], smoothly mixed with the strained juice of the lemon (with or without the addition of a little orange juice); take the sauce from the fire, throw in nearly half a glass of pale French brandy, or maraschino or any delicately flavoured liqueur.

(Eliza Acton, *Modern Cookery for Private Families*, 1845)

Chapter 6

OSCAR WILDE

After a good dinner, one can forgive anybody,
even one's own relatives.

A Woman of No Importance, 1894

If Dickens' world was that of the middle and professional classes,
Oscar Wilde's was much more exclusive. In general, it might be
described as 'society London', embracing certain writers, actors and
artists as well as the wealthy and well born. It was a community
based on the government and the civil service, but its substructure
was dinners and balls, theatre parties, Ascot, Cowes, weekends in
the country, and shoots in Norfolk or Scotland: all events which
defined the participants' fortune and position. According to one
calculation, in the 1890s, 30.7 per cent of Londoners were living in
poverty (defined as 'earning insufficient to obtain the minimum
necessities for the maintenance of mere physical efficiency'); the
remainder, especially the middle classes, were getting richer. At the
top of the scale the landed aristocracy, whose fortunes might have
been expected to decline as cheap food from abroad toppled
farmers' monopoly of the food supply, had begun to marry wealthy

industrialists, and its abler members were pursuing careers. A private income was no longer a necessity for admission to this powerful group – one had to have money, but it was allowable to earn it oneself. A condition of entry, however, was what might be called conspicuous expenditure; a large house (or preferably two), many servants, beautiful furniture and ornaments, and frequent parties demonstrated one's fitness to be part of the fashionable scene. It was a world which even obscure young men could join if they were brilliant enough. John Buchan, a poor minister's son from Scotland who ended his life as Governor-General of Canada, is one example. Oscar Wilde too entered it for a brief period and depicted it in his plays.

He was born in Ireland on 16 October 1854. His father was a leading surgeon, his mother a writer and Irish patriot. Except for the death of a much-loved younger sister at the age of nine, which affected him deeply, his childhood seems to have been uneventful. At public school, he far outstripped his peers and was awarded an entrance scholarship at Trinity College, Dublin, to study classics. In due course, a further award enabled him to go to Magdalen College, Oxford. Friends from this period of his life recalled him as a kind, rather indolent young man of prodigious memory, with an unusual gift for telling romantic or thrilling stories which were also wonderfully funny. Most dons and administrators thought him idle, impertinent, lacking in respect for authority. But he had philosophical leanings and a genuine love of beauty, and he found encouragement in the teachings of Ruskin and Walter Pater, who stressed the need to find or create beauty in every aspect of daily life.

At Oxford, he developed, quite consciously, a public identity and much to his satisfaction was dubbed an 'aesthete'. He grew his hair shoulder length, wore suits of a larger check and more extreme cut than those of his fellows and adorned his rooms with blue china, largely because it was cheap and pretty. In spite of his 'attitudes' he was far from being the effete, languid character later satirised by W.S. Gilbert in *Patience*. At Oxford as at school, he dealt easily, and if necessary physically, with 'sportsmen' who attempted to rag him, but he rarely lost his good humour; as at school, too, his charm, wit and sense of fun won him many friends.

In 1878, aged twenty-four, he came down with a First in classics and the prestigious Newdigate Prize for a poem on Ravenna. His father had died, leaving him a small legacy. He set his sights on becoming part of the London whose portrait John Buchan drew so accurately in *Memory Hold-the-door*:

> London at the turn of the Century had not yet lost her Georgian air. Her ruling society was aristocratic till Queen Victoria's death and preserved the modes and rites of aristocracy. Her great houses had not disappeared or become blocks of flats. In the summer she was a true city of pleasure, every window box gay with flowers, her streets full of splendid equipages, the Park a show ground for fine horses and handsome men and women. The ritual went far down, for frockcoats and top-hats were the common wear not only for the West End, but about the Law Courts and in the City ... Conversation was not the casual thing it has now become, but was something of an art, in which competence conferred prestige. Also Clubs were still in their hey-day, their waiting lists were lengthy, membership of the right ones was a stage in a career.

Wilde, despite his limited funds, had an entrée to this privileged class through several Oxford friends; he committed himself categorically to aestheticism, adopting the sunflower and the lily as his emblems, and appeared at evening parties in knee-breeches, silk stockings and a velvet coat edged with braid. His conversation was witty, his knack of turning an aphorism or a cliché upside down to reveal some unexpected truth refreshing, and he soon became a popular guest in the most sophisticated circles. 'To get into the best society nowadays,' he told a friend, 'one has either to feed people, amuse people, or shock people – that is all.' Women particularly enjoyed his company; he flattered and charmed them, and seemed genuinely interested in their views and feelings.

Probably he would have preferred to live, like so many of those he now met, in happy idleness, but to share their stylish world he had to supplement his income. He published a book of poems, which, though well received by the public, left reviewers unimpressed; and a play, *Vera*, dealing with the difficult subject of Russian nihilism, which, although accepted and scheduled for production, had to be abandoned when a relative of the Royal Family, Tsar Alexander II, was assassinated.

By the summer of 1881, his need of money was acute. Luckily for him, Gilbert and Sullivan's comic operetta *Patience* (for whose central character he was the model) was doing exceedingly well in the United States, and on the assumption that American audiences would like to see a real aesthete, *Patience*'s impresario, Richard D'Oyly Carte, offered Wilde a lecture tour. He was now twenty-eight years old and, apart from his poetry and *Vera*, had no claims to literary fame and no lecturing experience. However, years of preparation for the limelight had resulted in a polished, confident personality, and his quickness of mind allowed him to meet any situation with perfectly timed wit. His first remark on arrival in New York is typical. A customs official asked if he had anything to declare. 'Nothing,' he replied. A pause. 'Save my genius.'

Financially, the tour was moderately successful. Personally, it was a triumph. His lectures on 'The English Renaissance' were thoughtful but often amusing. He dealt firmly but good humouredly with those who came to mock, neatly turning the tables so that they, not he, looked ridiculous. He met and charmed most of the distinguished Americans of the day, and in his luggage when he returned to London was the manuscript of a sonnet by Keats, presented to him by a niece of the poet.

This American tour was followed by his first visit to Paris. Again he managed to meet most of the eminent men of letters: Zola, Victor Hugo (who, very old, dumbfounded him by falling asleep during the encounter), Alphonse Daudet, Verlaine and Mallarmé. An English friend who got to know him at this period described him as bubbling with new and joyous life, buoyantly scattering depression with his own exuberant vitality. Nevertheless, Wilde's writing was not going well. A new play, *The Duchess of Padua*, was turned down by the actress for whom it was written, and a major poem, *The Sphinx*, was still unfinished when he returned to London after three months. When a New York production of *Vera* failed, Wilde signed an agreement to tour Britain with three lectures: 'The House Beautiful', 'The Value of Art in Modern Life' and 'Personal Impressions of America'.

At about this time he got to know the painter James McNeill Whistler. The two had much in common. Both were passionately interested in the theory of beauty, both were witty and enjoyed good food, good wine and good conversation. Each had strong opinions and tremendous egotism. Their friendship lasted some years, but gradually became less good-humoured. Whistler was jealous of the younger man's success in society and resented the fact that Wilde had set himself up as an art critic. (Wilde's comments on Whistler's own work were double-edged: he once declared publicly that Whistler was indeed 'one of the great masters of painting' – somewhat spoiling this generous praise by adding: 'In this opinion Mr Whistler himself entirely concurs.')

In 1884, Wilde's finances were stable enough to allow him to marry an Irish girl, Constance Lloyd, and the couple moved into 34 Tite Street, Chelsea. The marriage was happy at first, and two much-loved sons, Cyril and Vyvyan, were born, but the predictability of domestic life bored Wilde. His wife, like poor Kate Dickens, found it hard to live up to her husband's constant search for amusement and novelty. Increasingly, he accepted engagements without her, and although affection and consideration remained, in time their lives became as separate as those of any couple in his plays.

For the moment, he was editing a women's magazine and persuading all the famous women he knew to contribute: Princess Christian, Lady Archibald Campbell, the Queen of Roumania, Marie Corelli, Olive Schreiner, Ouida and many more. He was also reviewing exhibitions, books and plays, and in 1887 published his first volume of short stories, *Lord Arthur Savile's Crime and Other Stories*. This was followed in 1888 by a collection of fairy stories, *The Happy Prince and Other Tales*. People who had heard the same stories from Wilde's own lips were disappointed in the published versions. He was a storyteller of genius, but he himself once said that only talent went into his writing.

Another aspect of his nature appeared when he published what became his most famous story, *The Picture of Dorian Gray*, in 1891. Its plot – of a portrait which alters as its subject becomes ever more immoral and debauched, while the young man himself retains his innocent beauty – shocked many, and its extravagant dialogue aroused the hostility of some of the more conventional members of London society. Further prejudices were inflamed, in the same year, by a long essay, *The Soul of Man Under Socialism*. An impassioned argument for more social equality and the abolition of privilege, it antagonised the aristocracy, though Wilde was much too valuable a guest at house parties and dinner parties to be struck off any hostess's list.

1891 was artistically perhaps Wilde's most productive year. In the autumn he sent to the actor–manager George Alexander the manuscript of a new play, *Lady Windermere's Fan*, first produced on 20 February 1892, with Alexander playing Lord Windermere and Ellen Terry's sister Marion as Mrs Erlynne. Although the critics were not entirely favourable, the public was delighted with its highly moral plot and witty epigrams, some of which have passed into the English language for good. If the plot now seems contrived and the characters stylised, we should make allowance for both the social and the dramatic conventions of the day.

Wilde's new theatrical venture was a dramatisation, in French, of the story of Salome. Sarah Bernhardt was to play the lead, and rehearsals had already begun when, in June 1892, the Lord Chamberlain refused a licence. Wilde was deeply hurt. But the text was published the following year in France, and later translated and published in England. In the meantime, inspired by the success of *Lady Windermere's Fan*, he was writing a new comedy, which had its premiere on 19 April 1893. The sophisticated wit of *A Woman of No Importance* completely captivated London audiences. For the first time in his life, Wilde had everything he wanted – attention, praise and money. *Dorian Gray* and *The Soul of Man* were almost forgotten as he was lionised and invited to all the season's major social events. Among his friends, he could now count all the leaders of society, including the Prince of Wales and his entourage, known as the Marlborough House set.

Unfortunately, not all his friends were of such impeccable background. In 1891, he had met a young Oxford student, Lord Alfred Douglas, a spoilt, rather foolish young man with a beautiful face and a penchant for poetry. The mutual infatuation which fast developed would perhaps have done Wilde no great harm but that through Douglas a whole host of undesirable young men entered his life. Their admiration, genuine or fabricated, flattered his egotism, which throve unchecked. He was spending his new wealth on a prodigal scale, lunching and dining with his new acquaintance at the best restaurants, taking a suite at the Savoy Hotel whenever he was too much fatigued to return to his own home, travelling everywhere by hansom cab and lavishing presents on all his friends – especially Douglas. But his arrogance was alienating many who might have been his friends, and the homosexual element which Douglas had aroused was leading him into dangerous waters.

In the meantime, his theatre successes continued with *An Ideal Husband*, which was premiered in January 1895. Bernard Shaw, in a review, wrote that other critics 'laughed angrily at his epigrams like a child who is coaxed into being amused in the very act of setting up a yell of rage and agony'. But the play contained more than epigrams; it had emotion and a deeper characterisation than any of his earlier work. 'It contains,' said its author, 'a great deal of the real Oscar.'

Wilde's personal popularity was diminishing as rumours spread. Lord Alfred Douglas's father, the Marquis of Queensberry, a bully whose aggression constantly sought new targets, decided that Wilde was having a bad influence on his son. Douglas himself, feeling no doubt protected by Wilde's friendship, gave like for like in response to his father's insults, threats and general boorishness. Eventually, Queensberry goaded Wilde beyond endurance. He booked seats for the premiere of *The Importance of Being Earnest*, due to open at the St James Theatre on 14 February 1895, intending to disrupt the performance. Luckily, word got out; the theatre management cancelled the booking and thwarted his efforts to enter the premises. Three days later, his fury inflamed by the play's rapturous reception, he left a card at Wilde's club, the Albemarle, 'To Oscar Wilde, posing somdomite [*sic*]' with the hall porter. When Wilde saw the card twelve days later, he let Douglas persuade him to prosecute Queensberry for criminal libel.

It was virtual suicide. Queensberry, charged and released on bail, spent the time before the trial rounding up witnesses, both genuine and dishonest, to prove that Wilde was a practising homosexual and pederast. The outcome was that the defendant was acquitted, but Wilde was immediately arrested and charged with immoral acts. When a first trial ended with the jury disagreeing, a retrial was ordered. Wilde was found guilty and sentenced to two years' hard labour.

The privation, brutality and humiliation he endured in the course of his imprisonment he has told himself, in the long letter he wrote to Lord Alfred Douglas, *De Profundis*, and in *The Ballad of Reading Gaol*. To say that he emerged broken is no platitude. All that had given his life security, comfort, friendship, beauty had been stolen from him. His wife, though kind and compassionate until her death, was persuaded to divorce him for the sake of the children, who thenceforward, like her, bore the surname Holland, and whom he never saw again.

Released from prison after completing his sentence (there was no remission for good behaviour despite several appeals to the Home Office), Wilde ended his life in exile, chiefly in France but occasionally visiting friends in Italy or Switzerland. He adopted the pseudonym Sebastian Melmoth, except where he was well known. He had had to pay the Queensberry costs of the libel trial and lived chiefly off the charity of a small band of loyal but far from wealthy friends. Apart from *The Ballad of Reading Gaol*, he wrote nothing more for publication; most of his energy indeed seems to have been expended on letters to anyone who might advance him a sum of money. He saw Douglas occasionally – they attempted to live together for a while – but despite protestations of love on both sides, the relationship had died, and only a curious impersonal friendship remained.

In October 1900, Wilde was living in Paris. An operation for ear trouble, a direct result of his imprisonment, failed to relieve severe pain, and he declared to his friends that he felt very ill and would soon die. Whether or not he had contracted syphilis as a young man and was now in its final grip is not clear; in any event, cerebral meningitis was the immediate cause of his death on 30 November 1900, a few hours after his reception into the Roman Catholic Church.

Two themes in London's gastronomic history were becoming prominent and indeed intermingling in the second half of the nineteenth century: the importance attached by high society to food, and the rise of restaurants and clubs. Their origins antedate Wilde's London years (1878–1895) by two to three decades, but because his own lifestyle is closely linked to both, it provides a convenient platform from which to view them. Wilde's London is above all the London of dining out: at society dinner parties or in the great restaurants, West End clubs and fashionable hotels.

There is a sense of déjà vu about society dinner parties of this period. The lavish quantities of food, the sophisticated and recherché delicacies, the fanciful shapes and elaborate garnishes – where has one seen it all before? The answer is, of course, in the food of the Middle Ages. This is no coincidence. Just as in the fourteenth century, food was being used as a symbol of wealth and power. And as Richard II's fondness for good eating had set a fashion, so once again royalty was exerting its influence. Albert Edward, Prince of Wales, born in 1842, coming to maturity in the '60s and '70s, was a man whose powerful appetites were not to be confined by a strict and repressive upbringing. His mother's dominant hold on all the functions of the Crown frustrated his active, genial spirit; denied all the work of a king, he could nevertheless live like one and put into the pursuit of pleasure the energy of a restless temperament.

In the matter of food at least, he did not lack for opportunity. Although his mother as she grew older preferred plain fare, a little book of handwritten recipes proves that when young she had been interested in cookery; and she felt it her duty, befitting her position at the head of a great Empire, to keep a lavish table. Five courses for breakfast, ten or twelve for luncheon and the same for dinner were the standard menu; there was every opportunity for the young Prince's unhappiness under the strict routine devised by his parents to be expressed in bouts of compulsive eating. Thus were established the habits of a lifetime, and in later years, the Prince became a renowned epicure. According to Anita Leslie in *The Marlborough House Set*:

> The Prince demolished an enormous breakfast as well as a vast lunch and dinner every day of his life. When in the country he tucked into a hearty tea of scones and cake as well, and during the season he could cheerfully consume a fifth meal – midnight supper.

His other appetites equally powerful, it was natural that he should surround himself with a group of like-minded friends, wealthy young men and their wives. When he married Princess Alexandra of Denmark in 1863 and the young couple set up home in Marlborough House, they became leaders of fashion in everything from dress to house decoration and dinner parties. Some of the most beautiful and well-connected young women in London – all married, to avoid scandal – belonged to the Prince's set: Georgiana, Countess of Dudley; Gladys, Countess de Grey; Daisy, Countess of Warwick; and the American beauty Jennie Jerome (Lady Randolph Churchill). Even without connections, a woman of exceptional looks could enter the circle for a time, as Lillie Langtry, the ravishing young wife of a quickly forgotten husband, proved. Shortly after her arrival in London, Lord Randolph Churchill wrote to his wife: 'I dined with Lord Wharncliffe last night, and took in to dinner a Mrs Langtry, a most beautiful creature, quite unknown, very poor, and they say has but one black dress.' Wilde too met her when she was quite unknown, in the house of an artist. They became friends and may have been lovers, but the Jersey Lily's ambitions were set higher, and Wilde helped her by teaching her fashionable manners and advising her on dress. When she became the Prince's mistress, she brought him to Wilde's house in Tite Street, at his request: 'I do not know Mr Wilde, and not to know Mr Wilde is not to be known.' Thus Wilde entered the highest society in London, and he became a frequent dinner guest at epicurean tables. He was also at home in political circles, among people like Gladstone and Disraeli, A.J. Balfour, and the Asquiths, with whom he often lunched or dined.

The style of the Edwardian dinner party was sharply elegant, extravagant but sophisticated, with a delicacy of approach lacking in earlier times. The Prince of Wales himself, according to Sir Harry Luke (*The Tenth Muse*, 1954), simplified private dining in England by causing champagne to be served throughout the meal in the place of a different wine to each course. He also initiated the practice of serving the joint immediately after the fish and before the entrées, though this was by no means universally copied. But the biggest change was in the way the courses themselves were presented. The new fashion was for *Diner à la Russe*, in which all the dishes of each course were no longer placed simultaneously on a great wide table before the diners. Instead, according to Mrs Beeton:

> the table is narrow, the ladies all walk in together and are followed by the gentlemen, who sit opposite them. The servants come and hand round every dish, the vegetables are served in separate compartments of a large round dish. When the dessert is handed round, the guests help themselves to all they are likely to require at once.

The fact that Mrs Beeton takes such trouble to describe *Diner à la Russe* indicates what a novelty it was in 1869, the date of the edition from which this passage is taken. It did not enter general usage until the '70s and '80s, but then it had numerous consequences. Meals became shorter, courses smaller (sometimes consisting of only two or three dishes), tables narrower, sideboards larger. And the duties of host and hostess became less onerous. Lady St Helier described in 1909 how in her youth:

> One had always the most profound pity for the host and hostess, who were obliged to carve the joints at their

respective ends of the table, the duty in the hostess's case generally falling to the unhappy man who took her in to dinner, and, consequently, got no dinner himself.

But under the new method, it was the butler who carved at the sideboard. Consequently, conversation at meals was easier and more relaxed. Moreover, no longer was one confined by the width of the table to talking only to those sitting on either side, nor was one responsible for satisfying their gastronomic needs by passing what they could not reach.

Surviving menus for private dinner parties at this level of society are hard to find. The dinner given by an unnamed hostess, cited by Sir Harry Luke in *The Tenth Muse*, may serve as an example. The dinner, 'in a private house in London in King Edward's cosy reign', was attended by Sir Harry's father:

148, Piccadilly
Diner du 22 juin, 1904

Tortue Liée
Consommé de Boeuf froid
Whitebait à la Diable et au Naturel
Pain de Saumon à la Riche
Sauces Genevoise et Hollandaise
Cailles Braisées Printanières Demi-Glace
Cotelettes d'Agneau Rachel
Canetons à la Voisin au Coulis d'Ananas
Salade des Gobelins
Hanche de Venaison à l'Anglaise
Sauces Porto et Cumberland
Granités au Champagne
Poulardes roties flanquées d'Ortolans
Asperges d'Argenteuil, sauce Mousseline
Oeufs de Faisan Parmentier
Croutes à l'Ananas
Coupes Petit-Duc
Petites Friandises
Fondants au Chester
Petites Glaces au café et Pain bis Vanillées
Petites Gaufrettes

The way the menu is set out obscures the fact that this dinner is modestly composed of only eight courses (soup, fish, entrées, joint, game, hors d'oeuvre, sweets, dessert), but it does give some indication of the pressure put on the cook on such occasions, however good the back-up from other kitchen staff. No wonder contemporary mythology portrays cooks as often bad tempered or drunk. (Whistler once told a friend that, when interviewing a prospective cook, his last question was always, 'Do you drink?' If the answer was 'No', he did not engage her.)

For more elaborate parties, professional caterers were often brought in. Thus did the legendary Rosa Lewis, owner of the Cavendish Hotel, begin her career, cooking ten-course dinners for hostesses like Mrs Murray Guthrie and Lady Randolph Churchill. 'Often enough during the past quarter of a century,' wrote Colonel Newnham-Davis in 1914 (*The Gourmets' Guide to London*), 'I have heard some hostess say reassuringly to someone whom she had asked to a dinner-party, "Mrs Lewis is coming to cook the dinner."' Slim and graceful, with a pretty oval face and charming eyes, Rosa had a quietly single-minded approach which inspired confidence. She would go to Covent Garden Market at 5 a.m. to choose her vegetables, then return to prepare what she could in her own kitchen. In the late afternoon, she and her 'girls', dressed like her in white with tall chefs' hats and high laced black kid boots, moved into the kitchen of the house where the dinner was to be held, banishing the regular servants. She commanded her own price, for her cooking pleased the Prince of Wales (he was especially fond of her quail puddings), and it was considered essential to engage her when he was on the guest list. (Among her other talents, she understood the need for discretion at certain times; she never 'told', and when she bought the Cavendish and turned it into a series of suites, each with its private dining room and bathroom, the hotel was furnished with four exit doors at the back.)

If few private-party menus survive, recipes from this spectacular age of gourmandise abound and reinforce the comparison with medieval gastronomy: dishes like croustade of larks, stuffed cock's-combs, chartreuse of hare, breast of pigeon in a mould with sauce supreme, lobster timbale, and a galaxy of foods in aspic; any number of sauces to accompany roasts and grills, including one specially named for the Prince; and dazzlingly colourful sweets and desserts: ices, sorbets, jellies and creams, all designed to delight the eye with gorgeous colour and intricate garnish. The imagination must be dazzled too: no society hostess worth her tiara dared overlook the earliest asparagus, the tiniest petits pois, the out-of-season strawberries, the fresh winter truffles from France ('as big as your fist' according to Rosa, and at their best in January), the poussins, ortolans and guinea fowl, the plovers' eggs, the hot-house peaches and the hot-bed pineapples. Sad to say, all was not always what it seemed. *Law's Grocer's Manual* for 1901 remarks that:

> Gourmets have for years been eating eggs never laid by plovers, and paying fancy prices for them. A large section of the gull family, who are farinaceous rather than fishy in their diet, lay eggs precisely similar to those of the plover. These are collected in hundreds on the small islands in the inland lochs of north Scotland and sent to London. They are ridiculously cheap (to the collectors) and require no dye or flavour to give them artistic verisimilitude.

All fashionable London imitated the dinners and supper-balls of the Marlborough House set, but not everyone was confident of behaving correctly. As the author of *The Diner's-out Vade Mecum* (not dated, about 1904) pointed out, rapidly acquired wealth 'often places small men in large positions, and thus opens the door of hospitality, without having first graduated host and hostess in the art of entertainment'. And only recently had it become acceptable to invite theatrical people to the 'best' houses; they, like writers and artists, however amusing or eminent, might come from any background. The *Vade Mecum*, a slim volume designed not to alter the set of a pocket in a dress-coat, was full of excellent advice on minutiae – when to bow, when to shake hands, how to accept or refuse an invitation to dinner, what to wear ('The dinner jacket is not admissible except on informal occasions . . . all display of jewellery is vulgar'), how to take a lady in to dinner (a new custom initiated in the 1880s) and how to cope with the cutlery:

> A well-ordered table is a pretty sight, with its white cloth, its bright silver, and shining glass, to say nothing of the dainty flowers and the varicoloured fruit . . . and yet when one descends from the general to the particular, and squarely faces one's own small portion, it presents, at least to the

novice, a somewhat formidable appearance. In the forefront he is faced with a dinner napkin folded maybe mitre-fashion, a loaf already in its mouth waiting the arrival of the fishes. On the left of his plate he will find a fair array of forks, and on the right a complementary equivalent of knives. There are probably more tools required daily for the feeding of a man's body than would be needed for its surgical dissection.

But one also needed to be able to converse with one's fair partner, and on occasion, a joke or a speech was called for. The *Vade Mecum* provided for all contingencies. How difficult to be a man in those Edwardian days! Only the most wealthy and the most titled dared be unconventional; others must conform exactly to all the rules of polite behaviour. Women were more fortunate. They needed only follow the man's lead when in society.

But, as we saw in the last chapter, dining out was no longer confined to visits to private houses. If a man had no other engagement, he might go to his club, or meet friends in a restaurant or hotel. It began with the clubs, but not the sort of clubs (best defined as groups of people who agreed to meet regularly because they enjoyed each other's company) with which Johnson and his friends were familiar. The kind of which I am now speaking evolved in some cases out of such meetings; in others, however, it developed in parallel. Many began as gaming clubs, for coffee-house rules were strict, and there was a desire for premises where people could play cards for high stakes without interference. Others were a response to a need for private rooms where one might relax in congenial company. The oldest such club, White's, founded in 1693 as a chocolate-house, still exists today. In this case, some of the clientele paid a subscription for the use of a room or rooms to which casual customers were not admitted. In time, these subscribers took over the entire building; thus the first club with its own premises came into being, the date being probably 1736. It remained a proprietary club with a single owner until 1923 when it became a members' club. Other early clubs were Boodle's and Brooks's.

Johnsonian-type clubs became defunct when the last member died, but clubs with their own premises and a turnover of subscribers gained in popularity. New ones continued to be founded throughout the eighteenth and nineteenth centuries. Subscribers had a common interest, perhaps an amusement such as gambling or sport (Boodle's, Brooks's, Pratt's, Lord's), a profession like the theatre or the army (the Garrick, the Guards) or a hobby (the Travellers', the Beefsteak), so that recruits were not difficult to find.

By the 1840s, one club in particular, the Reform, had become famous for its good food. The Reform's premises had been built by Sir Charles Barry for the Whigs, after their great Bill to reform Parliament had been safely seen onto the statute books; but Barry turned over the design and fitting-up of the club's kitchen to the prospective chef, a remarkable young Frenchman called Alexis Soyer. As a trainee in Paris, Soyer had had the unfortunate experience of being mobbed in his kitchen during the July Revolution of 1830. He had been quick-witted enough to leap onto a table and sing 'La Marseillaise' with an enthusiasm born of sheer fright, and the crowd, after chairing him round the kitchen, let him alone. Soyer concluded that France was not the place to pursue a peaceful career and moved to England, where his older brother was chef to the Duke of Cambridge. His genius was soon recognised, and after a succession of posts in various aristocratic establishments, he was engaged by the newly founded Reform. The custom-built kitchen he installed there caused something of a stir and was written up by journalists and travel writers. Soyer's main innovation was the substitution of gas and steam for coal, so that the premises remained 'as white as a young bride'. On entering, the visitor's notice was immediately engaged by the noise of the steam keeping plates and dishes hot, and whose power turned the spit. The whole kitchen was so well planned that however busy the chefs, all remained in the most perfect order.

Perhaps Soyer's greatest triumph at the Reform was the banquet he cooked for Ibrahim Pacha, the celebrated Ottoman general, on 3 July 1846. One hundred and fifty guests worked their way through an eight-course meal comprising forty-nine different dishes, which culminated in La Crème d'Egypt à l'Ibrahim Pacha. For this, an edifice two and a half feet high made of meringue cut to represent the stones of a pyramid enclosed a pineapple-flavoured cream, surmounted by a round satin carton on which was carefully drawn a highly finished portrait of the Pacha's father, Mehemet Ali, the whole just visible through sheets of finely spun sugar and garnished with grapes and other fruit.

Soyer resigned from the Reform for unspecified reasons in 1850, but we cannot leave him without mention of some of his other achievements. He invented the bain-marie, which by keeping water at boiling point in a large container allows food in an inner saucepan to cook at very low heat. He also wrote three books, the first of which, *The Gastronomic Regenerator*, contained over two thousand recipes. His second, *The Modern Housewife*, was directed at the middle classes, and his third, *Shilling Cookery for the People*, aimed to help the poor make the best use of cheap ingredients. He was much moved by the plight of the poor in London and later in Ireland at the time of the potato famines and not only set up model soup kitchens but also invented several recipes for soups which, he claimed, would feed large quantities of people at minimum cost. (They seem sensible and nourishing, but provoked much criticism on the grounds that a liquid diet must necessarily be debilitating and lacking in 'goodness'.) He also turned his attention to creating bottled sauces and relishes, which were so successful that he was able to sell the recipes to Messrs Crosse & Blackwell. After leaving the Reform, he took advantage of the Great Exhibition at the Crystal Palace to open a restaurant (modestly named the Gastronomic Symposium of All Nations) just outside the gates. When this failed, he was quiet for a while, but the Crimean War gave fresh spur to his energies, and he first designed a portable field-stove and then went personally to the battlefront to teach the soldiers how to use it and how to formulate diets for sick soldiers. It was during a visit to the Crimea that he contracted illnesses which eventually proved fatal. He died in August 1858. For so restless a man, the headstone above the grave he shares with his wife is singularly apt: it reads '*Soyez tranquilles*'.

Soyer's success at the Reform undoubtedly influenced the food of other clubs, so that two distinct themes developed in clubland catering. On the one hand, Victorian chop-house cookery, with its juicy kippers, well-grilled steaks and tender cutlets was turned into an art; on the other, classics of French cooking like crème Argenteuil, sole Duglère, lobster thermidor, veal sauté Marengo and crème brulée found a permanent home in the hands of competent chefs. For men who wished to dine well away from home, clubs offered the ideal solution.

They also provided an excellent locale for entertaining a friend or acquaintance whom one did not wish to bring into the family circle, at the same time signalling the status of both host and guest. To be a member of a club was a sign of exclusivity, since to join one must be elected, or at least approved by all the members. Some were easier to get into than others. Wilde, for example, was a member of the Albemarle, but he had also been put up for the Crabbet and the Savile. (Both applications were opposed. Lunching at the Savile as a guest one day, he said he felt 'like a lion in a den of Daniels'.) By the 1890s, it was rare to find a Londoner of any social standing who was not a member of at least one club.

The monopoly of clubs as fashionable eating places was, however, short-lived. For over 200 years, modest restaurants like the Huguenot establishment which so pleased Samuel Pepys and his wife had existed in or near the centre of London. Succeeding generations of French refugees continued to earn their living from such small eating-houses. None, however, made such an impact on fashionable London as the Café Royal, opened by Daniel Nicols and his wife Célestine in 1867.

Nicols (his real name was Daniel Nicolas Thévenon) was a man of high ambition, whose ventures into the wine-shop business in his native land had ended in bankruptcy. Rather than spend the next few years in prison for debt, he had packed up his belongings and come to London with Célestine at his side and five pounds in his pocket. After fifteen months, thanks to excellent cooking, his knowledge of fine wine and Célestine's thrift and good management, the couple had saved enough to set up the Café-Restaurant Nicols in Glasshouse Street. Two years later, they were able to open much larger premises in Regent Street.

Fashionable London had never seen anything quite like the Café Royal, with its painted ceilings, gilded caryatids and mirrored walls. Strollers along London's most elegant street noted the tasteful 'N' surmounted by a crown which was the restaurant's emblem and saw through the plate-glass windows choice foods, beautifully displayed on ornamental pedestals flanked with stuffed game birds. Once inside, they were not disappointed. Not only was the cuisine superb, but the wine was astonishing. This was largely thanks to Nicols' cousin, who bought with impeccable judgement and the abandon of a true enthusiast, choosing wines for immediate consumption but also laying down fine vintages for the future. Unfortunately, his extravagance all but ruined the Café Royal; to avert bankruptcy, Célestine had to produce £60,000 from her secret savings. The problem of cash flow was then dealt with by putting some of the wine up for public auction, and so high were the bids that only one-eighth of the stock needed to be sold. To make more room in his cellars, Nicols then decided to let his regular customers benefit from his cousin's twenty-year spending spree. For several months, superlative wines were charged to favoured tables at the price of vin ordinaire. A friend of Wilde's and notable bon viveur, Frank Harris, described the wine list in his usual moderate terms: 'Even in 1884–5 the Café Royal had the best cellar in the world. Fifteen years later it was the best ever seen on earth.'

The glittering brilliance of Café Royal society in the 1890s was a match for its wines. Artists, writers, musicians and actors flocked to play dominoes, eat breakfast, take coffee or luncheon, or dine. At any time one might see Whistler, Shaw, Beerbohm Tree, Max Beerbohm, Augustus John, Sir William Orpen, George Moore, Aubrey Beardsley – the names a veritable roll-call of bohemian London at its scintillating best. Wilde went there almost every day, for he loved the genuine French atmosphere, the blend of informality with meticulous regard for quality of service and excellent food and drink. Long afterwards, the staff remembered the gravity and concentration he brought to choosing his meals, discussing each course with the chef; then the sommelier would be summoned, and the question of suitable wines would be lovingly enquired into. To Wilde, white wine was never white – he always talked of yellow wine. One of his favourite champagnes was Clicquot vin rosé.

Wilde's last visit to the Café Royal was a poignant occasion. In a private room, Frank Harris was lunching with Bernard Shaw. Knowing that Wilde was contemplating taking out a warrant for libel against Queensberry, Harris had invited him to come in after lunch to discuss it. Shaw was still there when he arrived, and both he and Harris tried to persuade Wilde to drop the case and go abroad for a while. Wilde seemed influenced. Then Alfred Douglas came in. His little, white, venomous face distorted with rage, he told Harris his advice was not that of a true friend. Wilde repeated the accusation sadly, and left. Shortly afterwards, the worst of Harris's predictions were fulfilled.

During Wilde's London years, his love of wine and food had led him into many restaurants, a number of which are described in *Dinners and Diners: Where and How to Dine*, a series of newspaper articles by Col. Newnham-Davis, published in book form in 1899. (It was in reviewing this book that Wilde attacked the British cook for 'her entire ignorance of herbs, her passion for extracts and essences, her total inability to make a soup which is anything more than a combination of pepper and gravy'. He continued: 'The British cook is a foolish woman, who should be turned, for her iniquities, into a pillar of that salt which she never knows how to use.') Newnham-Davis used the device of characters belonging to standard types – the actress, the old-fashioned country squire, the maiden aunt, the sister-in-law who is the daughter of a dean, the old school friend down on his luck, the man-about-town – and found for each an appropriate place to eat. His sketches are vivid and often amusing, and since he presents us with not only the food but the decor, the atmosphere and even the head waiter, a very clear picture emerges.

The Florence, a small Italian restaurant in Rupert Street, Soho, was one of Wilde's early haunts, well known to theatre-goers. For two shillings (ten pence) you could have a good meal: antipasto assortito, ravioli, scallopine di vitello alla Milanese and zabaglione, with good Italian wine. The rooms were small but luxuriously furnished, with frescoed walls and ceiling. Pagani's, in Great Portland Street, also offered Italian food and initially catered for the modest purses of journalists, artists and singers, but by 1899, it had gone upmarket and was almost as grand as Romano's in the Strand, which shared with the Café Royal the custom of the most celebrated artists, writers and musicians. Wilde was also very fond of Kettner's, which had a German proprietor and specialised in after-theatre meals. He dined there with Aubrey Beardsley in December 1893, probably to discuss the illustrations to *Salomé*. Newnham-Davis describes Kettner's as a snug little restaurant with comfortable nooks and crannies. It had three or four public dining rooms below and a network of passages and rooms above. Private parties might dine in:

> a little room, with a paper in which old gold and soft browns and greens mingled . . . [It had] three windows with warm-coloured curtains to match the paper, bronze ornaments on the mantelpiece, oil paintings of Italian scenery on the walls, a tiny sideboard, and a square table lighted by gilt candelabra holding electric lights.

Newnham-Davis's sample menu from Kettner's includes caviar, consommé à la Colbert, fillets of sole à la Joinville (stuffed with shrimps, mushrooms and truffles), tongue with mushrooms, poulet à la Parmentier, asparagus, biscuits glacés (Neapolitan ice cream) and dessert.

One of the very few explicit references to food in Wilde's work occurs in *De Profundis*, when he reproaches Douglas for extravagance. Besides telling us more about where the two men liked to eat, it demonstrates that even in his anguish, he could not help using words beautifully, tonguing them as in happier days he had savoured the delicate flavours of food and wine.

> The Savoy dinners – the clear turtle-soup, the luscious ortolans wrapped in their crinkled Sicilian vine-leaves, the heavy amber-coloured, indeed almost amber-scented champagne – Dagonet 1880, I think, was your favourite wine – all have to be paid for. The supper at Willis's, the special cuvée of Perrier-Jouet . . . the wonderful pâtés procured directly from Strasbourg, the marvellous fine champagne served always at the bottom of great bell-shaped glasses that its bouquet might be better savoured . . . These cannot be left unpaid.

In another passage, he speaks of Douglas's preferred way of spending an evening: champagne dinner at the Savoy, a box at a music hall, then a champagne supper at Willis's. Newnham-Davis thought the latter was:

> as close a transcript of a Parisian restaurant as could be found in London. The white walls, with great mirrors let into the shining wood, the scarlet couches by the wall, the chairs with their quaint backs and scarlet seats all savour of Paris.

In the centre of the room stood a dumb-waiter piled high with fruit and bunches of asparagus, and a great clock of enamel and ormolu added another French touch. The effect was completed by the black leather apron worn by the sommelier. Newnham-Davis is silent about suppers, but dinner for two at Willis's could cost almost as much as at the Savoy, for the menu listed all the fashionable delicacies, from plovers' eggs to truffles and early strawberries.

The Savoy was the grandest of all of Wilde's haunts. The hotel had been bought by Richard D'Oyly Carte who, following Lillie Langtry's suggestion, persuaded César Ritz to manage the new restaurant which opened in 1889. Ritz brought with him a chef of outstanding brilliance and originality, Auguste Escoffier, and together they turned the Savoy into one of the greatest hotels of its time. Ritz realised that if he could get women to dine in his public restaurant, he could gather in all the fashionable world, so he began with private dining rooms where famous hostesses like Lady de Grey, Lady Randolph Churchill and the Duchess of Marlborough (Consuelo Vanderbilt) could give dinner parties. He then persuaded them that the public restaurant, with screens discreetly placed, might provide a pleasant atmosphere for small groups of diners. Gradually, the screens were removed. As Escoffier wrote later, 'since restaurants allow of observing and of being observed, since they are eminently adapted to the exhibiting of magnificent dresses, it was not long before they entered into the lives of Fortune's favourites'.

Great care was taken with the ante-room of the restaurant. With its two great fireplaces, white-and-gold-papered walls, comfortable armchairs and Satsuma china, it offered a welcoming but luxurious atmosphere, and on Sunday nights, the company was 'as fine a society salad as any capital in the world can show'. In the dining room, Monsieur Ritz, with his short whiskers and carefully clipped moustache, hands clasped almost nervously behind his back, went from table to table with a carefully graduated scale of acknowledgement of the patrons. Hot dishes were served unadorned at the Savoy, but the cooking was far from plain. One of Escoffier's favourite maxims was '*faites simple*'; nonetheless, the recipe Newnham-Davis extracted from him for Timbale de Filets de Sole Savoy is far from simple, consisting as it does of a pastry case lined with a layer of macaroni in sauce Béchamel, surmounted by fillets of sole cooked in white wine, the whole covered with a sauce of crayfish and truffles and garnished with more crayfish. This was a hot dish, but when dining at the Savoy, it was the custom to include at least one cold dish in the menu, 'to give M. Escoffier and his staff a chance of showing what they can do in the way of decoration'.

The Savoy staff considered it had a mission. M. Joseph, the then manager of the restaurant, wrote to Col. Newnham-Davis:

> The *maître d'hôtel* should be an adviser, tempter, theatrical producer . . . he must act on the diner's imagination to make him forget the machine which is being refuelled – in a word, he must conceal the physical aspect of eating . . . the pleasing

array of hors d'oeuvre, the salad to accompany the roast, the elegant way he carves that roast, quickly and well . . . placing himself not too near and not too far from the diners so that their interest may be aroused and they can see how tastefully he attends to each detail, in order to continue enticing appetites which, though almost satiated, are rekindled by the desire he has been able to arouse, tempting imagination although the stomach has almost acknowledged defeat . . . is the art of the *maître d'hôtel.* After providing a good meal he is satisfied, because he has given a little happiness to some poor folk who are not always happy.

Among the Savoy's many devices to give happiness to poor folk, two especially have proved memorable. Pêche Melba was created by Escoffier to soothe and relax the throat of the great soprano when she was singing in *Lohengrin*; and some genius behind the Savoy bar invented the whisky sour.

Escoffier left the Savoy in 1898 and moved to the Carlton. Like Soyer, he was an inventor and proselytiser, but also something of a self-publicist. How far he was prepared to take the latter instinct may be seen from what is probably his most minor work, a fifty-page pamphlet entitled *A Few Recipes by A. Escoffier, of the Carlton Hotel, London.* By following his instructions, he declared, 'the most unpretentious of cooks will . . . be enabled to prepare delicacies calculated pleasurably to excite the most refined and dainty palate.' A large claim, perhaps. One 'recipe' suffices to show how it could be realised:

CRÈME DE TOMATE AU RIZ (THICK)

This is a very nourishing soup, rich in cream, and thus most useful to yachting or exploring parties, expeditions, &c. . . .

To prepare: Pour the contents into a saucepan, bring to boiling point, and serve immediately. Should the soup be too thick, a few tablespoonfuls of water, milk, or stock, may be added.

Escoffier, in short, like Soyer, had gone into the canning business, with eight different varieties of soup and nine sauces. The twentieth century had arrived.

RECIPES

CRÈME PINK 'UN

This recipe comes from Romano's in the Strand. It is, as will be evident, not a dish for every day. Rather than spoil the impact of the recipe, I have not adapted the quantities. As given, it should feed 8–10 people.

1 lb (500 g) pearl barley
1 glass cognac
2 bay leaves
thyme, parsley, tarragon, chervil
8 oz (250 g) butter
2 tsp olive oil
1 carrot
1 onion
24 crayfish
1 lb (500 g) prawns
6 fresh tomatoes
½ bottle Chablis
salt and cayenne pepper
1¾ pts (1 l) stock
sippets of fried bread

Put the pearl barley to soak overnight. Next day, put it into a pan with cold water or stock and simmer for 3 hours. Set aside. Put the herbs to steep in the brandy and set aside. Melt 2 oz (60 g) butter in a heavy pan and add the olive oil. Cut the carrot and onion in small pieces and cook gently in the butter and oil for about 5 minutes. Then add the crayfish (the original recipe calls for them to be alive, but in these days of fast freezing there is no need for this), prawns and peeled tomatoes. Pour in the wine, season with salt and cayenne pepper, cover the saucepan and simmer for 20 minutes. Remove from the pan and (says the original) pound in a mortar with the barley (use the food processor). Dilute with the stock, and pass through a fine sieve. Put on the soup to warm again, without letting it boil. Add then the cognac, from which you have removed the bay leaves and other herbs. When the soup is thoroughly heated, cut 6 oz (175 g) butter into small pieces and drop them in, then serve with sippets of fried bread.

(from Newnham-Davis, *Dinners and Diners*, 1899)

SOUPE AUX FOIES DE VOLAILLES
(Chicken-liver soup)

This, one of Escoffier's easier soups, is rich and delicious. The restaurant would of course always have white consommé or brown stock to hand for the making of soups and sauces. You could substitute a good strong-tasting chicken stock, or a mixture of stock and tinned consommé.

1½ oz (45 g) butter
1½ oz (45 g) flour
2 pts (1.2 l) chicken or beef consommé
¾ lb (375 g) chicken livers
1 glass Madeira wine

Make a roux from the butter and flour. When it has acquired a nice, light-brown colour, moisten it with 1 quart of white consommé or brown stock, and set to boil, stirring the while. Add ½ lb (250 g) raw chicken livers rubbed through a sieve, and set to cook for 15 minutes. Rub the whole through a tammy; season strongly with pepper; heat, and complete the preparation, at the last minute, with ¼ lb (125 g) sliced chicken livers, tossed in butter, and 1 wineglass of good Madeira.

(Escoffier, *Ma Cuisine*, 1907)

CONSOMMÉ AUX PAILLETTES D'OR

Another simple recipe, included for its medieval overtones.

Take a very superior chicken consommé; add thereto, per quart, a glass of excellent liqueur brandy, and in the same proportion, one gold-leaf cut into small spangles.

(Escoffier, *Ma Cuisine*, 1907)

LOBSTER SOUFFLE – A COLD SAVOURY

Lady Clark of Tillypronie, from whose collection this recipe is taken, was the daughter of an English judge and wife of a Scots laird who spent some years abroad in the diplomatic service before settling in Britain, where the couple divided their time between Birk Hall, Bagshott Park, London, and Tillypronie, north of the Dee in Aberdeenshire. While not one of the great London hostesses, Lady Clark had a wide circle of friends, including royalty, and entertained a great deal at both her homes. She took a keen interest in food and her book represents Edwardian cooking at its domestic best.

Aspic jelly can be bought in packets from many delicatessen shops. If you wish to make it yourself, however, you will find a recipe at the end of the chapter. Lobster spawn, sometimes known as coral, may be difficult to find, but you could substitute a very little caviar.

Mayonnaise Sauce (see below)
1 cold boiled hen lobster
aspic jelly
lobster spawn (optional)

Stiffen the sauce if necessary with whipped aspic jelly. Mince a cold boiled hen lobster into tiny dice, mix it with the sauce, whisk all to a froth over ice, and pour quickly into little soufflé cups, which have had a paper band previously secured round them, standing up 1 inch high above the cup. Dish the cups on a napkin, remove the paper bands, sprinkle a little spawn on top, and add a little chopped aspic jelly. Garnish with parsley.

MAYONNAISE SAUCE

Put a yolk of egg into a basin, pour into it gently, drop by drop, a little very fresh olive oil; whisk all the time with an iron whisk, season with a little white pepper; when the mixture becomes thick, add a few drops of vinegar, then a few drops of oil, and so on alternately, till you have enough. Then add about ¼ pint (150 ml) of good thick cream and ½ teaspoon of French mustard.

(from *The Cookery Book of Lady Clark of Tillypronie*, 1909)

FILETS DE SOLE PAGANI

8 fillets of sole
8–10 mussels
1 pt (600 ml) fish stock made from heads and bones of sole or other fish
together with
1 small onion
1 bay leaf
parsley and thyme
1 small carrot, chopped
for the sauce
2 glasses dry white wine
¼ lb (125 g) chopped mushrooms
1½ tbsp butter
1½ tbsp flour
salt and pepper
2 tbsp cream
½ oz (15 g) butter
salt and pepper
1 tsp lemon juice
2 tbsp Parmesan cheese

Begin by making the stock: simmer the fish bones with the onion, carrot, herbs, bay leaf and about 1¼ pints (700 ml) water for 20 minutes. Strain this through a cloth. Set aside half of it, and to the rest add the wine. Tap the fillets of sole with a wooden spoon, then fold them and place in a large wide pan (a deep frying pan with a lid is ideal) and put the well-scrubbed mussels on top. Pour over the stock/white wine, cover, and simmer for a few minutes. When the mussels have opened, remove the pan from the heat. Now make a velouté sauce by melting the first quantity of butter in a heavy pan and adding the flour. Stir well and cook for 1–2 minutes but do *not* allow to brown. Bring the fish stock you set aside to the boil in another pan, then gradually stir it into the butter and flour over medium heat. Add salt and pepper, and leave to simmer, skimming occasionally. Meanwhile, carefully lay the sole in a fireproof dish (a silver dish, says the recipe, but then you would need a salamander) with the mussels, each in half its shell. Cover with a buttered paper and keep in a warm place. Bring the liquor in which the fish was cooked to the boil and add the chopped mushrooms. Boil hard until reduced to about ½ pint (300 ml). Add to it your velouté, the cream, the second quantity of butter, pepper and salt, and the lemon juice, and put into a liquidizer. You should now strain it, but this is optional. Pour the sauce over the fish, sprinkle with Parmesan cheese, brown under a hot grill and serve.

(from Newnham-Davis, *Dinners and Diners*, 1899)

Omelette Arnold Bennett

Like Wilde, the author of the 'Five Towns' novels was a noted gourmet. This recipe serves four, and the omelettes are best made individually.

½ lb (250 g) smoked filleted haddock
1 oz (30 g) grated cheese
6 eggs
salt and pepper
1 oz (30 g) butter
1 tbsp double cream

Poach the fish in water or grill it, flake it and add the cheese, salt and pepper. Melt a little butter in an omelette pan, pour in enough lightly beaten egg to cover the bottom, and stir gently for a few minutes. Put some of the fish mixture on top of the omelette and pour on a little cream. Put the pan under a hot grill for about 1 minute. Serve without folding. The omelettes should be eaten immediately.

Oeufs Brouillés for Breakfast

6 eggs
2 middle-sized truffles
salt, pepper, cayenne pepper
1 oz (30 g) butter

Break 6 eggs into a basin. Chop up small two middle-sized truffles to the size of fine capers and add them to the eggs. Season with salt, pepper, and cayenne.

Whilst you are seasoning, a little butter should be browning in a frying-pan over the fire, watched by the kitchenmaid. Add the seasoned eggs to the butter, stir gently with an iron or silver spoon till the mixture is sufficiently cooked. Of course, if you don't think truffles an improvement, the buttered eggs are very good alone.

(*The Cookery Book of Lady Clark of Tillypronie*, 1909)

BEEFSTEAK AND OYSTER PIE

Lady Clark gives a recipe similar to this and claims it is a Cornish dish. In Scotland, mussels are sometimes used and the dish becomes Musselburgh Pie. I have halved the number of oysters, since they are now more expensive than in Edwardian days, and also – because modern ovens are much more efficient – suggested cooking the meat before adding the pastry. An onion, a carrot and a bouquet garni cooked with the meat are an improvement.

1 lb (500 g) rump steak cut into 12 slices
12 oysters
¾ lb (375 g) rough puff pastry
salt and pepper
½ pt (300 ml) water or beef stock
1 egg

Set the oven to 350°F/175°C/Gas Mark 4. Open the oysters and blanch them in their own liquor. Put an oyster onto each piece of meat, roll up and pack the rolls into a pie-dish. Season with salt and pepper, and moisten with the water/beef stock. Cover with foil and bake for about 1½ hours. Remove from the oven and leave to cool. Set the oven to 425°F, Gas Mark 7, and roll out the pastry to make a lid. Use the trimmings to make pastry leaves or other ornaments. Brush over with beaten egg. Make some holes in the top to allow steam to escape, then bake the pie for 30 minutes.

(from *Mrs Beeton's All About Cookery*, 1909 edition)

TOURNEDOS BALTIMORE

This makes a pretty, if costly, dish, since tournedos are small thick slices taken from a fillet of beef. Each should weigh 3½–4 oz (90–125 g). They should be fried very quickly, at high heat, so the butter must be clarified to prevent it burning. Alternatively, use a mixture of butter and oil. The tartlet cases should be the same size as the tournedos, which will shrink slightly when cooked. Bake the cases blind and keep warm. For the maize, drain a can of sweetcorn and heat the contents in 2 tablespoons of single cream. If you intend to serve Chateaubriand Sauce, make that first.

6 beef tournedos
6 tartlet cases to fit
2 small green capsicums (peppers)
6 tomatoes the same size as the tournedos if possible; cut a thick slice from the middle of each

Season the tournedos, and fry them in clarified butter. Set them in the form of a crown on small tartlets garnished by means of maize with cream. Upon each tournedos set a roundel of tomato, seasoned and tossed in butter, and a smaller slice of green capsicum, also tossed in butter, on each roundel of tomato. Accompany with:

CHATEAUBRIAND SAUCE

1 oz (30 g) shallots, chopped
1 sprig thyme and a bit of bay leaf
1 oz (30 g) mushroom parings
¼ pt (150 ml) white wine
½ pt (300 ml) veal gravy (béchamel cooked with lean cubed veal in it)
4 oz (125 g) maître d'hôtel butter (butter pounded with chopped parsley and a drop of lemon juice)

Stew the shallots, herbs and mushrooms in the wine until the latter has almost disappeared. Add the gravy and reduce again until the liquid measures only ¼ pint (150 ml). Strain through muslin, and finish the sauce away from the fire with the Maître d'Hôtel butter.

(Escoffier, *Ma Cusine*, 1907)

Birk Hall Excursion Pie

Again, this recipe has been adapted so that the pastry only cooks for 30 minutes. It calls for 'first stock', which is concentrated and would turn to jelly when cold. I have substituted tinned consommé.

4 grouse or 6 partridge
1 onion, sliced
½ pt (300 ml) tinned beef or chicken consommé
truffles (or mushrooms) to taste
¾ lb (375 g) rough puff pastry

Set the oven at 350°F/175°C/Gas Mark 4. Use the fillets of the birds only, in as large pieces as you can. Put them in a pie-dish with the onion, consommé and chopped truffles or mushrooms. Cover with foil, and bake for about 1½ hours. Remove from the oven and cool. Set the oven to 425°F/225°C/Gas Mark 7. Roll out the pastry and cover the pie with it. Bake for 30 minutes. Allow to get quite cold, then leave in the refrigerator overnight.

(from *The Cookery Book of Lady Clark of Tillypronie*, 1909)

Reform Cutlets

This recipe was invented by Soyer at the Reform Club, then widely copied. Lady Clark's version is very close to the original but easier to follow and a little more showy.

8 lamb cutlets
1 beaten egg
1 oz (30 g) boiled ham, finely chopped
an equal volume to the ham of dried breadcrumbs
2–3 tbsp oil
'Reform chips' (see recipe)
'Reform sauce' (see recipe)

Having trimmed them, dip each cutlet in beaten egg, and then crumb them with equal parts of dried breadcrumbs and finely chopped boiled ham, ham and crumbs being previously well mixed.

The cutlets must be fried on both sides, and when thoroughly done, dished in a circle with sauce under them, and 'Reform chips' filling up the centre.

'Reform chips' for the centre of the dish are made of the *red* part of boiled carrots, black truffles, some lean cooked ham or bacon, the whites only of hard-boiled eggs, cut in strips, and the outer part only of Indian mountain green gherkins. All cut in needle shape, like Julienne vegetables, say ½ an inch long and the 12th of an inch broad.

Make all hot in a basin in the screen [use a double boiler], toss them up lightly to mix them, and pile them in the hollow centre of the cutlets.

For Sauce: Its foundation is 'Poivrade' [see below]; to this add a glass of port wine or claret, half that quantity Hervey's sauce, a teaspoonful anchovy sauce, and 2 good tablespoonfuls of red currant jelly. Boil all together for 5 minutes, and pour into a clean small saucepan for use.

For Poivrade: Take the red part of carrots and 1 onion, a little lean ham, 1 bay leaf, and parsley, and fry all in as little fresh salad oil as possible. The quicker they are done the better will be their colour. Add a teaspoonful of sugar and a few peppercorns. Finish in a little stock, and when stewed soft enough, pass through a tammy.

(*The Cookery Book of Lady Clark of Tillypronie*, 1909)

POMMES IRÈNE

Again, an example of modular cooking, since it calls for sugar syrup, vanilla ice cream, a purée of plums, and Italian meringue as well as apples. Choose large firm Cox's for preference. Note that initially they must be peeled but kept whole. I have halved the quantities for the Italian meringue.

'Select some nice apples, peel them, and cook them in syrup, keeping them somewhat firm. When they are cold, carefully withdraw their pulp so that they may form a sort of case. Rub the pulp through a sieve, sugar it with vanilla sugar, and spread a layer of it on the bottom of each apple. Fill up the apple cases with vanilla ice, combined with a purée of cooked plums; the proportion being one-third of the latter to one of the former. Cover this ice with Kirsch-flavoured Italian meringue; set the latter to colour quickly and serve instantly.'

ITALIAN MERINGUE

½ lb (250 g) sugar
whites of 4 eggs
1 tsp Kirsch

Put the sugar in a pan with water to cover, bring slowly to the boil, stirring, then cook until it reaches the *large ball stage*. Test it by dipping a finger in cold water, then quickly into the sugar, then immediately into the cold water again. If you can roll the sugar on your finger into a firmish ball it is ready. Meanwhile whisk the whites of egg to a stiff froth. Pour the cooked sugar into the egg whites, slowly and without a pause, while someone else beats steadily. Add a teaspoon of Kirsch to flavour.

(Escoffier, *Ma Cuisine*, 1907)

RÖDE GRÖDE

This, still popular in Denmark today, is said to have been Queen Alexandra's favourite dessert.

1½ lb (800 g) redcurrants or blackcurrants
½ pt (300 ml) water
6–8 oz (175–225 g) vanilla-flavoured sugar (or more, to taste)
1 full tbsp arrowroot per pint (600 ml) fruit purée

Put fruit and water into a pan, simmer for an hour, and push the mixture through a sieve. Measure the quantity of pulp. Mix the appropriate amount of arrowroot in a cup with a little cold water, then add some of the purée. Put the rest of the purée into a thick-bottomed pan and add the sugar. Stir over gentle heat till the sugar is dissolved, then add the mixture in the cup. Bring to the boil, stirring thoroughly. Allow to boil for 2 minutes. Allow to cool, then pour into a pretty glass bowl and garnish with fresh berries and with whipped cream.

(Traditional)

PRINCE OF WALES SAUCE

For grilled or fried meat or fish:

herbs: 1 bunch each of tarragon, parsley and chervil, parboiled and drained
2 anchovy fillets
1 dsp capers
yolks of 2 hard-boiled eggs
1 tsp French mustard
salt, cayenne pepper
2 egg yolks
2 fl oz (60 ml) tarragon vinegar
6 fl oz (175 ml) olive oil

Chop the herbs separately so that you have one dessertspoonful of each kind. Pound them with the anchovies, capers and hard-boiled egg yolks. Add the mustard, salt and pepper. Beat in the raw egg yolks, then the vinegar and oil. Blend until smooth in the liquidizer.

(from Oswell Blakeston,
*Edwardian Glamour Cooking Without Tears,*1960)

ASPIC JELLY

2½ oz (60 g) gelatine
1½ pts (850 ml) chicken stock
2 fl oz (60 ml) malt vinegar
2 fl oz (60 ml) tarragon vinegar
4 fl oz (124 ml) sherry
1 tsp salt
1 tsp celery salt
1 blade mace
1 bay leaf
2 cloves
12 peppercorns
1 lemon, juice and peel, cut into thin strips
1 onion, peeled and quartered
1 carrot, scraped and quartered
2 whites of egg, whisked

2 eggshells pounded in the mortar

Put all the ingredients in a saucepan. Heat: and stir till the gelatine has melted. Now whisk till it all boils. Simmer for a quarter of an hour. Strain the jelly through a cloth.

(Oswell Blakeston, *Edwardian Glamour Cooking Without Tears*, 1960)

Chapter 7

VIRGINIA WOOLF

One cannot think well, love well, sleep well, if one
has not dined well.

A Room of One's Own

O scar Wilde died in 1900 and Queen Victoria in 1901. The
Victorian era, the Naughty Nineties and the nineteenth
century thus reached the finishing line more or less
together. Coincidentally, within the twenty years straddling the turn
of the century, the wireless, the telephone, the motor car and the
aeroplane either came into general use or were invented. It is truer
than usual therefore to say that with this new century a new way of
life began, at least in the large cities of the West. By good luck, we
are able to consider the food of London from 1900 until the Second
World War in the company of a writer who was almost an adult in
1900 and who began her professional career in 1907.

Virginia Woolf was born in 1882. Her father, Leslie Stephen, is
now chiefly remembered for his *History of English Thought in the
Eighteenth Century* and for the first *Dictionary of National Biography*. Julia
Duckworth, her mother, was Stephen's second wife, a widow with

three children of her own. The new marriage produced two sons and two daughters: Vanessa, Julian Thoby, Virginia and Adrian. All the family lived under one roof at 22 Hyde Park Gate, Kensington, with great comings and goings of aunts, uncles and friends.

As was customary, the two girls were educated at home, but in no sense were they intellectually deprived, for among their father's friends were many eminent writers and thinkers, and their mother's family was artistic. At fifteen, Virginia had free access to her father's excellent library and soon afterwards began private lessons in Latin and Greek (the latter from Walter Pater's sister) – for a girl, an unusually liberal education. From an early age, she wrote little stories and essays, producing with Thoby a weekly paper for the family, the *Hyde Park News*.

But if intellectually she was encouraged (although later she was deeply to resent not being sent to university like her brothers), her emotional and psychological needs were often ignored, especially after her mother's sudden death when Virginia was thirteen. Julia's twenty-six-year-old daughter Stella, who took over the household, was kind, but ill-equipped to cope with a stepfather whose uncontrolled and self-absorbed grief took no account of the unhappiness of the rest of the family. It was now that Virginia had her first mental breakdown. A second collapse – again provoked by her father's behaviour – occurred two years later when Stella married. Three months afterwards, Stella's death from peritonitis left Vanessa and Virginia without female companionship or protection. The family now consisted of Leslie Stephen, Julia's two sons Gerald and George, Adrian, Thoby, Vanessa and Virginia. Only Thoby was away, first at public school and later at Cambridge. Gerald worked for a publisher, George at the Treasury. George was fond of society, and as the girls grew older, he tried to persuade them to accompany him to parties and dances, which neither enjoyed. Vanessa soon refused point-blank, but Virginia, younger and more timid, usually agreed. Nor dared she protest when, at night, George crept up to her room and into her bed. What occurred then remains in shadow.

When Virginia was twenty-two, Leslie Stephen died from cancer. In his later years, he had become increasingly self-centred and neurotic, but although at times Virginia had hated him, they had common ground in their love of literature and philosophy, and she had valued his intellectual companionship. It was she who, before his illness, went for long daily walks with him in Hyde Park; to him she had brought her literary discoveries and philosophical speculations. Sometimes, despite his self-absorption and ill-temper, she felt herself 'full of love for this unworldly, very distinguished, lonely man'. Inevitably, his death brought on another breakdown, the most severe so far. She became anorexic and physically violent, and imagined she heard the King shouting obscenities in the shrubbery and the birds talking in Greek. She also tried to commit suicide. She was prescribed milk, complete mental rest and outdoor exercise, and sent to stay with friends. Very gradually, she recovered. By the end of the year, she was able to rejoin her sister and brothers in their new home at 46 Gordon Square, Bloomsbury.

It was, she wrote later, a 'curious transition from tyranny to freedom'. For the first time, the Stephens were on their own, away from all their Kensington relatives. Vanessa, studying at the Slade School of Art, spent her days painting and drawing. Virginia began writing articles and reviews and took up part-time teaching. Adrian was an undergraduate. Thoby, just down from Cambridge, was reading for the Bar but keeping in close touch with his university set. In this way, the Stephen sisters met Clive Bell (later to become an art critic), Lytton Strachey (who revitalised the art of English biography), Saxon Sydney-Turner (whose ambitions to be a composer or writer were never realised) and Desmond MacCarthy (who became a distinguished drama critic). Another of Thoby's friends, Leonard Woolf, met Vanessa and Virginia briefly before going to Ceylon to become a civil servant. Much later he wrote down his memory of the occasion:

> to any superficial observer they might have seemed demure. Anyone who has ridden many different kinds of horses knows the horse who, when you go up to him for the first time, has superficially the most quiet and demure appearance, but, if after bitter experience you are accustomed to take something more than a superficial glance at a strange mount, you observe at the back of the eye of this quiet beast a look which warns you to be very, very careful. So too the observant observer would have noticed at the back of the two Miss Stephens' eyes a look which would have warned him to be cautious, a look which belied the demureness, a look of great intelligence, hypercritical, sarcastic, satirical.
>
> (Leonard Woolf, *Sowing*)

Thursday evenings at Gordon Square became dedicated to friends and conversation over whisky, buns and cocoa. This (although at this time there was no consciousness of the fact) was the foundation of that most nebulous of artistic fellowships, the Bloomsbury Group.

After two years, Vanessa and Clive Bell married. Thoby had recently and tragically died after a family holiday in Greece, so the Bells kept Gordon Square and Virginia and Adrian moved to 29 Fitzroy Square, where the Thursday evening conversations continued in an enlarged circle which included the young painter Duncan Grant and his friend Maynard Keynes, later to become an economist. Another addition to the group was the novelist E.M. Forster. Rupert Brooke also visited Fitzroy Square. Finally, there was the extraordinary Lady Ottoline Morrell, who did not so much belong to Bloomsbury as try to possess it, for she collected creativity as a naturalist collects butterflies or fossils.

By now Virginia was twenty-five. She had published several articles and reviews and had begun a novel, *The Voyage Out*. But life in Bloomsbury had its lighter moments, and at about this time an episode occurred which shows another side of the Stephen character. On 10 February 1910, the officers of the warship *Dreadnought*, the Royal Navy's pride and joy, received a 'Foreign Office message' that they were to be visited by the Emperor of Abyssinia and his retinue. Naturally, when the gorgeously attired foreigners arrived with their 'interpreter' and 'Foreign Office attaché' they were received ceremonially, shown over the ship and royally entertained. A few days later, a deliberate leak to the press revealed the hoax, which had been instigated by one of Adrian Stephen's friends, Horace Cole. Adrian himself had played the interpreter, and Virginia, dressed in rich apparel and with face and hands suitably blackened, had been one of the retinue. The affair caused fury at the Admiralty, but – to quote the *Daily Mirror* – 'all England laughed'.

In 1911, Virginia and Adrian moved to a larger house, 38 Brunswick Square, which they shared with Duncan Grant, Maynard Keynes and Leonard Woolf (recently returned on leave). The household settled to a loosely communal routine allowing to each member the greatest possible privacy. Meals, served at set times, were put on trays in the hall. 'Inmates' carried their trays up to their rooms and later brought down the dirty dishes. There was much socialising and many spontaneous parties, but the wish to work was respected. Vanessa and Clive Bell were still within close reach, and they now brought Roger Fry, the painter, dealer and critic, into the group.

Even more important to Virginia was Leonard Woolf, who proposed to her in January 1912, shortly before he was due to return to Ceylon. Virginia asked for time to think. Leonard applied to the Ceylon civil service for an extension of his leave, but was refused. Rather than risk losing Virginia, he resigned his job. At the end of May, she told him she would marry him; the wedding took place on 10 August 1912 in St Pancras Register Office. The words 'till death us do part' were not spoken during the ceremony, but looking over the registrar's shoulder at the tombstones in the cemetery outside, Leonard felt that he heard them.

The Woolfs rented a little flat in the City at 13 Clifford's Inn, between Chancery and Fetter lanes, minutes away from Dr Johnson's stamping ground at Johnson's Court and Gough Square. The spirits of Chaucer, Shakespeare, Pepys and Boswell seemed to hover in the ancient, narrow lanes, and for a few months the couple was very happy. During the day, both wrote – Virginia was finishing *The Voyage Out* and Leonard had begun a novel, *The Wise Virgins* – and every night they dined at the Cock in Fleet Street, where Tennyson was still remembered and both furniture and food had an air and flavour of considerable antiquity. Leonard described it as:

> a real old city eating house. One sat in wooden partitions and at night it was almost always pretty empty, only journalists from the dailies and lawyers from the Temple dropping in until quite late. Henry was a vintage head waiter, belonging to an era and tradition which, even in 1912, one felt was passing. Large, white faced, redheaded, he was incredibly solemn, slow, unruffled. It was a great day when at last he recognised one as a 'regular'. He would greet one with the ghost of the shadow of a smile, and, as one sat down, he would whisper confidentially: 'I can recommend the devilled bone tonight, Sir,' or: 'I am afraid I can't recommend the steak and kidney pudding tonight, Sir; it's not *quite* as good as usual.'
>
> (Leonard Woolf, *Beginning Again*)

Despite their happiness, the strain of finishing *The Voyage Out* brought on Virginia's most serious collapse to date. In September 1913, she took an overdose of veronal and was only saved by Leonard's quick action. This breakdown lasted for two years. At the beginning, Virginia had been taken to the country, but when at last her health began to improve, she and Leonard moved into Hogarth House in Paradise Road, Richmond, in March 1915.

Virginia now started work on a second novel, *Night and Day*, but Leonard only allowed her to write for a few hours each morning. Early in 1917, a chance sighting in a shop window of a small hand-press inspired the Woolfs to teach themselves how to print books. After a month, both were sufficiently practised to set about producing a booklet containing a story by each. They printed about 150 copies, stitched the pages into gaily patterned paper covers and offered them for sale to friends and acquaintances. Thus began the Hogarth Press, which gained an importance quite incommensurate with its size, publishing early work by Katherine Mansfield, T.S. Eliot, William Plomer and Christopher Isherwood, and also the first translations into English of many Russian and German works, including some by Freud.

Night and Day was finished in 1919. A more experimental novel, *Jacob's Room* (1922), and a stream of essays and reviews, mostly for the *Times Literary Supplement*, the *Nation and Athenaeum*, and the *New Statesman*, testified to Virginia's real recovery. Once again, her love of life and people asserted itself. Leonard, fearing the effects of over-excitement, rationed lunch and dinner parties; nevertheless, the next fifteen years or so were happy ones of steady writing and socialising, interspersed with weekends in the country. The Woolfs took Monk's House, Rodmell, as a country refuge; it was near Charleston Farm, which Vanessa and Clive Bell shared with Duncan Grant. Sometimes there were visits to Garsington, Lady Ottoline Morrell's house in Oxfordshire. In most of the photographs from this period, Virginia's face has a luminous quality, the sensitive mouth half-smiling, the large intelligent eyes calm and lustrous.

Richmond no longer suited the Woolfs. Virginia missed London, and the Press needed to be more central. In 1924, therefore, the second and third floors of 52 Tavistock Square became their home. Once again, Virginia found herself in Bloomsbury, 'fierce and scornful and stonyhearted', but vital and exciting. In the basement was the Hogarth Press, and at the back, down a long corridor, Virginia made her writing room. Here *Mrs Dalloway*, which of all her books most expresses her intense feeling for London, was finished in 1924. Here Mrs Dalloway, going to buy flowers for a party, reflects on life:

> Such fools we are, she thought, crossing Victoria Street. For Heaven only knows why one loves it so, how one sees it so, making it up, building it round one, tumbling it, creating it every moment afresh; but the veriest frumps, the most dejected of miseries sitting on doorsteps (drink their downfall) do the same; can't be dealt with, she felt positive, by Acts of Parliament for that very reason: they love life. In people's eyes, in the swing, tramp, and trudge; in the bellow and the uproar; the carriages, motorcars, omnibuses, vans, sandwich men shuffling and swinging; brass bands; barrel organs; in the triumph and the jingle and the strange high singing of some aeroplane overhead was what she loved; life; London; this moment of June.

To the Lighthouse, published in 1927, celebrates the creative, orderly powers of the human mind, symbolised by the famous boeuf en daube dinner:

> An exquisite scent of olives and oil and juice rose from the great brown dish as Marthe, with a little flourish, took the cover off. The cook had spent three days over that dish. And she must take great care, Mrs Ramsay thought, diving into the soft mass, to choose a specially tender piece for William Bankes. And she peered into the dish, with its shiny walls and its confusion of savoury brown and yellow meats, and its bay leaves, and its wine, and thought: This will celebrate the occasion.

Orlando and *A Room of One's Own* followed in 1928 and 1929, the first an invented biography, the second – brilliantly cogent, direct and witty – one of the major texts of early feminist literature and a delightful piece of writing. Largely thanks to *Orlando*, by 1930 Virginia Woolf was a bestselling writer, able to buy a car, travel abroad, get books and furniture for Tavistock Square and Monk's House. Her next major novel, *The Waves*, was finished on 7 February 1931, but it was only thanks to Leonard's extreme care and insistence on complete rest while she waited for the proofs that another collapse was avoided. *The Waves* was well reviewed and was followed by a light work, the supposed autobiography of Elizabeth Barrett Browning's spaniel, *Flush*.

The Years came out in 1936, and when war broke out in September 1939, Virginia was working on *Between the Acts*. Early in the war, the Woolfs moved from Tavistock Square to Mecklenburgh Square, but in 1940 they were forced to leave London for Rodmell and the Press was transferred to Letchworth. Virginia was upset by what was happening to London and by having to leave it. She was also under stress because she had no confidence in *Between the Acts*. At the beginning of 1941, the dreaded symptoms of collapse appeared, and on 27 March, she mentioned her anxieties about becoming mad again to a friend who was also a doctor. Next day, she filled her pockets with stones and walked into the River Ouse. The letter she left for Leonard told of her love, her gratitude and her wish 'not to go on spoiling your life any longer'. Her body was not found for three weeks.

In the light of her genius, and her somewhat tragic life, it may seem inappropriate to choose Virginia Woolf as companion in our exploration of London's food from 1900 to 1941. But in many ways she is the ideal person. Chronologically, she fits neatly into the period. Her passionate love of London inspired much of her work. The 'capacity for joy' of which Elizabeth Bowen, who knew her well, speaks and the gaiety and sense of fun which endeared her to her nephews and nieces ('Virginia's coming to tea. What fun we shall have!') must have made her the most delightful of fellow-explorers. And it is clear from the evidence of friends as well as from her own writing that when in good health she enjoyed food. Her niece Angelica Garnett says she knew how to cook and could bottle fruit, taking great pride in her cupboard of jade-green gooseberries and sad-purple raspberries at Monk's House. Louie Mayer, the cook at Rodmell, says Virginia made beautiful bread.

> Mr and Mrs Woolf did not like me to cook large meals, but they lived well and enjoyed good food. They particularly liked game – grouse and pheasant with well-made sauces. Puddings had to be very light and newly made, they were mostly cremes and soufflés.

William Plomer says she liked 'good talk, good food (and plenty of salt with it) and good coffee'. And E.M. Forster observed that the passages in her books describing food were 'a sharp reminder that here is a woman who is alert sensuously' and speaks, in a happy phrase, of her 'enlightened greediness'. How responsive are her eyes and nose and palate to Mrs Ramsay's boeuf en daube! How sensuous the description in *A Room of One's Own* of two contrasting meals – ostensibly to boost a feminist message but really, one suspects, because the food and the words to depict it gave her such pleasure! She had been given lunch in a men's college in 'Oxbridge':

> the lunch on this occasion began with soles, sunk in a deep dish, over which the college cook had spread a counterpane of the whitest cream, save that it was branded here and there with brown spots like the spots on the flanks of a doe. After that came the partridges, but if this suggests a couple of bald, brown birds on a plate you are mistaken. The partridges, many and various, came with all their retinue of sauces and salads, the sharp and the sweet, each in its order; their potatoes, thin as coins but not so hard; their sprouts, foliated as rosebuds but more succulent. And no sooner had the roast and its retinue been done with than the silent serving-man . . . set before us, wreathed in napkins, a confection which rose all sugar from the waves. To call it pudding and so relate it to rice and tapioca would be an insult. Meanwhile the wineglasses had flushed yellow and flushed crimson; had been emptied; had been filled. And thus by degrees was lit, half-way down the spine, which is the seat of the soul, not that hard little electric light which we call brilliance, as it pops in and out upon our lips, but the more profound, subtle and subterranean glow which is the rich yellow flame of rational intercourse. No need to hurry. No need to sparkle. No need to be anybody but oneself. We are all going to heaven and Vandyck is of the company.

With this she contrasts dinner at 'Fernham', a women's college: plain gravy soup, succeeded by beef 'suggesting the rumps of cattle in a muddy market, and sprouts curled and yellowed at the edge, and bargaining and cheapening, and women with string bags on Monday morning'. Prunes and custard follow:

And if anyone complains that prunes, even when mitigated by custard, are an uncharitable vegetable (fruit they are not), stringy as a miser's heart and exuding a fluid such as might run in misers' veins who have denied themselves wine and warmth for eighty years . . . he should reflect that there are people whose charity embraces even the prune . . . One cannot think well, love well, sleep well, if one has not dined well. The lamp in the spine does not light on beef and prunes. We are all *probably* going to heaven, and Vandyck is, we *hope*, to meet us round the next corner – that is the dubious and qualifying state of mind that beef and prunes at the end of the day's work breed between them.

This is the writer in good health. It is she – who with Leonard ate six Belgian chocolate cream bars (three each) at a sitting, 'silently, almost reverently', to celebrate the ending of the Great War – whose spirit will shadow this chapter.

The development of steam power, which so dramatically influenced food transport in the nineteenth century, was the first technological innovation to affect the kitchen. Inventors, however, did not rate domestic needs very high; change proceeded at a dignified rate until the suffragette movement and the prominence of women during the First World War forced a greatly accelerated pace. If Mrs Beeton could have returned to earth, she might have felt reasonably at home in Lady Windermere's kitchen in 1895, but by the 1930s any inspection of 'below stairs' in South Kensington or the Edgware Road would certainly have amazed and bewildered her.

The most important development was the change in that fundamental piece of equipment, the cooker. 'I know of no apparatus so desirable,' Mrs Beeton had written firmly in 1842, 'as the common kitchen range, that which has a boiler for hot water on one side, and an oven on the other.' Behind that statement lay a deep mistrust for what was then an almost miraculous invention – the gas appliance. As early as 1824, a gridiron with small holes under which lay jets of gas had been proposed as an alternative means of frying or grilling food. To cooks who properly understood the management of a coal-fired range, it was obviously of limited practical use, but as we have seen, by 1841 the design of gas cookers had sufficiently advanced for Alexis Soyer to install them in the kitchen of the Reform Club. Despite this, ten years later, a domestic gas cooker on display at the Great Exhibition in the Crystal Palace was thought by most people to be smelly, noisy and dirty. When these problems were solved, cooking by gas made rapid progress, for it had many advantages. Although the 1901 edition of Mrs Beeton scarcely mentions gas in the text, an advertisement at the back makes impressive claims which must have influenced many readers. In any event, by 1914 most new London homes had gas cookers, and if gas was not replacing the coal-fired range, it was at least a recognised alternative. The changing status of women and the shortage of servants after the 1914–18 war rapidly increased its popularity, so that by the early 1920s it was considered the most desirable cooking method. Its disadvantages were that it was dangerous in inexperienced hands, and also expensive. (The *Daily Mail Cookery Book* for 1927 gives fourteen tips for gas-cooking economies; they include using three-tiered steamers to cook a whole meal on one burner, having only one or two 'cooking mornings' per week and just reheating food on other days, and deciding how much gas to allow per week for cooking and keeping a close eye on the meter.) Aware of consumer resistance, the industry met it by exploiting the wish to be up to date. 'British Housewives,' declared one advertisement, 'have Science for their servant. British Housewives are famed for the efficient running of their Homes. In the past the high standard has often been maintained by personal drudgery, but to-day Science is their Servant.' And it goes on to recommend gas for ease and cleanliness, offering at the same time a series of pamphlets on 'Gas Economy'.

Despite its drawbacks, then, for a short time it seemed as though gas might see off its rivals, oil and electricity. Oil was cheap and the stoves could be moved to any part of the kitchen or to another house without the problems of connection. On the other hand, it was smelly and sometimes provoked headaches; also, the stoves were large and unsightly because a burner and chimney were needed beneath each plate. By the late 1930s, oil stoves were only sold to country areas as yet unreached by gas or electricity. As regards the latter, the first electric ranges had actually appeared in the 1890s, together with a host of other appliances such as kettles, saucepans, frying-pans, toasters, hot-plates and coffee grinders. The big problem with electric cookers was controlling the heat; not until after the war was this resolved, although even in the late 1920s when electric stoves were beginning to be more generally used, getting and keeping the desired temperature could be difficult. It was a point which the manufacturers of gas cookers did not fail to exploit. The cost of electric current varied in different parts of Britain, but in London cooking by electricity was expensive. However, it was the cleanest method, and as thermostatic control gained in accuracy, electricity became, and remained, a real rival to gas.

Much slower to develop, but also important, was the domestic refrigerator. On country estates, ice houses and ice stacks had been built since the seventeenth century – Pepys was offered wine with ice in it on a hot summer's day and much enjoyed the novelty, and ices for dessert amounted almost to a craze in Georgian high society. Ice collected and stored in winter had long been used to pack salmon for its journey from Scotland down to London. In the late nineteenth century, ice was also imported in large quantities from Norway, and later from America. But the principles of mechanical refrigeration were not developed at any practical level until the 1860s, and the first consignment of frozen meat from Australia reached Britain in 1880. At this time, domestic refrigerators were hardly in question. Some London merchants set up refrigeration plants from which ice could be delivered to shops or homes. By 1900, we find *Law's Grocer's Manual* mentioning the refrigerator, or 'portable ice chest', for domestic use; it was to be found in the better hotels and restaurants, and very occasionally in the kitchens of the rich. Until well into the '30s, most households relied on the meat safe, a cupboard with walls of very fine wire mesh, keeping out flies but allowing cool air to circulate. One could also buy small portable cold chests, with thick walls of porous clay and a cavity on top into which one poured cold water. In this, milk, meat and butter could be kept cool for two or three days during hot weather. In *To the Lighthouse*, we first meet Mrs Ramsay's little boy cutting out a picture of a refrigerator for his scrapbook, and a 1927 advertisement (perhaps the same one?) for Servel refrigerators shows how much of a novelty they still were at that date:

> SERVEL makes all the difference! Every dish more fresh, more dainty and more appetising. A Servel in the home is an investment with a wonderful return in health and happiness – preventing food decay and the development of bacteria, automatically, without trouble or attention, all the year round

– making all kinds of frozen delicacies and delightful desserts
– providing dainty ice cubes for drinks and table use . . . Call
and see the Servel in operation at our showrooms.

Even in the '30s, fridges were unfamiliar objects to many people.
Monica Dickens, in her first job as cook-general (*One Pair of Hands*,
1939), could not understand why the ice in her employer's
refrigerator was always melting. The explanation came from a
friendly tradesman: it seems she had not realised the door had to be
kept shut.

In all the writing on domestic management published after 1918,
one term crops up regularly. That term is 'labour-saving', and it
shows clearly how much the war had affected the supply of domestic
servants. From 1914, young girls ready to go into service had
another option: they could work in the factories, taking the place of
the men at the Front. They found the work less irksome, less lonely
(usually a skivvy or an under-housemaid had few friends) and better
paid. Employers were satisfied too, for female labour was cheap and
women proved they could work as well as men. At the end of the
war, therefore, the below-stairs battalions had been depleted, except
on large country estates. In London, the largest houses were
renovated to make them easier to run, or divided into flats. But
domestic help was scarce, and employment agencies boomed. Even
the inexperienced found work easily, as Monica Dickens makes
clear. After a short spell at a cookery school, she took various jobs
as cook-general or parlour-maid, living at home and going to work
daily. All her employers had modern gas stoves, some had
refrigerators, and all expected a high standard of cooking. Usually
she was the only domestic apart from a daily cleaner, so she had to
do all the preparation and the washing up – a situation that would
have been unheard of in that social milieu before the war.

This 'servant problem' had important consequences for kitchen
design. In pre-war Britain, the principles of labour-saving and
convenience had little popular appeal. The virtual disappearance of
the live-in servant then forced a change of attitude, as it was
recognised that the housewife might have to do at least some of her
own cooking. Middle-class magazines such as *Good Housekeeping*
began to feature kitchen design, and in 1920 an article in *Ideal Homes*
described the average kitchen as 'a source of continual irritation'.
Dressers with narrow shelves for plates and dishes, scanty

accommodation for cutlery in ill-fitting drawers, free-standing cabinets with too little room for pots, pans, bowls and jugs, wooden tables which needed to be scrubbed at least once a day, and every cupboard standing at some distance from every other were the main complaints. Architects and manufacturers were forced to recognise the demands of women working, like Monica Dickens, single-handed at a job previously done by two or three people. The result was the replacement of the dresser and the haphazardly placed cupboards with kitchen cabinets designed specifically for the job, and wooden tables were ousted by ones with porcelain or enamelled metal tops. The man who led the revolution in Britain was a Canadian, Wilson Crowe, whose experience of transatlantic kitchen design allowed him to design for British housewives the ultimate in cabinets, or 'kitchenettes' as they were sometimes called. 'Scientifically designed', they were intended to be to the housewife what his businessman's desk was to her husband; the 'Easiwork Kitchen Cabinet', it was said, made the kitchen as efficient as any office. In addition to the shelves planned to hold specific items (including a fixed flour bin with rotary sifter, 'an invention which saves an incredible amount of waste and dirt'), it had drawers of different sizes (baize-lined for cutlery, tin-lined to hold bread and cakes), fitments inside the doors for small items and saucepan lids, and a fold-down porcelain table large enough for rolling pastry. It came with its own glass containers for storing groceries. 'So compact is it,' ran the advertisement, 'that it saves you the trouble of thinking.'

But if it was release from the trouble of thinking that the housewife sought, technology had come up with something even more compact, and cheaper, than the Easiwork kitchen – the tin. The principle of food preservation by heat-treating in glass jars had been discovered early in the nineteenth century in France, but it was an American who first used 'tin' (actually iron) cans for the process. Manufacturers soon exploited the idea in the United States; in Britain it was accepted more slowly, and at the turn of the century, canning was used mainly (though not entirely) for luxury foods. Escoffier's recipes (see previous chapter) are one example. *Law's Grocer's Manual* for 1900 provides others: jugged hare, mulligatawny soup, chicken gumbo, and French beans. Fortnum & Mason sold their tins of Scotch salmon and beef stew with clear (if hardly user-friendly) opening instructions:

To open the Canister, first stab a hole with the butt-end of a knife, near the upper rim. Then insert the blade as far as it will go. Draw the handle towards you and the blade will be found to cut through the tin with perfect ease.

Many tinned goods were imported: fruit from the United States, salmon from Canada, meat from Argentina, condensed milk from America and Switzerland. Only the last two came within the budget of the working class; even so, by 1914, Britain was the world's largest importer of tinned foods. As basic foods became cheaper in the prosperous years before 1914, food manufacture became increasingly lucrative; wartime shortages further stimulated research. By 1918, the industry was ready to build on that research, and within a few years, firms like Smedleys, Chivers and Hartleys were producing large quantities of tinned vegetables, fruit and jam. Now the working classes provided a ready market, for wages had risen, and they were no longer content to live on a diet of bread, bacon and potatoes. They wished for variety and (because women were often wage earners) ease of preparation. Among the upper classes too, inexperienced housewives or those with inexperienced cooks were grateful for products which saved work and eliminated mistakes. Monica Dickens finds it unnecessary to apologise or even comment when she describes opening tins of lobster to make lobster cocktails. Rose Henniker Heaton summed up the situation nicely in her book *The Perfect Hostess* (1931):

The Bride gives her First (and worst) Dinner Party
(She has an indifferent cook, and a single-handed house-
parlourmaid)

Menu
Caviare Freshly-made Toast
Consommé Royale
Soles in Aspic
Duck and Green Peas Apple Sauce
Gravy Seasoning Potatoes
Omelette en Flamme Soufflé au Fromage
Coffee (roasted and freshly ground at home)
Iced Burgundy Tepid Champagne

Her Second Dinner Party (A Month Later)

Menu
Lazenby's Julienne Soup
Fortnum & Mason's Tinned Duck
Petits Pois (bottled)
Lemon Cheesecakes from Harrod's
Vanilla Ice from Lyons in packets
Camp Coffee

Of all the canned foods ever sold in Britain, baked beans deserves a paragraph to itself on the grounds of its phenomenal popularity. Beans have a very minor place in British culinary tradition, and as a new food introduced by H.J. Heinz in 1905, they could hardly compete with the jugged hare and the mulligatawny soup; at a lower level, they were not cheap enough to appeal to the poorer classes. Their first appearance therefore flopped badly. Heinz waited twenty years and then made another attempt. This time, beans were to be the chief product of a new factory at Harlesden, on the outskirts of London, thus reducing the cost. Partly for this reason, partly because the British public was by now used to tinned food and becoming more adventurous, and partly also due to a massive advertising campaign, baked beans became a British staple (and are probably responsible for the fact that many of today's adults have a gastronomic age of nine).

If Mrs Beeton would have felt out of her depth in the Easiwork kitchen of the '30s, she might have found shopping a less disorienting experience. For people of her class, the mechanics of shopping had changed little. The milkman brought the milk to the door; other tradesmen sent boys to collect orders which were delivered by horse and cart – or perhaps motorised van – the same day. (Monica Dickens had never realised 'what a sociable lot of back-door traffic there is, especially in a house where the mistress doesn't order the things at the shops herself'.) Bigger changes had taken place in the shops, however. Although Fortnum & Mason was still the 'top people's' grocer, department stores like Harrods, the Army & Navy Stores and Selfridges also sold quality foods. The huge rounds of cheese on the counters, however, had probably been made in factories rather than on farms, and some came from Canada or New Zealand. Butter was still sold from tubs from which it was the apprentice's daily duty to cut and stamp prettily decorated pound or half-pound portions, but it was a rare grocer now who boiled or baked his own hams. The better shops still offered their own blended tea, and Mrs Beeton would have been able to take and sniff a pinch of her favourite blend, making sure it was up to standard before asking the assistant to scoop a pound or two from a huge tin-lined chest. At the biscuit counter, she would have been astonished by the variety; demand for factory-made biscuits had increased enormously since the war, and the manufacturers seemed to bring out a new type every month or two. Biscuits came to the shops in large tins with airtight lids and were sold loose by weight. Sugar would have been another surprise – where were the sugarloaves? she would ask, and be delighted to know that she could now buy granulated sugar which the assistant weighed out and put in a strong paper bag. (It was a standard complaint against grocers that they mixed sand into the sugar.) Even in 1925, few goods were pre-packed, though if Mrs Beeton had wanted to make a steamed pudding, packets of ready-grated suet stood on the shelves. If dried fruit was still sold loose, at least now it was washed and stalked before you bought it.

Far more significant changes – in that, in time, even quality shops would be forced to follow the trend – had taken place at a humbler level. The growth of population in towns like London and Glasgow, combined with the increased quantity of cheap food flooding into Britain from all over the Empire, put tremendous pressure on ordinary small grocers' shops in the early years of the century. Food distribution became a problem, and it was solved by the establishment on the one hand of co-operative retail societies and on the other of multiple-shop businesses. Both used the principle of bulk purchase, the goods then distributed to a number of outlets. Food bought thus cost less, and administrative costs were kept down by careful management, so that the less well off could buy food of reasonable quality at low prices. The Maypole Dairy, Home & Colonial Stores and Thomas Lipton Ltd are probably the best known of the multiple-shop retailing companies. Lipton, a colourful character from Glasgow, began his career in the 1870s using what are now classic business methods – undercutting his rivals by buying direct from manufacturers in enormous quantities instead of through agents, fitting out all his shops to a standard design, and using displays and stunts to gain public attention. (One of his stunts was to install distorting mirrors at the entrances and exits of each of his shops. Those at the entrance made people look thin, whereas when they left Lipton's they looked plump and well fed.) By 1890, he had established several shops in London and had hit on the bright idea of buying tea plantations in Ceylon. Under the slogan 'Direct from the Garden to the Teapot', he imported and blended his own tea and packed it in one-pound, half-pound and quarter-pound packets, thus providing consumers with a product of guaranteed standardised quality at low prices. His example was followed by many and marked the way for the large multiple stores we know today.

It was probably due to Lipton that British manufacturers and retailers after the First World War realised the importance of visual marketing. Bright, attractive advertisements and eye-catching packaging, as used in America, encouraged customers to choose a particular brand. An example is Bird's Custard, which, invented in the 1830s by Alfred Bird for his wife who liked custard but was allergic to eggs, became popular enough to generate a number of imitations and rivals; but it took the design of a colourful, distinctive packet almost a century later, plus an aggressive advertising campaign, to put Bird's into virtually every kitchen cabinet in the country. So, in the years between 1918 and 1939, the hoardings went up, the buses blossomed, the tube stations were enlivened with colour. Everywhere, Bovril prevented that 'Sinking Feeling', the Bisto Kids were lured home by the smell of dehydrated gravy browning, and the Ovaltine Maid held in her wheatsheaf the promise of health, beauty and happiness. Not all the advertisements were equally persuasive: 'COOK'S FARM EGGS have ever been a boon and blessing to Every Home. They are all-egg (only moisture and shell removed). One heaped tablespoonful equals two shell eggs, and the Price is ever low.'

From horrors such as this many households never escaped. Why, between the wars, did British cooking become so bad? The answer may be that it did not – that, paradoxical as it may seem, dried eggs, custard powder and gravy browning were a sign that some British cooking was improving. The fact is that when we speak of any national cooking, we are thinking of that portion of the nation which traditionally is able to choose food it enjoys. Thus British cooking in the eighteenth and nineteenth centuries is represented by the food of the middle and upper classes, together with that part of the rural community which was prosperous enough to be able to choose what it wanted to eat. The poorer working classes are omitted from the concept because they lived at subsistence level and had no choice. But when we speak of British cooking in the twentieth century, we include the working classes, because for much of the period their standard of living has been high enough to allow them to vary their diet and buy what pleases them. Consider H.G. Wells' Mr Polly, sitting dejectedly on a stile somewhere in Kent in 1910 and struggling with indigestion:

> There had been the cold pork from Sunday, and some nice cold potatoes, and Rashdall's Mixed Pickles, of which he was inordinately fond. He had eaten three gherkins, two onions, a small cauliflower head, and several capers with every appearance of appetite, and indeed with avidity; and then there had been cold suet pudding to follow, with treacle, and then a nice bit of cheese. It was the pale, hard sort of cheese he liked; red cheese he declared was indigestible. He had also had three big slices of greyish baker's bread, and had drunk the best part of the jugful of beer.
>
> (H.G. Wells, *The History of Mr Polly*, 1910)

Urban families with a background of deprivation and near-starvation may need generations of exposure to good food before they like it; but if in 1910 Mr Polly wanted pickled gherkin and cold suet pudding, if in the '20s the great-great-granddaughter of Mayhew's little watercress-seller enjoyed baked beans and processed peas, can we claim that 'national' cooking had deteriorated?

This move towards gastronomic democratisation had interesting consequences, in that now for the first time we find daily newspapers carrying recipes and even publishing recipe books. The *Daily Mail Cookery Book* (1927), from which most of the advertisements quoted above have been taken, is aimed at the young housewife of moderate means who may well be doing all her own cooking. It is written very simply and although it begins by describing the ideal kitchen of the future (dresser and cabinet on castors, all cooking done by gas and electricity, no shelves too high for convenient cleaning), it soon comes down to reality: 'in the meantime the average kitchen is built with plastered walls and ceiling, a boarded floor and skirting, and is supplied with a fixed open dresser and a coal range.' For those housewives fortunate enough to be able to plan their own kitchens, the *Daily Mail* writer has a word of advice: 'let your text be: *Everything in this Kitchen will have to be cleaned.*' The practical but sympathetic tone continues throughout, most manifest where, at the end of all but the simplest recipes, a short section suggests 'Reasons for failure'.

For whom was the *Daily Mail Cookery Book* intended? Primarily, it seems, for women of little or no experience, since all the basic methods are clearly and carefully explained. The simple recipes move from stock, steamed fish, and boiled vegetables to soufflés, mousses and casseroles, and include too a few foreign dishes: Sole à l'Italienne, Risotto (a rather unorthodox recipe) and Blanquette de Veau. Apart from a few general instructions, the only game recipe is for a Chaudfroid of Pheasant or Partridge. The oddest, or perhaps the wisest, feature of the book is the mix of genuine and spurious: from Fillets of Sole in Mayonnaise, which calls for sole, lobster stuffing, green peas and home-made mayonnaise, to something called Entente Pudding, for which the ingredients are one packet of tangerine orange jelly, one pint of custard made from powder, gelatine, sponge cake, sugar, unsweetened condensed milk or cream, angelica, glacé cherries and vanilla essence.

The *Daily Express Book of Home Management*, published a few years later (1934), is a rather different affair and has clearly set out to compete with Mrs Beeton. Its four colour plates are paintings of elaborate dishes complete with dainty garnish, its half-tone prints illustrate the 'best' way to set a table, decorate cakes, bring up children, furnish a sitting room. The cookery section takes up exactly half the book.

It is obvious at the start that this is aimed slightly higher up the social scale than the *Daily Mail Cookery Book*. The kitchen, it advises, must be well fitted-up, and 'if it is to be used as a servant's sitting room also it must be made comfortable for her leisure hours' with two basket-chairs, a cosy hearthrug, pretty curtains at the window, and a cover for the table out of working hours. As regards equipment, it is recommended that the old kitchen range be removed and replaced by a gas or electric stove. There is no mention of refrigerators (the book carries no advertisements), but a meat safe which can be fixed to the kitchen window ledge is advised. What of the recipes?

The surprise is that they are for the most part rather old-fashioned. Certainly there appears to be a direct line of descent from

Mrs Glasse through Miss Acton and Mrs Beeton to Margaret Garth, the author. Classic British dishes, from Almond Soup, Toad-in-the-Hole and Sheep's Head Pie to any one of fifty-six steamed or boiled puddings, form the backbone of the text. The book is none the worse for that, indeed a revival of such cooking in intelligent hands might be cause for pride rather than shame. But there has obviously been a desire to give the book a modern flavour, and various interspersed sections sit uneasily among the traditional fare. The first gives instructions for making the most popular cocktails – Bronx, Maiden's Blush, Sidecar, and the like – and also recipes for cocktails served as hors d'oeuvres. These are mainly of shellfish but include a particularly nasty-sounding concoction of grapefruit, sugar, chilli vinegar, paprika and tomato ketchup. The next gives four foreign soups, 'with which many of us are now familiar'. They are Bouillabaisse (certainly not authentic but probably very good, since it includes oysters, shrimps and lobster), Minestrone, Bortsch (*sic*) and Basque Cherry Soup. The final interspersed section is for 'Entrées and Made Dishes', defined as 'a light, delicate, daintily served dish, complete in itself'. 'Now that so many excellent commodities are canned,' writes Mrs Garth, 'it is sometimes easy to prepare an excellent entrée from tinned goods, but, generally speaking fresh meat or fish is used.' These recipes are elaborate and often, but not always, expensive – Oyster Kromeskies, for instance, Quails à la Biarritz, Fillets of Beef à la Béarnaise and Lamb Cutlets à la Mazarin.

Perhaps the best way to sum up the *Daily Express Book of Home Management* is with a quotation from the restaurateur Marcel Boulestin, who wrote that on his first visit to England, 'I took my meals in all sorts of places; hotels, restaurants, and taverns. The food seemed quite good when English, mediocre when it made the pretence of being French.'

Boulestin's was one of the best restaurants in London between the wars, and it is a paradox – because she disliked restaurants – that Virginia Woolf was in part responsible for its creation. Boulestin had come to England before the First World War and, being fully bilingual and of literary bent, worked as a theatre critic until he went to act as interpreter to the British forces. After the war, he lived rather precariously, giving French lessons, writing articles and reviews, advising people on wines and spirits, and occasionally cooking for other people's dinner parties. He also produced a little book of recipes called *Simple French Cooking for English Homes*. It so happened that in 1925 *Vogue* wished to commission Virginia Woolf to write an article which would be accompanied by photographs of her, her house and her friends. It was customary for the details of such commissions to be worked out over lunch with the author, but *Vogue*'s editor, Dorothy Todd, knew that Virginia hated going to restaurants. When she mentioned this to Boulestin, the latter suggested that he should arrange the whole meal and that the luncheon party should be held in his flat. Dorothy Todd agreed. Two more guests were invited, Boulestin, with the help of his friend Robin Adair, produced a splendid meal, and the party was a great success. Afterwards someone remarked that it would be wonderful if Boulestin had his own small restaurant to which his friends could go to enjoy his marvellous food. No sooner said than done – one of Virginia's fellow guests, a rich man, put up the money, and premises were found in Leicester Square and decorated by another guest, who was an artist. Robin Adair proved to have great managerial skill, the help of an excellent and experienced chef called Bigorre was enlisted, and very soon the fame of the restaurant spread, for it was the only place in London at the time to have genuine French cooking and a Gallic ambience. Madge Garland, then *Vogue*'s fashion editor, who tells this story, writes that Boulestin's 'was just for French food and was so small that it was really like a club; we never went there without knowing everyone, which was one of its great charms'. But it had no licence, and its size made it financially vulnerable, so in October 1926 the Restaurant Boulestin reopened in Southampton Street, not far from Covent Garden and the Royal Opera House. There were tables for eighty people, but Boulestin maintained his high standards and was enormously successful. He avoided all gimmicks except on one occasion: when Wagner's *Ring* was on at Covent Garden, he engaged a trumpeter to sound Siegfried's fanfare ten minutes before the end of the dinner interval so that his customers could get to their seats on time.

Boulestin was particular about his ingredients: he used English beef, mutton, cream and butter, but his vegetables, fruit, cheese and coffee were flown in from France. His approach to food was simple and unpretentious:

> Good meals should be the rule and not the exception.
> Economy is a basic rule in French cooking, which is rarely extravagant.

Try to balance rich and simple food.

When you cook *taste all the way.*

A good cookbook should illustrate the idea that *'On ne mange bien que chez soi.'*

He insisted on coal fires and charcoal grills, believing (most people would agree) that no oven could compare with an open fire for roasting meat or birds. Undeniably, here lay the secret of much of his success, together with his faithful adherence to traditional French dishes. Omelettes, poules au pot, carbonnades and ragouts stand in his pages unadorned and glorious, and he writes of the havoc caused by 'many who, disappointed at seeing that most French dishes are simple, complicate them purposely, probably adding other flavours detrimental to the taste'.

Without doubt, Boulestin exerted immeasurable influence on British gastronomy between the wars. Apart from his restaurant, his books were well known, and he was the first person to demonstrate cooking on television. Boulestin's was very much the kind of small establishment preferred by the Woolfs, where the food was interesting and the atmosphere informal, where good conversation counted for more than stage acts and the presence of *le tout Londres.* Even in such places, things did not always go their way. In *Beginning Again,* Leonard gives a very amusing account of a dinner to which he and Virginia were invited by Rose Macaulay in the late '20s. They had thought it would be a small informal affair and did not worry when, having spent most of the day printing, they discovered that they were going to be late. They dashed off without changing and arrived, dishevelled and probably still bearing traces of printer's ink, to find ten or twelve people, immaculate in evening dress, preparing to go to a restaurant across the street. Conscious of their appearance, and that they had kept everybody waiting, Leonard lost his nerve. His hand habitually trembled, but now it shook so badly that he could not eat, his spoon clattering against the plate and showering soup over the tablecloth. Suddenly, in one of those complete silences which fall upon even a literary dinner party, Virginia's clear voice was heard: 'What do you mean by the Holy Ghost?' To which her neighbour replied angrily, 'I did not say "Holy Ghost", I said "the whole coast".' Leonard, feeling that Virginia had disgraced herself, tried to hide his embarrassment by turning to speak to his neighbour and, noticing, as he thought, that she had dropped her white napkin on the floor, leaned down and picked it up to give to her. Unfortunately for him, it was her white petticoat which was hanging down below her skirt: 'She took it badly and we slunk away as soon as we could after dinner.'

To understand why Boulestin's became such a favourite in some London circles between the wars, it is necessary now to return to the restaurant scene as we left it at the end of the Naughty Nineties, characterised by large expensive places like the Savoy, and much smaller, rather exclusive ones like Willis's. The accession of King Edward VII with his huge zest for life and enormous capacity for enjoyment meant that a much greater range of pleasurable activities than before was deemed to be socially acceptable. The fact that 'nice' women could now be seen dining in public restaurants changed the entertainment scene and freed people from the narrow confines of the dinner party. The time was ripe, therefore, for an entrepreneur to give the fashionable public a meeting-place even bigger than the Savoy – not a hotel, but a whole group of restaurants of varying sizes and catering for different age groups and tastes under one roof. With this in mind, Joseph Lyons, already the owner of a successful chain of London tearooms, opened the Trocadero in Shaftesbury Avenue in 1903.

The 'Troc', specifically designed with women in mind, set new standards of opulence and enjoyment. Great attention had been paid to the interior architecture and the decor, as the essayist and theatre critic Clement Scott explained in an article called 'How they dined us in 1860 and how they dine us now':

> we took our so-called pleasures alone and moodily in the days before gaiety and electric light and flower decorated tables and stringed bands in gilded orchestras; we who were obstinately denied the priceless pleasures of woman's society, her voice, her sparkling eyes, the beauty of her dress, the sense of contact with all that is charming and elegance; what should we have thought in 1860 of the marble halls, the frescoes, the soft carpeted staircases, the courteous liveried attendants, the scent of flowers and the air of hospitality and opulence that distinguishes such a distinctly new departure in London life as the Trocadero.

Indeed the 'Troc' was amazing. The Golden Staircase, perfectly designed to display women's gowns to best advantage, led up to nine dining rooms, three of which had space for dancing as well as dining. In the Great Hall, the orchestra played in a gilded gallery beneath frescoed cupids. The more sober grill room (grey marble, gold and buff) provided simpler food than the main restaurant; it was not necessary here to wear formal dress, which American visitors appreciated. Parties of fewer than 20 people could hire a small room for the evening. The 'Troc' employed 7,000 staff, and its weekly shopping list set the mind reeling – 180 loins of beef, 400 chines, 1,500 fowls, 600 quail, 800 whiting, 14,000 oysters, 60 gallons of vinegar, 400 gallons of milk . . .

'The glittering comfort of the palatial restaurant' – to quote *The Caterer* of August 1902 – was not for everyone's pocket. Many people of more modest income, following at a humble distance the fashions of the great and affluent, would have liked to allow themselves an occasional small extravagance. Joseph Lyons realised that here was a large, almost untapped market; his Popular Café in Piccadilly opened in 1904, just a year after the Trocadero. Here one could choose from a mixed grill, a simple set meal (soup, whitebait, braised ham or mutton, mousse) or à la carte. To create an atmosphere of relaxed enjoyment, an orchestra played during supper, just as at the Trocadero.

A further untapped market was that of midday lunches. Dickensian chop-houses and pie-shops, often badly run, far from clean and offering poor-quality food, could no longer cater for crowds of shoppers and City workers. Low-cost but decent food was hard to find, until John Pearce, an ex-barrow boy, opened his first restaurant at Farringdon Street in 1892. The lunches were not exciting: steak puddings, Irish stew, roast beef, mutton or pork, or a pork chop served with potatoes. But they were reasonably well cooked and cheap, and the premises clean and comfortable. For young City clerks especially, the Pearce and Plenty shops were a blessing: by taking soup first and finishing with a pastry or a mug of tea, coffee or cocoa, they could have a cheap three-course meal at midday, which meant they needed but a light supper when they returned home at night. By 1905, the chain owned restaurants and tearooms all over London, and other firms were copying the formula.

One more change in the eating-out scene of this pre-war period should be noted, since it foreshadowed what is probably the most significant gastronomic development in London this century: the growth in the number of restaurants serving foreign food. The French, as we saw, got in first, 200 years ahead of the others; but between 1890 and 1910, Italian, Spanish, German, Jewish and Chinese restaurants all appeared, so that when Newnham-Davis revised his guide to London restaurants in 1913, he judged that an Englishman wishing to extend his gastronomic education need no longer travel abroad.

On this happy state of affairs the 1914–1918 war had the destructive force of an avalanche. Before the war, four-fifths of all bread baked in Britain was made from foreign wheat, and three-fifths of the butter spread on that bread was imported. Three-quarters of the cheese consumed came from the Continent. Suddenly supplies were cut off. Sugar, much of which had been imported from Germany, became as much of a luxury as in Tudor days; there were no more eggs from Russia, no more beef and mutton from Australia and Argentina. It was not even possible to get fish, since the North Sea fishing grounds were now closed.

To the restaurants, the most devastating blow of all was caused by the depletion of staff: so many men enlisted or were conscripted, so many more were interned as German nationals. The clientele too shrank. Of those who remained in London, many preferred to eat their meals at home; there was nothing festive now about the Savoy or the Trocadero, and once the air-raids began, gilt caryatids and marble walls could be positively dangerous. By 1916, it was more profitable to run a tea and bun shop than a restaurant; but there were still office workers and businesspeople who needed to be fed. For them, Joseph Lyons, making a bold decision, opened the Strand Corner House with seating for 1,000 in 1915.

It was just the right moment – a year later, with the shortage of labour and food, he could not have done it. As it was, he met both a material and an emotional demand, providing an eating-place in the heart of London where one could get a cup of tea and a bun or a quick meal in the reassuring company of 999 other people with the same needs. The Corner House became an institution.

The government's first measure to conserve food was to make it compulsory for restaurants to shut at 10 p.m. Its second was to fix the number of courses permitted at meals. Then, late in 1916, 'war bread' made from unrefined flour was compulsorily introduced. (One restaurant at least found a way round this particular restriction – the Café Royal went on serving white bread for some time, much to the fury of other restaurateurs. During an official investigation, the secret was revealed: someone was adding mashed potato to the flour.) As food stocks diminished, voluntary rationing was attempted, but by late 1917, compulsory rationing in public eating-places had to be introduced, and official meatless days – Tuesdays in London – were declared. By 1918, at the Savoy, they were substituting vegetables for meat, cornmeal for wheat, margarine for butter and saccharine for sugar.

At last the war ended. Very slowly, Londoners recovered, but nothing in their feeding would ever be quite the same. There was a shortage of fuel, whose most immediately noticeable effect was the disappearance of the coffee-stalls and street vendors of baked potatoes, eel pies, roast chestnuts, and cockles and winkles. The government set up National Kitchens to provide cooked food which people could eat at home; a number of private restaurants no longer able to stay in business took on this role, but after rationing had been revoked in 1919, National Kitchens gradually faded out. The street sellers did at last reappear, but their numbers were much reduced.

In their place came more large and inexpensive eating-places. Lyons' Corner House was extended and began to serve breakfasts from 7 a.m. It also sold ready-made meals to take home (the slogan was 'Bring a Lyons' chef to every home'). All the Lyons tea shops were decorated in white and gold, and served tea or a savoury drink called Celesco with rolls and butter, Bath buns, oatcakes, toasted muffins, or fancy cakes. The waitresses were dressed in black with white aprons; known affectionately as 'nippies', they became a byword for the speed and neatness of their service.

The snack-bar habit, a development of tavern food and once confined to City stockbrokers, also spread, to such an extent that by 1937 almost all restaurants in the centre of London had a snack-bar as well as a dining room. The first all-night snack-bar, Bogey's Bar, opened in Bloomsbury itself, in Woburn Place. Sandwich bars made their appearance; as early as 1919, one Bassett Digby, traveller and writer, was selling sandwiches of reindeer tongue, sheep's-milk cheese, tuna and other delicacies opposite the *New Statesman* office in Great Queen Street. And in 1921, the first self-service restaurant opened. It was run by ex-servicemen; you chose your dish and paid for a ticket which you surrendered at the service counter in exchange for the food.

When the more formal type of restaurant reappeared, a change of attitude was noticeable. The rich, multi-course meals of the Edwardians seemed irrelevant now. People ate less and they did not want their dinners to be long-drawn-out affairs. Cocktails were sometimes blamed for the diminished appetites, but the truth was that eating was no longer the only way to spend an evening. Upper-class women, accustomed now to managing their lives without the help of men, refused to abandon their new freedom, and above all things dreaded boredom. Everybody hungered for gaiety and the chance to be frivolous and irresponsible. Many restaurants translated this in terms of music and dancing. The Berkeley, as every P.G. Wodehouse reader knows, was one of the most popular places; when Bertie Wooster was not hiding from his aunts at the Drones club, he was likely to be found here, toying with a soufflé or dancing with a beautiful girl. The Berkeley's food was extremely good and also innovative: it was here that Prawns Mary Rose and Fraises Mimosa, to name but two dishes, were invented.

Other places offered cabaret. The Savoy, as so often, was the innovator here: it installed hydraulic jacks to raise the dance floor when required so that it could be used as a stage. By 1937, Thomas Burke, in his excellent guide to London restaurants, *Dinner is Served*, estimated that 80 per cent of restaurants in central London had a band or a cabaret act. One place became a great success simply because, while the diners ate, a man dashed round the place on roller skates, 'glancing from the tables by a quarter-inch, and never upsetting one of them'. 'A man may start out to be a restaurateur,' Burke wrote despairingly, 'but the taste of the age compels him to become a part-time music-hall manager.'

The true heir to the music halls, of course, was the cinema; and the builders of post-war cinemas, taking their cue from the fashionable restaurants, decided that they too would link entertainment and food. Quite apart from the pleasurable aspects, it made sense to provide somewhere where people could eat before or after a two-hour film. By the late 1920s, all the large picture palaces had restaurants and tearooms. Some went further: the Regal had a dance floor as well. Its decor carried on from where the Savoy and the Ritz left off, with the foyer a mix of Empire and Regency, the auditorium in Roman style and the attendants dressed in Victorian costume. In the restaurant, turquoise lamps illuminated lacquered tables flanked by coral-pink chairs, and golden silk curtains printed with red poppies framed the windows. Dancing was all the rage now. Flat-chested and Marcel-waved, young women danced the foxtrot or the Charleston with clean-shaven brilliantined young men, or with each other at the tea dances which were the latest craze.

But despite 'the taste of the age', some of the older restaurants did survive and thrive, right up to the outbreak of the Second World War. In their pre-war incarnations Prunier's (specialising in fish dishes), Kettner's (closed down in 1914 but triumphantly resurrected and enlarged), Claridge's, Frascati's, Gatti's, the Ivy and Quaglino's seem to have acquired almost mythological status. Also that most Wodehousian of eating-houses, Simpson's-in-the-Strand, described in *Something Fresh* as a 'restful Temple of Food', where 'no strident orchestra forces the diner to bolt beef in ragtime' and worshippers sit, 'in their eyes that resolute, concentrated look which is the peculiar property of the British luncher, ex-President Roosevelt's man-eating fish, and the American army-worm'.

From the international array of London restaurants, only the French were missing. Since the death of Mme Nicols the Café Royal had lost its French ambience. So too had Willis's. It was this vacuum which Boulestin so triumphantly filled. His contribution to the literature of English cooking is well known. Few people recognise, however, his modest but vital contribution to English literature itself: it is almost certainly due to him that the main dish at Mrs Ramsay's dinner table was not roast beef or braised leg of lamb, but rather boeuf en daube. Not only did he cook this in his restaurant, but, alone among contemporary English recipe books, his writings include at least two recipes for the dish.

RECIPES

LOBSTER COCKTAIL

Not the desperate invention of Monica Dickens, but a more authentic though humble recipe. Not to my taste, but typical of its time.

1 cup lobster meat
¼ cup lemon juice
½ cup tomato catsup
2 tsp Worcester sauce
½ tsp each Tabasco and finely chopped chives
salt and paprika to taste

Mix all the ingredients together, place on ice, and serve in glasses or in opaque glass cups of small size.

(Daily Mail Cookery Book, 1927)

POTAGE PRINTANIER

This soup is typical of the light, graceful dishes which were introduced by Boulestin.

2–3 young carrots
2–3 young turnips
1 white cabbage
3 leeks
1 oz (30 g) butter
1½ pts (900 ml) clear stock or consommé
1 lettuce (Iceberg or Webb's Wonderful)
½ lb (250 g) shelled peas
2 tbsp chopped chervil

This soup, which is an adaptation of the soup beloved of the French peasant of the South, will be found pleasant and comforting for a typical English summer day. Get some young carrots and turnips, wash them well and scrape them lightly; their skin is still very thin and will come off easily. Also get a white cabbage, remove all the outside leaves and use the heart only; cut it in four quarters and the other vegetables in thin narrow slices; add the white part only of two or three leeks and cook all this very slowly in butter in a fireproof dish, keeping the lid on all the time. When tender, add some good clear soup, the heart of a lettuce cut in four, a handful of small fresh peas and a little chopped chervil. You should add clear soup in sufficient quantity so that there is enough for your purpose when it has been reduced by one-third, on a slow fire.

Taste it to see if it is properly seasoned and, just before serving, add in the yolk of one egg well beaten and mix it well with this pleasant mixture of spring vegetables.

(Marcel Boulestin, article in *Vogue*, from *Food in Vogue*, 1976)

SPICED ONIONS

An interesting dish, harking back to the eighteenth century. The authors of *The Gentle Art of Cookery* were keen revivers of the best English culinary traditions, although their book does contain some foreign dishes. Mrs Leyel was a noted herbalist, and the book is particularly strong on vegetable cookery. I suggest that one clove would be sufficient for modern tastes.

6 small onions
2 anchovies
parsley
¼ pt (150 ml) claret
¼ pt (150 ml) stock
1 tbsp flour
1 tbsp butter
½ tsp capers
pepper, cloves, bay leaf and salt

Make a brown roux of the flour and butter, and add the wine and stock to it. Let it simmer for a few minutes, and then add the onions, which must have been cooked in boiling water for twenty minutes. Put in the parsley, cloves, and the bay leaf, and let the whole cook slowly. Take out the onions and put them on the dish in which they will be served.

Strain the sauce and reheat it, with the capers and the anchovies chopped fine. Bring it to the boil, and pour over the onions.

(Mrs C.F. Leyel and Olga Hartley, *The Gentle Art of Cookery*, 1925)

HARICOT BEANS À LA ROMAINE

Not an English recipe, but an excellent one.

1 qt (1 kg) fresh haricot beans
3 small onions
1 lemon
2 anchovies
grated nutmeg, pepper and salt

Cook the beans. In another pan cook the onions, cut into small pieces. When they are brown add them to the beans, with pepper and grated nutmeg to season, and the anchovies finely minced and passed through a sieve. Moisten with good brown stock. Cook the beans until they have absorbed all the stock.

Squeeze lemon juice over them, and serve hot.

(Mrs C.F. Leyel and Olga Hartley, *The Gentle Art of Cookery*, 1925)

BRUSSELS SPROUTS À L'ITALIENNE

Needless to say, this dish, like the other vegetable dishes given here, should be served on its own, before the meat course. Only thus can it be appreciated. Be very careful not to overboil the sprouts.

1 lb (500 g) Brussels sprouts
2 oz (60 g) butter
1 tbsp flour
1 pt (600 ml) milk
nutmeg, salt, pepper
1 lemon
about 2 oz (60 g) grated cheese

Wash and clean some Brussels sprouts, drain them well and cook them in boiling salted water on a quick fire for about a quarter of an hour. Meanwhile, put in a small saucepan a piece of butter the size of an egg, and a spoonful of flour, and cook this for five minutes, stirring and mixing well; add about a pint of milk, bring to the boil and let it thicken; it is then time to add seasoning, a little grated nutmeg, the juice of a lemon and grated cheese. Then put your sprouts (well drained once more) in the sauce and cook a little more on a slow fire, bringing to the boil.

(Marcel Boulestin, *The Best of Boulestin*, ed. Elvia and Maurice Firuski, 1952)

HOT CRAB

Another typical English recipe collected by Hartley and Leyel. Simple and good. Remember to keep some breadcrumbs to sprinkle on top. I should put the crab under the grill, unless the oven was on to cook something else.

1 crab
2 oz (60 g) butter
3 oz (90 g) breadcrumbs
2 tbsp vinegar
1 tbsp oil
pepper, salt, nutmeg

Put the meat from a boiled crab into a basin and stir the nutmeg, oil, vinegar and seasoning into it. Add the butter and the breadcrumbs.

Return it to the shell, strew it with breadcrumbs, and brown it in the oven.

(Mrs C.F. Leyel and Olga Hartley, *The Gentle Art of Cookery*, 1925)

HERRINGS AND MUSTARD SAUCE

A simple but pleasant dish, making the most of a sadly neglected fish. It is not unlike medieval recipes, except that there is no element of sweetness. A teaspoon of sugar does in fact improve the sauce. Do use cider or wine vinegar.

4 fresh herrings
1 oz (30 g) flour
½ pt (300 ml) vinegar
10 peppercorns
1 onion
1 tsp mustard

Cut the heads and tails off the cleaned fish. Wash and dry the fish with a cloth. Flour them and grill them. Serve the fish with the following mustard sauce. Boil the heads of the fish in the vinegar, with the onion and peppercorns, for 10 minutes; strain. Mix the flour and mustard, blend with a little cold water, strain the vinegar onto it. Return to the pan. Stir until boiling. Simmer 5 minutes.

How to Dish. – Dish the fish neatly on a hot dish and pour the sauce over and round the fish.

(*Daily Mail Cookery Book*, 1927)

AGNEAU RÔTI PROVENÇALE

The excellent sauce is the reason I have included this as an example of Boulestin's cooking.

1 leg of lamb
1 clove garlic
4 anchovy fillets
½ oz (15 g) butter
for the sauce
1 small onion
2 shallots
2 tsp flour
2 anchovy fillets
2–3 gherkins
1 dsp tomato purée
about 3 tbsp stock of any kind

Take a leg of lamb, insert one small clove of garlic near the bone, and lard it with small pieces of fillets of anchovy about one inch long, a dozen in all. Bake it in the ordinary way, basting often. When cooked, remove it, keep it hot, and skim the fat off the gravy.

Prepare the following sauce: Melt a small piece of butter in a pan, cook in it one small onion and two shallots finely chopped, and do this slowly, so that they are more melted than fried; sprinkle a little flour, stir, cook for one minute more; then add two fillets of anchovy, also finely chopped, with two or three gherkins, a puddingspoonful of tomato purée, the gravy from the lamb, and a little stock, if too

short. Mix well, cook for two minutes more, and serve. This sauce
should be highly seasoned.

(Marcel Boulestin, The Best of Boulestin,
ed. Elvia and Maurice Firuski, 1952)

BOEUF EN DAUBE

Which of Boulestin's recipes to use? I have chosen the one I think is
nearest to Virginia Woolf's description. Her 'savoury brown and
yellow meats' must use 'meat' in its older sense of 'food' (as in the
Scots grace, 'Some hae meat, and canna eat') since the only yellow
thing in the dish is the carrots. Since a calf's foot is difficult to buy,
I suggest a pig's trotter instead. There is no need to cut it up. Notice
that there are no olives – was Virginia mixing this up with
Boulestin's Ragout de Boeuf? Or was her famous imagination at
work here?

1 piece silverside or rump, weighing about 4 lb (2 kg)
4 pieces streaky bacon
1 bottle claret
2 oz (60 g) butter
1 liqueur glass brandy
1 cup consommé
a little nutmeg
1 bouquet garni
2 lumps sugar
3–4 small onions
1 calf's foot or pig's trotter
5–6 small carrots

Take a piece of beef, lard it with strips of bacon sprinkled with salt
and pepper, season it on all sides and soak it in claret (about three-
quarters of a bottle would do for a piece of beef weighing about four
pounds) for a couple of hours. Drain it well and fry it in butter so as
to close the meat, which should retain its juice during the lengthy
process of braising. Put it in a saucepan, pour over it the wine used
before, a liqueur glass of brandy, a cup of consommé, add a little
grated nutmeg, a bouquet (one clove, parsley, thyme and bay leaf),
two lumps of sugar, and bring to the boil. Then add a few onions
cut in quarters, one calf's foot cut in small cubes, and let it simmer

very slowly for at least eight hours; at 'half time' put in a few carrots cut in slices and previously fried in butter. When the cooking is finished put the beef on a serving dish, arrange the carrots round the meat and pour over it the gravy from which the fat must be carefully removed. It should be so soft that you can use a spoon for serving it (hence its other name: boeuf à la cuiller). It is equally good hot or cold.

(Marcel Boulestin, *The Best of Boulestin*,
ed. Elvia and Maurice Firuski, 1952)

Bananas au Café

Very '20s, this use of banana with what is really a basic rice pudding. Very good, too.

6 bananas
2 oz (60 g) rice
2 tsp instant coffee
sugar candy (the brown coarse coffee sugar does perfectly)
sugar
curaçao

Boil two ounces of Carolina rice in a double saucepan with a pint of milk very slowly until all the milk has been absorbed and the rice is well swollen. Flavour strongly with coffee and sweeten with six or nine lumps of sugar, according to taste. Remove it from the fire.

Cut up the bananas, cover them with a little sugar and leave them in a basin for an hour or more, then add two tablespoonfuls of rum.

Take six or more custard glasses; put in them alternate layers of the banana and the coffee rice, finishing with the rice, and thickly sprinkle with dark brown crushed sugar candy.

(Mrs C.F. Leyel and Olga Hartley, *The Gentle Art of Cookery*, 1925)

Geranium Jelly

Very typical of the authors, even to the extent of getting the instructions out of order. Heat the sugar in the oven and put the pulp on to boil *before* you combine the two with the geranium leaves. I have not tried it, but intend to – it sounds delicious.

2–4 pounds (1–2 kg) apples
sugar (see recipe)
sweet-scented geranium leaves

Fill an earthenware jar with apples, rub them but do not cut or peel them. Set the jar in a pan half filled with water, and let them simmer all day until the juice is extracted. No water should be put with them. When the apples are reduced to pulp, strain them through a jelly bag, and add a little water to extract the utmost from the apples. To each pint of juice allow one pound of sugar, and boil together in a preserving pan with a handful of sweet-scented geranium leaves. Heat the sugar in the oven and do not add it to the juice until the pulp has boiled for twenty minutes. Cease stirring when all the sugar is melted, and let the liquor come to the point of rapid boiling for one minute only. Take it off the fire and immediately fill the moulds or pots, which should be already standing in boiling water. Remove the geranium leaves and tie down the pots [i.e. cover with rounds of greaseproof paper and tie down squares of cotton over all]. This should be served in jelly glasses with Devonshire cream.

(Mrs C.F. Leyel and Olga Hartley, *The Gentle Art of Cookery*, 1925)

A London Menu

Ruth Lowinsky and her husband wrote *Lovely Food*, 'For each other and our greedier friends'. They entertained a great deal and planned menus for various occasions. This is a typical one, which I give with its recipes. Note that for the salmon, you will need extra cream and anchovy essence for the garnish. The spring chickens are what we now buy in supermarkets under the name of poussins. For the Glace aux Fruits you will need glacé cherries, angelica, raisins, glacé fruit and brandy, as well as the ingredients listed.

Menu 14

A dream party of some of the most celebrated people of the day, whom one can never hope to meet or, if met, be remembered by: Einstein, Mr Charles Chaplin, Freud, Virginia Woolf, Stella Benson, Mussolini, P.G. Wodehouse, Minstinguett, Lydia Lopokova and Jean Cocteau.

Tomates à l'Espagnol

Consommé à l'Indienne

Saumon en Surprise

Poulet aux choux

Glace aux fruits

Tomatoes à l'Espagnol

Cut in strips some cheese, tongue, apples, celery, truffles. Mix with mayonnaise and fill the tomatoes.

Consommé à l'Indienne

One quart of good stock. Slice into it two onions, one large cooking apple, and add one tablespoonful of desiccated coconut, one dessertspoonful curry powder (more if liked hot), and bones of roast chicken or game. Simmer one hour, strain, clarify, reboil; serve pieces of game or chicken and a little plain boiled rice.

Saumon en Surprise

2 lb (1 kg) salmon
4 yolks of egg
¼ lb (125 g) butter
½ pint (300 ml) cream

Cook the salmon in water with oil and pass through a sieve. Mix well with ingredients. Put in soufflé case and stand on ice before serving. Decorate with whipped cream flavoured with anchovy essence. Enough for six people.

Poulet aux Choux

3 spring chickens
1 large white cabbage
½ lb (250 g) ham or bacon
1 pt (600 ml) consommé
pepper and salt
2 oz (60 g) butter

Fry in a stewpan a large white cabbage, half a pound of ham or bacon cut in squares and three chickens for ten minutes. Add a pint of consommé, a little pepper and salt, and let the whole stew for an hour or, if *old* chickens, an hour and a half. Take out the cabbage and chickens, cut up the cabbage and add two ounces of butter, pepper and salt to taste, reduce the stock, put the chickens in the stock to get thoroughly hot, place the cabbage in the centre of the dish, cut the chickens in half and place round the cabbage and pour the stock round the dish. Enough for five or six people.

Glace aux Fruits

3 eggs
1 lb (500 g) castor sugar
1¼ pts (725 ml) milk
1 pt (600 ml) cream

Make a custard with eggs, sugar and milk, and let it cool. Cut up some glacé cherries, angelica, raisins and glacé fruit and sprinkle with brandy. Whip cream very thick, add some custard and sufficient good rum to flavour. Put the mixture alternately with fruit into an ice mould and freeze for four hours.

> *From Leonard Woolf, Monk's House, Rodmell, Lewes, Suffolk*
> 'Many thanks for the delicious cake which we both enjoy every day at tea. Could you be so good some time as to write out the recipe, as I can't get any cakes made except yours that I like to eat?
> We go to London tomorrow.
> V. Woolf.'

Virginia's letter to Grace Higgens, who cooked for Vanessa Bell at Charleston, brought in response these recipes for:

DUNDEE CAKE

5 oz (150 g) butter
5 oz (150 g) sugar
3 eggs
8 oz (250 g) plain flour
2 tsp baking powder
6 oz (175 g) currants
6 oz (175 g) sultanas
2 oz (60 g) cherries
grated orange and lemon peel
2 oz (60 g) peel
Put almonds on top. 325°F/150°C/Gas Mark 3, 2½ hours.

CHOCOLATE ROLL

6 eggs
5 oz (150 g) castor sugar
2 oz (60 g) cocoa

Whip egg whites till stiff. Whip yolks. Add sugar to yolks. Whip cocoa in yolks mixture. Fold egg white into mixture.

Put in oblong tin lined with greased paper. 350°F/175°C/Gas Mark 4, for twenty minutes. Turn out on paper sprinkled with icing sugar. Spread with whipped cream and melted chocolate. Roll up.

Chapter 8

THE CHANGING LARDER
1939–2005

Eating and drinking in London, despite old-fashioned rumours to the contrary that still persist, can be all right.

David Piper, *Companion Guide to London*, 1964

Saturday 13 May: Sharon and Jude . . . brought a little extra something from M&S. Therefore, in addition to the three-course meal . . . I had already bought from M&S (I mean prepared by entire day's slaving over hot stove) we had:

1 tub hummus & pkt mini-pittas
12 smoked salmon and cream cheese pinwheels
1 raspberry pavlova
1 tiramisu (party size)
2 Swiss Mountain Bars

Helen Fielding, *Bridget Jones's Diary*, 1996

In the years between the wars, there had been great changes in eating and cooking, in kitchen design and in food marketing. What had changed less was the difference between the meals of the rich and those of the poor. If the London rich ate more lightly than in Edwardian days (and this was not invariably true), they still ate luxuriously and well. If the London poor had access to a greater variety of food (and this also was not always true), their diet was still, in general terms, nutritionally poor, because deficient in the elements essential for good health. In 1901, when men were being recruited to fight in the Boer War, medical screening showed that two-thirds of British adult men were physically unfit. Again in 1917, only one-third of men medically examined for active service was deemed healthy. Research during and after the war illuminated the dietary deficiencies of the majority of Britain's urban population: not enough protein, too few vitamins and minerals, too little roughage. The urban poor (almost by definition the ill-educated) suffered the consequences of their ignorance as well as their poverty, and during the years of the Depression (1927-1930) when work was hard to find, their diet was reduced almost to Victorian level: white bread, margarine, jam, tea and fried fish. An Advisory Committee on Nutrition appointed in 1931 to give the government some guidelines was quite specific:

> Probably if the diet contains per person one pint of milk per day, if cheese is partaken freely, if one orange or one tomato or a helping of raw salad is taken daily, if 30 g [1 oz] of butter (or of vitaminized margarine) is given, and if some sort of fat fish, such as herring, appears on the winter menu once a week (or if in default of such fish half a teaspoonful of cod liver oil is taken once a day) the mineral matter and the vitamin content of the diet is satisfactory.

Londoners on the breadline – evocative phrase – could hardly follow such well-intentioned advice. Nevertheless, as the economic situation improved, it became clear that even when choices could be made, knowledge and incentive were lacking.

In an effort to improve public health, the government set up bodies like the National Milk Publicity Council, which promoted its product by offering all children in grant-aided elementary schools half a pint of milk daily either at a reduced price or free, depending on parental income. By 1939, over half the children in these schools were drinking school milk, and in that year a survey of twelve-year-old London boys showed that on average they were three inches taller and eleven pounds heavier than their fathers had been.

In the main, the national diet was beginning to improve. Great poverty still existed in London and other cities, but the Depression was over, the number of unemployed had fallen considerably and enormous progress in the canning and refrigeration industries had brought down food prices to a level which allowed most people to feed adequately, though not always healthily. The way in which researchers found their samples is sometimes open to question, but the Bermondsey housewife who in the late '30s described her family's diet to a team from the London School of Economics could almost be described as a model provider. For breakfast, her husband (a docker) took a cup of tea and bread and butter or dripping, and the children had boiled eggs or porridge on alternate days; no details were given of her husband's packed lunch, but the children came home from school for minced meat on Mondays, gravy (*sic*) on Tuesdays, a small meat pudding on Wednesdays, baked lamb chops, potatoes, cabbage and Yorkshire pudding on Thursdays and fish on Fridays. Saturday dinner consisted of braised steak, potatoes and cabbage, or liver and bacon, and on Sundays they ate a small piece of beef or half-shoulder of lamb with baked potatoes, Yorkshire or suet pudding, and vegetables. Each day's dinner was rounded off with a small milk pudding, so that the children needed very little 'tea', and if any pudding was left over from lunch they had that before going to bed. Her husband came home from work at five o' clock for *his* tea: eggs and bacon on Mondays, lamb chop on Tuesdays, steak and onions on Wednesdays, ham or leftover meat on Thursdays and fish or eggs and cheese on Fridays. It was a high-protein diet, with no mention at all of fruit and little of vegetables; significantly, the housewife did not describe her own meals, which almost certainly consisted largely of leftovers and 'bits and pieces' to make sure that nothing was wasted. But despite its inadequacies, this family's food cannot be described as desperately unhealthy.

Thus when war was declared in September 1939, many Londoners were actually perhaps better off nutritionally than they had ever been. Lord Woolton, the new Minister of Food, and his adviser Sir Jack Drummond, a biochemist and the co-author of the classic *The Englishman's Food*, were nevertheless very conscious of malnutrition and its attendant effects. They also knew that either the war itself or the conditions of poverty which might occur when the war was over could once again reduce working-class diet to a Victorian level. They were far-sighted enough to realise that only a healthy nation could hope to win the war and that a healthy nation would be needed, too, to cope with peace. Paradoxically, war itself was presenting an ideal opportunity to improve the nation's diet.

There had not been time for the lessons learnt in the First World War to be forgotten. The government's approach to food organisation was complex. As soon as it became evident, in 1937, that Hitler's ambitions might lead to conflict, the Food (Defence Plans) Department organised the printing of ration books. By August 1939, these were stored in warehouses round the country, and at the beginning of 1940, the packages were unsealed. It had been obvious that Britain would be blockaded, and one of Woolton's main principles was that farmers must produce as far as possible the essentials for the nation's healthy survival. Reliance on imported food must be cut to a minimum, but he was determined somehow to keep bread off the ration. Milk too was considered an essential food; a milk allocation scheme ensured that pregnant women, children and adolescents received their necessary daily requirement. Dried imported milk, known as Household Milk, supplemented fresh. (Remarkably, despite a scarcity of animal feedstuffs, total milk production and consumption actually rose during the war years.)

By 1943, the pattern of rationing and food supply was well established. Some food, mainly dehydrated or in tins, was reaching Britain from the United States and the Colonies, but at irregular intervals. Bread and potatoes were the main prop of every meal. Fish was unrationed but scarce, game was also unrationed. For the rest, each adult's *weekly* entitlement was about 1 lb (500 g) meat (it is impossible to be more precise, because meat was unique in being rationed by cost rather than by weight, but the allowance included bone and offal, and sausages – however high their content of bread – counted as meat), 2 oz (60 g) butter, 2 oz (60 g) cooking fat, 4 oz (125 g) vitamin-enriched margarine and 3 oz (90 g) cheese – vegetarians were given extra. Eggs (one a week), tea, sugar and sweets were also rationed. Pregnant and nursing women and children under five were given cod liver oil and concentrated orange juice to boost their vitamin intake. The lack of fresh eggs was a particular hardship. People with suburban gardens tried to keep their own hens, but poultry feed was hard to come by, and with kitchen scraps being turned wherever possible into something the family could eat, fresh eggs became a black-market commodity. The deficiency was made up, theoretically, by importing spray-dried eggs from America, but what could be produced from them hardly amounted to a gastronomic treat. Reconstituting dried eggs required patience and skill; few people in those stressful days had either. Many cooks also mistakenly believed that the more dried egg one used for a dish, the better it would be, but if contemporary accounts are to be believed, it was the nastiness, not the 'egginess', which was increased.

As well as ration coupons, people were allocated 'points' for tinned and imported foods. These could be spent at discretion – on a tin of sardines, say, worth six points, or two tins of fruit worth three points each. This frustrated hoarders, and much time-wasting bureaucracy was avoided; psychologically too, even a limited ability to choose was important, relieving the monotony of total predictability.

Parallel with all this, the government mounted a massive campaign to encourage the cultivation of fruit and vegetables. With the brilliant slogan 'Dig for Victory', people were persuaded to turn every available piece of land to productive use. The response beat all expectations. Parks, front gardens, even newly bombed sites were dug over and turned into allotments. Londoners discovered in themselves unsuspected talents and, just like their Elizabethan predecessors, took pride in growing cabbages, leeks, carrots and early peas.

In the wartime diet, monotony, rather than scarcity, would be the enemy. Woolton and Drummond, luckily, understood the importance of direct explanation in simple terms. Their messages, conveyed through advertisements, broadcasts and music-hall sketches, were phrased in sympathetic language with a touch of humour and implicit appeals to patriotism, and in this way they were able to persuade people to accept with relative cheerfulness rationing, shortages, even the National Loaf – a major triumph achieved by no previous wartime government. (According to Woolton, his deliberately high profile occasionally led to confusion. The story goes that one little girl saying her nightly prayers looked up at her mother after repeating 'Give us this day our daily bread' and asked, 'Mummy, why do we have to have both God and Lord Woolton?')

On this diet of milk, dehydrated eggs, home-grown vegetables and the National Loaf, Britons grew healthier and children's diseases caused by malnutrition were virtually eradicated. But in the cities especially, there was little to alleviate the dreadful boredom of meals. Food became an obsession, the stuff of daydreams. Some people were lucky enough to receive an occasional parcel from abroad which was usually shared with friends or neighbours; always one or two items were put aside – a tin of fruit or ham, a packet of dried apricots – to be brought out triumphantly at Christmas or on someone's birthday. Country people could sometimes get a hare, a pheasant, a rabbit, a trout; they could gather rowans, blackberries, mushrooms, rosehips; they had room to grow off-beat vegetables like artichokes and asparagus as well as everyday ones. In London, there were few such dietary diversions. There is a limit to what can be grown on an allotment, particularly when time is divided between normal work and other duties such as fire-fighting, hospital portering or being an air-raid warden. A joke in *Punch* shows an upper-class woman in hat and high-heeled shoes working with her husband in their allotment. She is saying, 'I shall celebrate Victory Day by switching over to asparagus.'(In fact, the allotments continued to be worked long after the war, but eventually many became neglected and overgrown with brambles and rosebay willow-herb. Recently, however, borough councils have increasingly come to realise that they are a valuable green resource. In 2004, twenty-one London boroughs are offering allotment plots, sometimes renamed Leisure Gardens. Here, for a rent of between twelve and twenty pounds a year, people get not only a plot but the help of a volunteer manager, who will advise on cultivation, use of pesticides and fertilisers, how to encourage – or discourage – wildlife, and the best sustainable use of garden materials and resources. Unfortunately, demand exceeds supply and in some boroughs land is scarce – Lambeth, for instance, can only offer 0.2 plots per 1,000 homes, whereas Sutton provides 29.3 plots per 1,000 homes.)

Wartime recipe books, pamphlet-sized and printed on shoddy paper, are often undated, though from internal evidence one can roughly guess the year of publication. The *Stork Wartime Cookery Book* must have been brought out very early. Its most remarkable feature is photographs of three beautifully iced and decorated cakes which readers are recommended to make and send to friends or relatives at the Front. Calling as the recipe does for 1½ lb (750 g) dried fruit,

4 eggs, 8 oz (250 g) margarine and 8 oz. (250 g) sugar, it seems fairly obvious that the book was written during the time of the 'phoney war'. Historically its interest lies in the short section on feeding London children who had been evacuated to the country, pointing up the vast dietary differences current at the time: a major complaint by those who took in the children was that they would not eat 'proper' food. 'They don't like vegetables and they won't eat soup, in fact, they don't seem to like anything but fish and chips and bread and jam.' Women's Institute reports from all over the country told the same story: some children hardly knew how to eat with a knife and fork – they were used to being given pennies to buy fish and chips or biscuits, which they ate in the street, and preferred sitting on the doorstep to eating at a table. Almost all disliked fresh vegetables and fruit. One little girl of five asked for beer and cheese for supper. The *Stork* author suggested giving the children 'a good hot dish with plenty of gravy, and a good thick slice of bread and Stork to eat with it'.

An early, dated (1940) recipe book with its own dust jacket is *A Kitchen Goes to War*, to which famous people in all walks of life – politicians, music-hall performers, radio celebrities – contributed recipes. The tone is optimistic, with the emphasis on a well-balanced diet and a few party dishes 'because every household feels the need to celebrate now and then, even in wartime'. It must already have been with the printers when rationing began in January 1940, for sugar and dried fruit, meat and eggs are freely recommended. The first recipe, for 'An excellent cake for the troops', comes with an account of how a slab of it, sent to the Front, travelled round France and returned to Britain still in good condition after ten weeks. When it finally caught up with the addressee, it 'was much appreciated'. Some more realistic contributors seemed to be using their experience of the previous war: Viscountess Hambledon offered a recipe for something called Siege Cake, pointing out that it needed no eggs and little sugar. Another early booklet, put out by the North Middlesex Gas Company in April 1940, warned that supplies of unrationed foods such as offal, rabbits, fish, poultry, eggs, vegetables, syrup, cereals and dried fruits would fluctuate. It gave hints for rendering fat and suet ('avoid putting onions or stuffing in the baking tin, if you want to use the dripping for cakes'), making breadcrumbs, pickling eggs and cooking with a hay box to save fuel. (The food was brought to boiling or simmering point in the usual way, then put in a box thickly lined with hay and covered with a felt pad or old cushion. Left overnight or all day, enough heat was retained to continue the cooking very slowly, so that the porridge, soup or stew would be ready when wanted.) The Gas Company also offered demonstrations of wartime cookery at all its main showrooms.

By 1941, shortages were really beginning to make themselves felt. The phrase 'The Kitchen Front' was coined to encourage housewives to feel that theirs too was a heroic battle. As Ambrose Heath, a popular pre-war writer and broadcaster, expressed it in *Kitchen Front Recipes*:

> to carry on, as her husband, perhaps, and her kin are carrying on, *is no mean contribution* towards those days when our homes and kitchens will be normal once again . . . what you are doing, quietly, in your homes is very often as much – and sometimes even more – than is given to a great many of us to contribute towards the better times that are ahead.

A radio programme called *The Kitchen Front* brought together housewives, home economists and food writers to broadcast recipes approved by the Ministry of Food; thousands of listeners appealed for them to be published, and the first edition appeared in August 1942. The second, a year later, shows just how difficult things had become. A Mainmeal Salad required among other things 'two hard-boiled eggs' made from reconstituted dried eggs poured into greased eggcups and steamed until set.

It was now that dishes like Woolton Pie (cooked mixed vegetables covered with pastry), Lentil Roast and Carrot Pudding were introduced to the British public. Sceptical as to their nutritional value, most people regarded them with suspicious hostility. There were few conversions to vegetarianism during the years 1939–1945, yet vegetarian meals were often all that was offered in the canteens set up by government order in factories round the country. Providing workers with meals on the premises saved time, food and fuel; it also ensured that at least once a day they got something hot and filling to eat, cooked by somebody else. In the same mode, the British Restaurants which the government ordered local authorities to set up were really community feeding centres. Churchill himself had chosen their name on the grounds that 'everybody associates the word "restaurant" with a good meal, and they may as well have the name if they cannot get anything else'. Here office staff, refugees and those made homeless by the Blitz could get hot meals of varying quality. The Restaurants were manned largely by volunteers, for whom the *Daily Telegraph* produced a recipe book called *Good Fare*. It included Mock Turtle Soup (using a few bones, mixed vegetables, bacon rinds, herbs, gravy browning and water), Eggless Toad-in-the-Hole, and Steak, Kidney and Vegetable Pie, which astonishingly turned two pounds of steak and kidney into a pie for twenty people.

If the domestic kitchen had difficulties, for caterers the position was bleaker still. With enormous effort, most of the London restaurants kept going, but they had to change their attitudes and their self-image. Very early in the war, an anonymous diarist recorded how one evening after fire drill he took his wife for a meal in Frith Street. With the greatest reluctance – the management objecting to his fireman's uniform – they were given a meal and a bottle of wine. A year later, at the height of the Blitz, they returned to the same restaurant. This time they were ushered to the best table, waited on personally by the manager and had their request for a bill refused. Nothing, they were assured, could be too good for a London fireman. Somehow the mood was different from that in the First World War. Even through the appalling experience of the Blitz, people wanted to lunch and dine out, and the restaurants converted their cellars into air-raid shelters and managed with a skeleton staff, for, as in 1914, enemy aliens were deported, and Italy's entrance into the war decimated London's catering workforce. Tragically, some of the most famous chefs and restaurateurs died when the *Arandora Star* was torpedoed on its way to Canada.

But if the restaurants were being forced to adapt, so were the customers. Near the beginning of the war, a fashion photo in *Vogue* showed a couple in evening dress sitting at a table flanked with sandbags piled up to the ceiling. The caption read: 'On leave, he likes to dine against the sophisticated decor of La Popote du Ritz. You in his favourite black, his favourite lace, feminine to the last flounce.' But as the war continued, sophisticated clothes and decor were less on the diners' minds than decent food. A maximum permitted charge of five shillings per three-course meal (if bread was served it counted as one course) increased the clientèle while restricting its gastronomic pleasure. By rising early and being at the markets when they opened, chefs sometimes managed to get unrationed delicacies: fish, shellfish, onions (very scarce right through the war) or game. Often the wine, drawn from stocks laid down over previous years, was far better than the food. Even the famous Ivy restaurant sometimes only had tripe and onions and Spam on the menu.

The story of food in wartime London would not be complete without mention of the Women's Voluntary Service and its mobile kitchens. The WVS had been established shortly before the war to back up the ARP (Air Raid Precaution) services in their expected duties. But from 1939 its major role was to help local authorities cope with every kind of social problem from homelessness to school transport. The mobile kitchens the women took to bomb-damaged areas – over 300 in London alone – were financed by various organisations such as trade unions and businessmen's clubs at home and abroad. Many of the London ones were built by Wilson Crowe who, now that the market for his Easiwork kitchens had collapsed, used his experience to fit out mobile canteens with pressure cookers and everything necessary to provide quick hot meals for Blitz victims and their rescuers.

Peace returned in 1945. Photographs of the celebrations and street parties show cheerful people – mainly women and children – gathered round tables decked with streamers and flags but little food. Whatever people's hopes may have been, rationing was not to end for quite some time. Even in 1949, some London children had never seen an orange, a banana, a real egg, a shop window full of buns or sweets. It was, however, their elders who had cheerfully borne the queues, the shortages and the substitute foods, who were most discouraged by the slow pace of recovery. Several more years of belt-tightening were ahead. What war had not achieved, peace did: a bread ration was introduced in 1946 because British wheat was being sent to starving Europe. In 1948, after one of the severest winters on record followed by spring floods and a diabolically hot summer, meat and cheese rations were actually smaller than they had been in 1945. Demobilisation had swelled the civilian population and the total quantity of food available was less than it had been in the middle of the war. Why had recovery been so slow? Mainly because Britain was not able to adapt to peace as rapidly as less industrialised, more rural nations. Farmers who had concentrated on cereals, milk and vegetables had to begin from scratch if they wished to breed and raise cattle. Land which had been given over to factories was not returned to farming. And the necessity of feeding Europe as well as Britain made the government's job even more difficult than it had been in wartime.

P.G.Wodehouse, living in France, had trouble with authenticity in his latest work. He wrote to a friend:

> In *Joy in the Morning*, Bertie speaks of himself as eating a steak and Boko is described as having fried eggs for breakfast, and Grimsdick of Jenkins [his publisher] is very agitated about this, because he says the English public is so touchy about food that stuff like this will probably cause an uproar. I have changed the fried egg to a sardine and cut out the steak, so I hope the situation is saved.

Even fish was scarce. The protein ration was eked out first by whalemeat (bought from whalers who killed the whales for their blubber) and second by a long, slender but tasteless fish called snoek, caught in South African waters. It was imported in tins and provoked a reaction disproportionate, one would have thought, to its dullness. But as Christopher Driver has remarked in *A Hundred Years' Eating*, many English words beginning with 'sn' convey dislike or disparagement, and snoek was a gift to cartoonists and versifiers. The public, hard-pressed though it was, rejected the tins and they ended up as cat food.

Scanning *Punch* and food articles in *Vogue* from 1945 to 1949, one can see how gradual recovery really was. Sweets came off the ration in 1949; there was an immediate stampede and the shops were cleaned out within two days, forcing the government to reinstate the ration. (A cartoon in *Punch* showed a signwriter making dozens of 'Sorry, No Sweets' notices while telling a friend, 'Business has doubled ever since sweets came off the ration.') *Punch* sighted the first Breton onion-seller in 1949, and thereafter onions are a more frequent ingredient in *Vogue*'s recipes. Later, fish dishes became more interesting as the fleet went out again for shellfish, haddock and Dover sole. By 1950, imported luxuries like French cheeses – Roquefort, Brie, Camembert – were appearing in shops and on menus. Many shop assistants had never seen them before, as is shown by a little poem in *Punch*:

The Carnivorous English

The fact that it is spelt e m
has no significance for them;
suavely they ask if one would care
to have a little camel-bear.

If margarine still served where butter was once used, and dried eggs continued to replace fresh, now Londoners at least could sometimes find olives, tomatoes and wine. In *Vogue*, a recipe for Corned Beef Hash was flanked by one for Boeuf en Gelée calling for cinnamon, cloves, ginger 'and if available some red wine'. The Camembert rhyme in *Punch* is about the only food joke in that periodical for the whole of 1950, and in the 29 March issue, an interesting feature on Westminster Technical College makes it clear that, while the students 'rarely see more than a few ounces of meat at a time' and have to learn butchery from drawings on a blackboard, the public restaurant attached to the college serves grilled steaks and carbonnade de boeuf à la flamande – still subject of course to the five shilling rule. (Another *Punch* joke, the previous year, showed the interior of a restaurant with large windows, through which crowds of people, noses pressed against the glass, can dimly be seen. At one of the tables, a man says to his companion, 'I know it's a bit embarrassing by the window, but we do get larger helpings.')

By 1951, although rationing was not over (it ended in 1954, the last item to come off being those re-rationed sweets), there was a real improvement. A couple of New Yorkers reported in American *Vogue*, 'hunger-pinched Britons are not fainting in platoons in Trafalgar Square. Almost everything is available in good supply now, though napkins are still not as plentiful as they should be, and meat and eggs are still short.' A poem in *Punch* in January 1951 summed up the meat situation and what people felt about it:

Conversation with a Butcher's Cashier

Lady in the glass gazebo,
Overalled in sober green,
What departed glories haunt you
On this modern, meatless scene?

'Sometimes on a winter's evening
When the power is ebbing low
Phantom porkers, pale and portly,
Dance before me, row on row.

Legs of lamb are seen suspended
Where the alien rabbit hangs;
Sides of beef crowd in upon me
In phantasmagoric gangs.

Ectoplasmic steaks and sirloins
Fill the air, while on the phone
Ghostly voices ask for "Something
Nice for Sunday – not much bone."

Briskets bloom in plump profusion,
Kidneys overflow their bowls;
Spectral chauffeurs shuffle past me,
Carting cutlets to the Rolls.'

Lady in the glass gazebo,
Come, I pray you, back to earth;
Give me change and let me hurry
Home with my tenpennyworth.

To boost confidence, the government decided to hold a Festival of Britain in 1951. Unlike the unfortunate Britain Can Make It exhibition a few years earlier, this mammoth event was proof that Britain really was recovering. British *Vogue* entered into the spirit with an article entitled 'Bounty of Britain', advising readers to give visitors 'only dishes that are typically British, the things our grandsires relished and that our countryfolk still delight in'. As examples, the article listed Isle of Wight Crab, Scotch Barley Broth, Sussex Game Pudding, Oxford Hare (aka stuffed shoulder of mutton) and Lancashire Hot Pot.

The sad truth was that, grandsires and countryfolk excepted, the majority of the population, especially in cities like London, seemed to have lost both knowledge of and interest in good food, so much so that the writer and historian Raymond Postgate had proposed in 1949 founding a Society for the Prevention of Cruelty to Food. In an article in *Leader* magazine, he reflected on the standard fare currently offered in the average London eating-house:

> Sodden, sour, slimy, sloppy, stale or saccharined – one of these six things (or all) it certainly would be, whether it was fish, flesh, vegetable or sweet. It would also be over-cooked; it might be reheated. If the place was English, it would be called a tea-shop or caffy; if foreign it would be called a restaurant or caffy. In the second case it would be dirtier, but the food *might* have some taste.

From this article, *The Good Food Guide* eventually developed, the first issue published in 1951. The fact that 5,000 copies sold shows that if professional cooks were demoralised by the war and its effects, consumers were recovering their aspirations and eager to encourage a gastronomic revival. The Wine and Food Society (founded by a Frenchman, André Simon, before the war) was also anxious to raise standards in hotels, restaurants and private homes.

But British food would never be the same again. As had happened after the First World War, technology took a huge leap, profiting from wartime research. To begin with, the discovery that food could be fast-frozen to keep for months or even years had limited impact, although in 1948 a *Vogue* article recognised that: 'The new look has spread to the larder, insomuch that "quick-freeze" methods have come to stay, turning our bill of winter fare topsy-turvy.' Since no housewives had freezers, frozen fruit and vegetables were for immediate use only. They came unwrapped in large tubs, from which shoppers helped themselves with a scoop, and although Doris Lytton Toye's article stressed the saving in time and the elimination of waste, they were expensive. Freezing remained at a fairly primitive stage for several years. Poor home storage and careless cooking, especially in restaurants, contributed to a backlash, but as more and more women went out to work, the social value of frozen food became assured. Packaging and advertising improved, and when home freezers appeared on the market in the 1970s, the most significant development in the sociology of eating since the war was well on its way, with consequences which could hardly be foreseen even by the most imaginative of supermarket managers.

Meantime, the '50s, like the '20s, were a period of adaptation. Servants and cooks were in even shorter supply, and as food trickled back into the shops, women whose only experience of cooking had been dishes like Spam hot-pot and mayonnaise of dried eggs were bewildered when confronted with real ingredients. Huge numbers, from women who before the war had always had a cook to girls straight from school, needed to be told how to make a stew or a sponge cake. At this elementary level, the best advice probably came from Bee Nilson. Her *Penguin Cookery Book* appeared in 1952. She took no skill for granted, describing with care how to whip cream (and which kinds of cream *will* whip) and how to make simple pastry; she was not extravagant, and her recipes accommodated dried milk, dried or fresh eggs, and corned beef, as well as 'real' ingredients. Some of her recipes, although simple, were interesting enough for any dinner party; and they always worked.

Once the new cooks had gained some expertise, they looked for books with more challenging or interesting recipes. Immediately to hand they found two recently published works, already acclaimed by the older generation for their 'knowledgeable aid in reviving the happy past here and now' – to quote a *Punch* review. Both were by Elizabeth David. The first, *A Book of Mediterranean Food*, had come out in 1950; it was followed in 1951 by *French Country Cooking*. Much as Boulestin had done thirty years earlier, much as Eliza Acton had tried to do a century before, these two books opened the shuttered windows of British gastronomic imagination and let in the glorious light of a culture which placed food near its centre. It is not too much to say that they and their author's later work changed the direction of serious cooking and eating in Britain. For four reasons, David's influence was to be stronger and further-reaching than either Acton's or Boulestin's. First, her recipes were subordinate to the feeling for food that lay behind them; she recalled to readers what many had forgotten or never experienced – the visual, olfactory, tactile, sometimes even audible attributes of good cooking and good food. She reminded them that between the high art of haute cuisine and the drab meals of the caff ('caffy' was soon jettisoned by popular agreement) lay a world of imaginative but simple cooking, close to soil and sea. Secondly, she did not confine herself to the cooking of France. Italy, Spain, Greece and Egypt were also within her compass. In many of the middle-class families which bought her books, there was at least one person who had served in these countries during the war, and David had the knack of identifying and reproducing dishes which stood at the heart of each nation's traditions. Furthermore, her splendid easy style and superbly evocative writing presented readers with a text fully as memorable for the historical, literary and autobiographical passages as for the recipes. And fourthly, her passion for perfection in simple things ensured that her instructions, like Boulestin's, were both authentic and, if properly followed, productive of delicious meals. To post-war readers in a country only beginning to emerge from the nightmare tedium of austerity, her books were like rain after years of drought. What was more, the dishes in them were not expensive. The English dinner party suddenly, almost overnight, abandoned roasts, grill cuts and complicated sauces, and substituted dishes which needed long, gentle stewing; boeuf en daube was back in fashion, and navarin of lamb entered the repertoire of every sophisticated hostess.

There is no doubt that the war had dented the British xenophobic armour. Britons eagerly travelled abroad as soon as currency regulations allowed - at first, it must be admitted, principally to eat. They went to Ireland, Norway, Holland, France – wherever food was plentiful and cheap, for the fifty pound travel allowance was a distinct limitation. Writers in *Punch* and *Vogue*, clearly overwhelmed by the unfamiliar sight of well-stocked tables, described with almost hysterical fervour Irish steaks, Dutch butter, Norwegian lobsters. Travellers brought back booty: cheese and butter, garlic and olive oil, tinned anchovies and pâté de foie gras. And when the fifty pound limit was eventually abolished, they travelled further, motivated by a curiosity to see in peaceful conditions places they had dimly apprehended through the smoke and dust of battle.

Later, with the growth of industry, a return to full employment, and cheaper air fares, more and more people sought holidays in Greece, Spain or Italy. The motives now were beaches and sunshine rather than food. Ironically, many Britons reverted to type and complained bitterly about foreign cooking.

But the traffic was by no means all one way. London in the '50s took up again its traditional role as foreigners flocked to study or work in this most international of cities. From Italy came a new contingent of waiters, chefs and café workers, bringing with them what was to become one of the symbols of London in the late '50s and early '60s: the Gaggia espresso coffee machine. Just why espresso coffee bars achieved such huge popularity is not entirely clear. Certainly they formed part of a general craze for Italian culture, manifested also by the popularity of Italian films and film stars, food and hairstyles. Partly it may have been also because alcohol was still in real terms quite expensive, and a cup of coffee took a much smaller proportion of the weekly wage than a pint of beer. Most influential of all, perhaps, was the fact that pubs were still the predominant preserve of the older generation of men – some indeed excluded women altogether. For the younger, mixed society which was pushing to the fore, coffee bars formed ideal meeting places. Of the best ones, each had its own character: El Cubano on the Brompton Road was brash, lively and noisy, whereas the Partisan on Carlisle Street, with the offices of the New Left Review above, was mostly frequented by young left-wing intellectuals. There were establishments to suit existentialist students or teddy boys, artists or spivs. Decor varied, but most were well painted and brightly lit, and often decorated with trellises from which hung artificial plants, and/or paintings of gondolas or other typically Italian scenes.

When the existentialism of the fifties was replaced by the frenetic trendiness of the Swinging Sixties, coffee bars lost their cult status. In that prosperous era, music and clothes, not food or drink, signified participation in the culture of the day, and first the Beatles, then Carnaby Street and Mary Quant became the new icons. In your local caff, you could eat tinned spaghetti or leathery fried eggs. Round the corner there was certain to be a Golden Egg or a Quality Inn, or perhaps an Angus Steak House (whose steak, no longer rationed, probably came from anywhere but Angus, the Trade Descriptions Act being as yet unborn). Lyons Corner Houses and the old ABC chain catered for tired shoppers and people in a hurry. In all these places, the tables were furnished with bottles of tomato ketchup and HP sauce. And this was perhaps what many young Londoners preferred; it was certainly a slight improvement on the caffs so criticised by Postgate fifteen years previously. But the real improvement was in the standard of restaurants targeting more sophisticated tastes. It is instructive to read the section on 'Eating and Drinking' in David Piper's *Companion Guide to London*, published in 1964. After a quick run-through of chain restaurants and London pubs, some of which provided simple, straightforward and sometimes very good dishes, he moved to the better restaurants. For 'the tuned palate in expectancy of the subtle ranges of all kinds of European and Oriental cooking', London, he believed, could supply most requirements; moreover in many top-class London restaurants you could get the best French wines, better and cheaper than in France. He advised consultation of Egon Ronay's new *Guide to 1,000 Eating Places in Great Britain* as well as *The Good Food Guide*, but he himself managed to list 104 restaurants, varying in price from modest to expensive, which tourists might try. There were a few familiar names: Bertorelli, Boulestin (Marcel Boulestin had died in Paris in 1943 but the restaurant continued to bear his name), the Connaught Hotel, Isola Bella (described as 'expensive; pre-war Soho style'), Rules ('Edwardian décor'), the Savoy Grill, Simpson's-in-the-Strand, the Trocadero; for late-night dancing and cabaret, one could still go to the Savoy or Quaglino's. At the other end of the scale, he recommended places like Manzi's House of Hamburger (actually fish specialists), the Piccadilly Lyons Corner House ('American-style snacks') and the British Overseas Airways Terminal, praised for its modern decor and English cooking. One restaurant he did not mention, but which caused some stir because of its innovative cuisine and excellent value for money, was Cranks, Britain's first vegetarian restaurant, which had opened in Carnaby Street in 1961.

The growing popularity of oriental food is reflected in Piper's list. *Vogue* too noticed that Chinese and Indian restaurants in London were flourishing as never before. Jamshid's, Veeraswamy's (actually founded in 1925 and enjoying a surge in popularity), Choy's, Shangri-La, Star of India, the Canton and the China Garden took their place among the other recommended restaurants by virtue of quality. So did the Asiatique (Chinese and Japanese food) and the Ox-on-the-Roof (French, Japanese and Indonesian). But neither Piper nor the *Vogue* journalists could have foreseen the explosion in popularity of foreign food which was to take place over the next thirty years – one of three major changes which, as we shall see, would make the London of the twenty-first century as different from the London of only fifty years earlier as Elizabethan London was from the medieval city.

Two major new writers on food – writers who had at least as much influence as Elizabeth David had had a decade earlier – began to publish in the late 1960s and early '70s. Jane Grigson was one, Claudia Roden the other. Their interests were very different, as was their approach, for while Grigson concentrated enthusiastically on the traditional recipes of Britain (chiefly England) and northern France, Roden concerned herself first with the food of North Africa and later extended her palette to encompass Italy and all the Mediterranean countries. Grigson's intense love of history, literature and the arts pervaded her writing – her recipes sit like little coloured flags on a map of European culture. Her style of writing was direct, friendly and unpretentious; she wore her considerable knowledge lightly and had the pleasant ability to make the reader feel knowledgeable too.

Claudia Roden's first volume, *A Book of Middle Eastern Food*, appeared in 1968 in hardback. Two years later it was reissued by Penguin Books and quickly became one of the most popular books on their list. No wonder. The food in it was delicious, the recipes easy to follow and patently authentic. Stories, anecdotes, proverbs enlivened the text. Above all, the writing was, like Grigson's, unpretentious and serious. The reader is in the presence of someone whose concern is for quality without fuss.

It is interesting to read on Roden's website her own evaluation of London food in the '50s. It was, she says, horrifyingly bad. There was very little in the shops and no way to reproduce the tasty Middle Eastern dishes she was used to. She notes that in the first edition of *Middle Eastern Food* she had to explain ingredients and suggest substitutes for almost everything.

And here we meet the first of the factors which have changed London eating so dramatically. Today, says Roden, London is one of the food capitals of the world. 'Going to Stoke Newington and Green Lane is like stepping into Turkey or Cyprus. The East End and Southall and Wembley in north London are our Little India and Little Pakistan.' It is true that the development most closely linked with London has been the growth in 'ethnic' food. Throughout this book, the city has continually appeared in her role of workplace or second home to immigrants seeking religious freedom, further education, political asylum, jobs or simply more money. One of the strongest links between an exile and his homeland is through his native food, and inevitably where a community shares the same background and traditions, restaurants open. But never has London had such a multiracial mix, and never have there been so many 'ethnic' restaurants. In 1999, consumption of ethnic foods eaten outside the home reached ninety grams per person per week, higher than in any other part of Britain. At the top level, on that page of the 2005 issue of *The Good Food Guide* which classifies restaurants according to predominant cuisine, we find one Australian, seven

British, twelve Chinese, one Danish, three East European/Eurasian, forty-eight French, five Fusion/pan-Asian, two Greek, twenty-one Indian/Pakistani/Bangladeshi, three Indian vegetarian, three Indonesian/Straits/Malaysian, twenty-nine Italian, fourteen Japanese, five North African/Middle Eastern, three South American, four Spanish, two Thai, two Turkish, one Vegetarian and one Vietnamese. And these are only the best; to them one must add the many 'ethnic' restaurants never likely to make it into *The Good Food Guide* but which offer simple, unpretentious dishes to homesick immigrants.

But not to immigrants alone – nor are the dishes always simple, let alone authentic. Britons had been familiar with Indian food in its various forms since the days of the British East India Company, and mulligatawny, kedgeree and curries, however corrupted, have figured in English recipe books for well over a century. Moreover, as we have seen, there were Indian restaurants in London before the First World War. No one, however, could have forecast the boom which began in the 1970s as thousands of Asians, chiefly Bangladeshis escaping from a murderous civil war in their own country, came to Britain and set up small eating-houses and takeaway outlets. Many had not been cooks at home, but they reproduced as far as they could the food that they knew, for themselves and others, despite the difficulty of sourcing spices and other ingredients. Often they used a formula, adding ready-blended curry powder and a standard sauce to varying main ingredients, producing something spicy and hot, pleasing to the palate but unauthentic; a bewildering mixture of the traditional, the invented and the historic British curry. Costs and prices were kept low. The novelist Amitav Ghosh, in his book *The Shadow Lines* (1988) has his characters, who have come to London from Calcutta, eating in an 'Indian' restaurant some time in the 1970s:

> 'Chicken Singapore?' he said under his breath.
> 'Prawn Bombay?' responded . . . Ila.
> . . . Ila . . . leant towards us and whispered: 'Treat it like something exotic – like Eskimo food – and you'll enjoy it.'
> . . . when the food came, everything fell just beyond the border of familiarity, – the usual taste of spices transformed by stock and cream and Worcestershire Sauce. But the food was delicious in its way.

This type of Indian restaurant has persisted all over Britain. But in London (and elsewhere), the last few years have seen the emergence of establishments whose sophistication in the matter of menus, quality, service, and decor is a world away from what Ghosh describes. Some concentrate on authentic regional recipes, others use the style and ingredients of a region to create new and subtle dishes which owe nothing to so-called fusion food, others again claim the freedom for the chef to experiment with Western ingredients. Their aim has been to be thought of as top London restaurants rather than top Indian ones – with some success.

London's Chinese community, based largely in the Gerrard Street/Shaftesbury Avenue/Leicester Square area, has a more ancient history. They had come originally as sailors and dockers towards the end of the nineteenth century, but soon a few began to settle in and around Limehouse, where they set up eating-houses and laundries for their compatriots. It's surprising to realise that at the turn of the last century there were still only 545 Chinese, mainly men, in the whole of Britain. Popular fiction and films of the period presented the Chinese as smugglers, opium addicts, gamblers and peddlers of the worst kinds of vice, and there was also a language barrier, so the community kept to itself and grew but slowly until after the Second World War. Then several things happened. Limehouse had been bombed out of existence during the Blitz. New laws within the Seamen's Union made it much harder for foreign sailors to work on British ships. The introduction of launderettes and, later, domestic washing-machines caused the collapse of the laundry business. And soldiers returning from the Far East began to seek out restaurants where they could enjoy Chinese food. The Chinese community, looking around, discovered that short leases in the shabby, run-down Gerrard Street area of Soho were available for next to nothing. At the same time, thousands of agricultural workers from Hong Kong, out of work because of a collapse in the price of rice, arrived in Britain and began to work in the catering trade. As a result, south Soho became and remains the centre of the London Chinese community. Many of the workers still live in tied accomodation, and working seventeen hours a day leaves little time to learn English let alone attempt to integrate. So Soho now has its own Chinese supermarkets, dentists, lawyers, doctors, even estate agents, and in 1984 Westminster City Council officially recognised it as 'Chinatown'. Outside Soho, it is possible to 'get a Chinese' in at

least twelve thousand restaurants and takeaways, and five London
boroughs have Chinese supermarkets. The effect on the food of
other communities? Negligible so far. Many people enjoy Chinese
food, but few cook it for themselves.

Restaurants, of course, bear only a tenuous relationship to the
daily food of ordinary people. But immigration has had other
interesting consequences. Consider the West Indians who flooded
into Britain in the 1950s and 1960s. They have had very little impact
on the restaurant scene (I can find only twelve eating-houses
claiming to offer Caribbean food in the 2004 *Yellow Pages*), but what
Jeremy Round wrote in *The Independent* in 1988 is true today: a visit
to Brixton Market on a winter afternoon is London's cheapest route
to the tropics. Just off Electric Avenue in the Granville Arcade, one
of the market's two covered sections, the senses are assaulted by the
vibrant colours, strange smells and odd shapes and textures of
plantains and mangoes, yams and okra, pumpkins and gourds,
sugar cane and breadfruit which lie heaped on the stalls, while at the
fishmonger's or butcher's you can buy blue crabs, Trinidad shrimps,
bonito, cow heel and pig's trotters. (the two last to make English
dishes introduced into the West Indies two centuries ago, and now
largely forgotten in their country of origin). It is the children and
grandchildren of the original immigrants who shop in such markets
now; it is they who have kept the market alive.

Londoners themselves vary in their reaction to this
internationalism. Claudia Roden approves wholeheartedly, saying
that it has been to London's advantage, making it one of the food
capitals of the world. Jonathan Meades, food writer and television
journalist, is less happy. He welcomes the variety but claims that
London is in thrall to the easily exotic, to the detriment of native
produce: 'London has effectively seceded from the country of which
it is the capital.' This is true, insofar as the number of traditional
London eating-houses, like the George and Vulture and Simpson's-
in-the-Strand, has diminished. Worse, to find the authentic cockney
fare of jellied eels and pie-and-mash, one must now go out of central
London to Greenwich or the East End.

Meades' other complaint, that London has very few German,
Middle European or Scandinavian restaurants, perhaps overlooks
the fact that restaurateurs from prosperous countries can make a
living in their native land and are not likely to emigrate. In fact,
London may see a good many more Middle European restaurants

in the coming years, as a consequence of the breakdown of Communism and the expansion of the European Union. As another Londoner put it, 'We are undergoing an exciting shift in ethnicity as Eastern Europeans arrive from a wide variety of countries.'

A second, equally dramatic change in London eating has been the growth of supermarkets and the decline of the small independent shop. *The Alternative Census*, published by the London School of Economics towards the end of 2004 and based for the most part on a study of the *Yellow Pages*, records the changes countrywide over the last ten years. Unfortunately it does not give separate figures for London.

> Listings for supermarkets increased 8 per cent.
> Those for individual butchers fell almost 40 per cent
> Those for greengrocers and fruiterers were down 59 per cent
> Those for bakers and confectioners fell nearly 20 per cent
> In 2003, 76 per cent of bread was bought in supermarkets.

The trend is very clear, the question of cause and effect less so. What supermarkets offer, more than anything else, is convenience. Next to that comes cost, and these two factors alone may account for the figures for bread, for instance. Again, greengrocers and fruiterers with limited storage space and facilities for keeping produce fresh and selling it cheaply now find themselves in competition with large companies with dedicated warehouses, excellent transport and access to fruit and vegetables from all over the world at low prices.

The case with butchers, however, is a little different. In the 1960s and 1970s, the food at Cranks might have been delicious, but it hardly changed public perception of vegetarians and Soil Association members as – well, cranks. But the BSE crisis of the late 1980s, when thousands of cattle were slaughtered and a hideous illness which affects humans (CJD) emerged, sparked a movement to vegetarianism which rapidly gained momentum. In December 1994, BBC Radio Four put the number of conversions per week at 2,000. Then in 2001, a serious outbreak of foot-and-mouth disease caused further problems for butchers despite the fact that the illness posed no danger to humans. The cattle crisis has undoubtedly hit hard, for a second effect has been to increase squeamishness; far fewer people eat offal nowadays, and younger meat-eaters prefer to buy their meat ready cut, boned, rolled, prepared, so that they need to touch it themselves as little as possible. Supermarkets have understood this – the meat is presented in neat polystyrene trays with clingfilm wrap, ready-cut into portions and requiring only to be tipped into the pan. A press release from Tesco in 2003 claimed that only 17 per cent of customers aged between 21 and 35 had heard of common cuts of meat such as brisket, fore rib, chump and loin.

The small shops – butchers and others – which *have* survived have done so for a variety of reasons. In a city as large as London, with an ever-shifting population, anonymity threatens, and the friendly service of a local grocer or butcher acquires added value, particularly for people from immigrant communities. Then again, some shop owners have changed their approach and concentrated on a specific niche. There is an almost medieval feel about the specialist shops which have arisen – the delicatessens, the shops selling only Middle Eastern or Italian produce, only jam, only coffee, only cheese.

If the meat crisis was the most dramatic of the health scares, there have been many others since the 1970s. Salmonella in eggs, carcinogenic pesticides and herbicides, the dangers inherent in cholesterol-rich animal fats, and the addition of salt and sugar to most manufactured foods all received wide press publicity. The result has been an increased desire for 'natural' food. Recent figures from the Soil Association show an increase of 10 per cent in sales of organic food in the year 2003–2004 – a modest figure and not exactly a breakthrough considering that it still accounts for only 2 per cent of food sold in the United Kingdom. Nevertheless, what was once considered an eccentric whim has now turned into a trend whose importance is demonstrated by the fact that in London as elsewhere Farmers' Markets – defined as markets in which producers from a demarcated local area (for London the radius is one hundred miles) sell their own products directly to the public – have become so popular.

Most Farmers' Market stallholders (but not all) concentrate on the organic side of the business; the emphasis is on freshness and quality and most particularly the farmer-to-consumer link, in a concept borrowed from the United States. The first weekly Farmers' Market in London was set up in Islington in 1999. It has since been joined by twelve others – the number limited by the reluctance of producers to travel into London and by the availability of good sites. But Jonathan Meades rightly points out that the so-called 'gastronomic revolution' affects only a minority of the population – indeed the location of the Markets and the cost of the produce make them socially divisive. Just over three-quarters, 76 per cent, of customers come from socio-economic groups A, B or C, and 40 per cent are aged 55 or over.

It yet remains that the shift to organic food and to the small specialist shop has stimulated reaction from the supermarkets, almost all of which now have shelves for organic food. Indeed, as early as 1999, the Soil Association estimated that 69 per cent of organic food sold in the UK passed through supermarkets. They also have counters for delicatessen, foreign cheeses and fresh fish, and many have in-store bakeries. Whether this is evidence of an opportunistic leap onto the bandwagon or an assumption of responsibility for the nation's health and gastronomic sensibilities need not concern us here; any shopkeeper must respond to consumer demand if he is not to go out of business.

Quite as dramatic as the impact of foreign flavours and the rise of supermarkets has been the change in cooking and eating habits over the last thirty years. The domestic refrigerator, deep freeze and microwave oven have so altered cooking that it is hard to remember what life was like without them. In 1977, the London market for refrigerators was already approaching saturation point, but only 14 per cent of households in the whole of Britain owned a deep freeze, and statistics don't even mention microwave ovens. In contrast, in 2002, 87 per cent of households owned a microwave, and there is no figure for fridges or freezers, only the vague statement that most households own them – which suggests that they are so common that researchers considered it not worthwhile to ask.

The result has been a huge increase in the consumption of frozen vegetables and, more recently, pre-prepared chilled dishes, needing only to be finished in a microwave or conventional oven. (It's worth noting that on most packets, instructions for putting in the microwave precede those for conventional cooking.) Dishes range from Italian and French to Middle Eastern, Chinese, Caribbean and Indian. There are very few British dishes. In a parallel development, firms are now producing freeze-dried foods such as cooked rice or couscous to which herbs, chopped vegetables and perhaps shellfish or bits of chicken have been added. No need to measure out spices or chop the onion here, though in more sophisticated form these dishes may require the addition of an ingredient such as chopped tomatoes or an egg so that the consumer feels she is actually cooking something.

Here, in a word, is the Easimeal, a boon to busy workers and those living alone in cramped flats with tiny kitchens, often to be eaten on the living-room sofa, in front of a television screen on which a charismatic chef demonstrates exotic, sophisticated cooking. In the quotation from Helen Fielding's *Bridget Jones's Diary* at the head of this chapter, the entire three-course meal has been prepared not by Bridget but by Marks & Spencer. But Bridget does have some knowledge of cooking. Here, inspired by a conversation with a 'green' friend, she plans a birthday party:

> *Sunday 19 March*: . . . These nineteen people are my friends; they want to be welcomed into my home . . . with simple homely fare . . . am going to cook shepherd's pie for them – All British Home Cooking.

Next day she has second thoughts:

> *Monday 20 March*: Have decided to serve the shepherd's pie with Chargrilled Belgian Endive Salad, Roquefort Lardons and Frizzled Chorizo, to add a fashionable touch (have not tried before but sure it will be easy), followed by Grand Marnier soufflés. V. much looking forward to the birthday. Expect to become known as brilliant cook and hostess.

Needless to say, Bridget is unable to cope with the demands of this preposterous, television-inspired menu. The birthday party is only saved because her friends have taken the precaution of booking a meal at a nearby restaurant. In another attempt to entertain, she again turns to television for her menu, but blue dye gets into the soup, she has forgotten to buy tuna steaks and a confit of oranges turns into marmalade.

Thus the picture that emerges of London today is of a multicultural megalopolis, in which the link between producer and consumer is tenuous at best; in which, too, more meals are eaten outside the home than in any other part of Britain. Technology has enabled people to eat a huge variety of food at low cost and with the minimum of effort, but it has turned cooking into a rather mysterious art practised by a diminishing number. In *Bridget Jones's*

Diary Helen Fielding has given us an authentic portrait of the young, single, working Londoner, grazing on sandwiches, wraps and takeaways, falling back on restaurants and supermarket food for social meals. It's a bizarre echo of medieval days, for though the range of food and the level of hygiene might astound Hodge of Ware and the hero of 'London Lickpenny', they would be quite at home with many of today's eating habits.

Modern eating in London – three approaches:
One: A day in the meals of Bridget Jones

Breakfast: hot-cross bun (Scarsdale Diet – slight variation on specified wholemeal toast); Mars Bar (Scarsdale Diet – slight variation on specified half grapefruit)

Snack: two bananas, two pears (switched to F-plan as starving and cannot face Scarsdale carrot snacks). Carton orange juice (Anti-Cellulite Raw-Food Diet)

Lunch: jacket potato (Scarsdale Vegetarian Diet) and hummus (Hay Diet – fine with jacket spuds as all starch, and breakfast and snack were all alkaline-forming with exception of hot-cross bun and Mars: minor aberration)

Dinner: four glasses of wine, fish and chips (Scarsdale Diet and also Hay Diet – protein forming); portion tiramisu; peppermint Aero (pissed)

Two: Eels and Mash in the East End
Interview with Robert Cooke, 9 Broadway Market,
Hackney. 2 November 1989.

[This interview was conducted for the first edition of Londoners' Larder. *It is sad evidence of how culinary traditions can disappear before our eyes.]*

My great-grandfather started in the eel-and-pie business in 1862. My grandfather bought this shop in 1900, then he opened a second one in Kingsland Road in 1910. The Kingsland Road shop still has its original appearance and fittings. It's been in lots of books on architecture. The dining room has a huge Victorian dome – spectacular. It's run by my cousins. This shop was refurbished in 1930: tiled walls and terrazzo floors and marble tables. Before that, we had an extra dining room in the basement, but now it's a cellar. It's just as it was in the '30s, except I've changed the lighting to fluorescent. Maybe one day I'll change it back again – I think the traditional lights were better.

I helped my Dad here from a boy. Then when I left school I just naturally worked here. I've no hang-ups – never thought really about doing anything else. I must say that although we make our living, it's not what it was in the '50s. Then the eel trade was cracking on. There was no McDonald's and no Wimpy. I can remember the first Wimpy Bar in London, it was in Lyons Corner House. My Dad used to take us to the panto at Christmas, and I remember one year – 1960 – we saw Harry Secombe in *Humpty Dumpty* at the Palladium, then we went to the Wimpy Bar in the Corner House as a special treat. Now they're everwhere – Wimpys, McDonald's, Greek places, Indian places – it's a lot of competition. But we make a living.

Our main trade nowadays is in meat pies, which we make with minced beef. We use a fatless dough for the bottom and a lovely pastry with margarine and beef suet for the top. We make everything ourselves. There's a bakehouse at the back, all terrazzo floor and wall tiling.

We get through a lot of eels, though. They're quite expensive now. I buy them live at Billingsgate. English eels finish in October, then it's imported ones from New Zealand, then Canada and America until April. We sell stewed eels and jellied eels. Eels-and-mash is very traditional. We stew them with pimientos and a little salt in the water, then we skin them and cut them up. A portion is five pieces. We make a special gravy to go with them, with lots of parsley. Parsley sauce should be *green*, not white with little green dots. In the winter, I have to use a bit of dried parsley as well as the fresh stuff from France. We also have a market stall outside the shop to sell live eels, and in the summer we can sell them through the open front windows. There's more trade in cooked eels, but the older generation still likes to do its own. The young ones don't know how to cook them. You choose your eel and we'll kill it, cut off the head and tail, gut it and send you home with a nice bit of parsley for the gravy as well.

My grandfather died in 1959 aged about 80. He was the man who thought of putting jellied eels on the street; before him the stalls only sold shellfish. There's a number of other eel and pie shops now, more people are doing it. We're mostly related. The Manzi's and us have intermarried a bit.

I think if we can keep going family-wise we'll be all right. People are coming back to eels. We get local shoppers but also people from right across London. We're right by Regent's Canal, so we get quite a lot of people from City offices in for their lunch. When this new development of luxury flats is finished, I think we'll get the yuppies too. Maybe I should start laying down some Chablis! Eels are a good food, and people know it. They were a fast food before fast food was invented; you come in here and give your order, and you can be served and sitting at your table in ten seconds. But the business must be run properly. I don't skimp, and I'd never, for example, use the Japanese frozen eels. If it's done properly the trade will go on for a long time yet. I've got two daughters, and my wife's pregnant again. I'd like a boy. I'd never force anybody, but it'd be nice if he came into the shop after me. . .

Postscript, December 2004: *The shop in Kingsland Road became a Chinese restaurant in 1997, but as it is a Grade II listed building, its appearance is unchanged.*

Mr Cooke's main trade now is in pies and mash, still made on the premises, still popular with City workers and, as predicted, the residents of the luxury flats. The demand for live eels has practically vanished, although he will get you one within twenty-four hours. His stewed eels and jellied eels are now made using eels from Danish farms, which export all year round.

His wife did have a boy, who is now fifteen and helps in the shop on Saturdays.

Three: Rules restaurant, the oldest in London:
Rules has been owned by only three families since it opened in 1798. It has a well-defined approach to its position as purveyor of traditional British food at affordable prices, and strong connections with literary and theatrical London from its earliest days. Writers ranging from Dickens and Thackeray to Graham Greene, Dick Francis and Penelope Lively

have enjoyed its food. In 1971 when a demolition order to make way for the development of the Covent Garden area threatened, the then Poet Laureate John Betjeman successfully led a campaign to preserve it. Today as ever, it is a favourite with writers, actors, artists, lawyers, journalists and businessmen, serving meals to over 100,000 people per year.

Interview with Julian Payne, business director of Rules,
35 Maiden Lane, London, 7 December 2004

A lot of regulars come in at lunch-time; in the evening, we may have more overseas visitors. I always say that Rules is the world's club. They come from all over – at present, we get many people from Russia and the Eastern bloc. They find Rules fits their idea of what London is like – a sort of Dickensian picture. As well as the restaurant, we have four dining rooms for private parties – the John Betjeman Room, the Dickens Room, the Edward VII Room (he used to entertain Lillie Langtry there) and the Graham Greene Room. Anyone can book them, from children wanting to treat Mum and Dad (or vice versa) to companies or literary societies. The Noel Coward Society is having its annual dinner in the Graham Greene Room on Saturday. We also do children's parties. I think children who come to Rules tend to come back later – it has a happy resonance in people's culinary experience. It's like a favourite aunt or uncle, always there and always dependable.

The menu hasn't changed greatly over the last fifty years, although our chef Richard Sawyer, who started with us last summer, brought a wonderful pastry chef with him, so the range of puddings has enlarged a bit. We do a lot of game – venison and wildfowl – but our most popular dish has to be steak and kidney (pie or pudding). We serve an awful lot of potted shrimps, smoked salmon, Stilton and watercress soup, that sort of British food. Our menus change four times a year with the seasons – including the puddings. At present, we do a very nice baked rice pudding with damson jam.

John Mayhew, the owner, has an estate in the high Pennines, which is let out to shooting-parties on a very low-key basis, it's not one of your smart estates. We source very little game from it, because the supply is erratic and moving food from north to south is a nightmare. But we do use the estate to train our staff. We take them up in parties and show them how the game is managed and teach them to stalk and shoot, so that they are knowledgeable about the food they serve.

A man called Paul Coppen grazes a herd of about ninety Belted Galloway cattle on adjoining pasture land, and we do buy three or four carcasses from him each year. The cattle are slaughtered in Darlington, then sent down to our London butcher who trims it and hangs it for us. We use Sussex lamb and get meat from Cornwall too.

As far as possible, we use vegetables in season and try to keep things British, although in winter we do have to extend our sourcing a bit; winter vegetables here are a bit monotonous. But we never buy forced vegetables or fruit. My philosophy is, 'If you shut your eyes, you should be able to identify and enjoy what you're eating.' So definitely no strawberries in winter.

Our wine list changes all the time, and we like to offer a different champagne from time to time. At present, it is Veuve Clicquot, poured into your glass in front of you so you see exactly what you are getting. Our wine is better than ever. Obviously, with the kinds of meat we serve, we have a bias towards red wines, but they come from a wide variety of countries. We have some good reds from small producers in the Southern Rhône region. We don't only sell it in bottles, we sell six or seven white wines by the jug and ten red wines. People don't always want a full bottle. We also sell draught beer, in rather nice silver goblets.

We feel it is important to keep doing what we do well. I like to say that we try to preserve our DNA. Tinker with that, and you never recover your identity. Having said that, one continually has to work at it, buff it, *never stop polishing*. In this trade, you can't rest on past achievements. One thing has changed: since 2000, we don't allow smoking in the restaurant. It was unfair to the staff and non-smoking customers. There was a bit of protest, but people didn't stop coming to eat here.

ACKNOWLEDGEMENTS

Constable Publishers for permission to quote an extract from *Food and Drink in Britain* by C. Anne Wilson.

Reinhardt Books for permission to quote a passage from *Lovely Food* by Ruth Lowinsky.

Messrs Chatto & Windus for permission to quote extracts from books by Leonard Woolf and Virginia Woolf.

The Directors of *Punch* for permission to quote the two poems in Chapter 8.

Messrs Holtzmann & Holtzmann for permission to quote an extract from *The Marlborough House Set* by Anita Leslie.

Messrs A.P. Watt Ltd for permission to quote an extract from *Memory Hold-the-door* by John Buchan and from a letter by P.G. Wodehouse.

The Rev. Kirk for permission to use a quotation from an unnamed Lord Mayor of London in *Tried Favourites Cookery Book* by Mrs E.W. Kirk.

Messrs B.T. Batsford Ltd for permission to use the illustration of seventeenth-century sellers of live fish.

The Trustees of the British Museum for permission to reproduce *Cries of London*, as well as the woodcuts from *The Roxburghe Ballads* used as a recurring motif.

The Museum of London for permission to reproduce the painting of Covent Garden by Collett on the front cover.

The Directors of the Reform Club for permission to reproduce the illustration of Soyer in the kitchens of the club.

The Pepys Library, Magdalene College, Cambridge, for permission to reproduce the illustration of a seventeenth-century dinner party from *The Gentlewoman's Delight in Cookery*.

Alice and Frank Prochaska for permission to quote recipes from *Margaretta Acworth's Georgian Cookery Book*.

The Bodley Head for permission to quote from *The Tenth Muse* by Sir Harry Luke.

Macmillan Ltd for permission to quote from *Bridget Jones's Diary* by Helen Fielding.

BIBLIOGRAPHY

Chapter One
Austin, Thomas (ed.), *Two Fifteenth-Century Cookery Books*, Harleian
  MS 279 and 4016 (Early English Text Society, O.S. 91, 1888)
Bagley, J.J., *Life in Medieval England* (London, 1960)
Baker, Timothy, *Medieval London* (London, 1970)
Book of Ancient Cookery, A, in Rev. Richard Warner (ed.), *Antiquitates
  Culinariae* ([1791] facsimile edn, Prospect Books, London, n.d.)
Brewer, Derek, *Chaucer and his World* (London, 1978)
Brooke, Christopher, and Keir, Gillian, *London 800–1216: The
  Shaping of a City* (London, 1975)
Chaucer, Geoffrey, *The Canterbury Tales*, tr. J.U. Nicolson (London,
  1988)
Chute, Marchette, *Geoffrey Chaucer of England* (London, 1951)
Drummond, Sir John, and Wilbraham, Anne, *The Englishman's Food*
  (London, 1957)
Forme of Cury, The, in Rev. Richard Warner (ed.), *Antiquitates Culinariae*
  ([1791] facsimile edn, Prospect Books, London, n.d.)
Hieatt, Constance, and Butler, Sharon, (eds.), *Curye on Inglysch*
  (London, New York, Toronto, 1985)
Hieatt, Constance, and Butler, Sharon, *Pleyn Delit: Medieval Cookery for
  Modern Cooks* (Toronto, 1976)
Mead, W.E., *The English Medieval Feast* (London, 1931)
Rickert, Edith, *Chaucer's World* (New York and London, 1948)
Sass, Lorna, *To the King's Taste* (London, 1976)
Wilson, C. Anne, *Food and Drink in Britain* (London, 1973)

Chapter Two
Chute, Marchette, *Shakespeare of London* (New York, 1949)

Drummond, Sir John, & Wilbraham, Anne, *The Englishman's Food* (London, 1957)

Fettiplace, Elinor, *Elinor Fettiplace's Receipt Book* (London, 1986)

Harrison, Sir William, *Description of England 1587* (Ithaca, NY, 1968)

Jonson, Ben, *Works of Ben Jonson* (London, 1838)

Lupton, D., *London and the Countrey Carbonadoed* (London, 1532)

Markham, Gervase, *The English Hus-wife* (London, 1675)

Mendelsohn, Oscar, *Drinking with Pepys* (London, 1963)

Murphy, N.T.P., *One Man's London* (London, 1989)

Murrell, John, *A new Booke of Cookerie* (London, 1638)

Pearson, Lu Emily, *Elizabethans at Home* (California, 1957)

Platt, Sir Hugh, *Delightes for Ladies* (London, 1609)

Rowse, A.L., *The Elizabethan Renaissance: The Life of the Society* (London, 1971)

Rye, W.B., *England as seen by Foreigners in the Days of Elizabeth and James the First* (London, 1865)

Stow, John, *Survey of London* (London, 1598)

Wilson, C. Anne, *Food and Drink in Britain* (London, 1971)

Winchester, Barbara, *Tudor Family Portrait* (London, 1955)

Youings, Joyce, *Sixteenth Century England* (London, 1984)

Chapter Three

Bell, W.G., *Where London Sleeps* (London, 1926)

Berry, George, *Taverns and Tokens of Pepys' London* (London, 1978)

Blencowe, Mrs Ann, *The Receipt Book of Mrs Ann Blencowe AD 1694* (London, 1925)

Borer, M.C., *Covent Garden* (London, New York, Toronto, 1967)

Bowle, John, *John Evelyn and his World* (London, 1981)

Cromwell, Joan, *The Court and Kitchen of Elizabeth commonly called Joan Cromwell* (London, 1664)

Digby, Sir Kenelm, *The Closet of the Eminently Learned Sir Kenelm Digby Knight Opened* (London, 1669)

Driver, Christopher and Berriedale-Johnson, Michelle, *Pepys at Table* (London, 1984)

Evelyn, John, *Acetaria* (London, 1699)

Evelyn, John, *Diary*, 3 vols (London, 1906)

May, Robert, *The Accomplisht Cook* (London, 1664)

Mendelsohn, Oscar, *Drinking with Pepys* (London, 1963)

Morshead, O.F. (ed.), *Everybody's Pepys* (London, 1926)

Murphy, N.T.P., *One Man's London* (London, 1989)

Ponsonby, A., *John Evelyn* (London, 1933)
Shaw, R.A., Gwynn, R.D., and Thomas, P ., *Huguenots in Wandsworth* (Wandsworth, 1985)

Chapter Four
Acworth Margaretta, *Margaretta Acworth's Georgian Cookery Book*, ed. Alice and Frank Prochaska (London, 1987)
Ashton John, *Social Life in the Reign of Queen Anne* (London, 1882)
Borer, M.C., *Covent Garden* (London, New York, Toronto, 1967)
Boswell, James, *Life of Samuel Johnson*, 2 vols., ed. Roger Ingpen (London 1907)
Drummond, Sir John and Wilbraham, Anne, *The Englishman's Food* (London, 1957)
Ellis, Aytoun, *The Penny Universities* (London, 1956)
Letts, Malcolm, *As the Foreigner Saw us* (London, 1935)
Mitchell, R.J. and Leys, M.D.R., *A History of London Life* (London, 1958)
Murphy, N.T.P., *One Man's London* (London, 1989)
Pearson, Hesketh, *Johnson and Boswell* (London, 1958)
Pullar, Philippa, *Consuming Passions* (London, 1970)
Old English Coffee-Houses (Rodale Press, London, 1954)
Raffald, Mrs Elizabeth, *The Experienced English Housekeeper* (London, 1789)
Roche, Sophie von La, *Sophie in London*, trans. C. Williams (London, 1933)
Sheppard, R. and Newton, E., *The Story of Bread* (London, 1957)
Smollett, Tobias, *The Expedition of Humphry Clinker* (London, 1771)
Stead, Jennifer, 'Quizzing Glasse: or Hannah Scrutinized', in *Petits Propos Culinaires*, 13 and 14 (London, 1983)
Steele, Sir Richard, *The Tatler*, 1710
The Spectator, 1712
Stout, Adam, 'Three Centuries of London Cowkeeping', in *Farmers' Weekly*, 18 August 1978, p.p. v–xii
Wilson, C. Anne, *Food and Drink in Britain* (London, 1973)

Chapter Five
Acton, Eliza, *Modern Cookery for Private Families* (London 1845)
Beeton, Mrs, *The Book of Household Management* (London, 1861)
Burnett, John, *Plenty and Want* (London, 1979)
Clutterbuck, Lady Maria, *What shall we have for Dinner?* (London 1865)

Dickens, Charles: Works

Dodd, George, *The Food of London* (London, 1856)

Forshaw, Alec and Bergstrom, Theo, *The Markets of London* (Harmondsworth, 1983)

Hibbert, Christopher, *The Making of Charles Dickens* (London, 1967)

Lewis, R.A., *Edwin Chadwick* (London, 1952)

Mayhew, Henry, *London Labour and the London Poor: The Street Trader's Lot* (London, 1862)

Mitchell, R.J. and Leys, M.D.R., *History of London Life* (London, 1958)

Murphy, N.T.P., *One Man's London* (London, 1989)

Rundell, Mrs, *A New System of Domestic Cookery* (London and Edinburgh, 1807 and 1850)

Stout, Adam, 'Three Centuries of London Cowkeeping' in *Farmers' Weekly*, 18 August 1978, pp. v–xii

'S.W.', *The New London Cookery* (London, 1836)

Timbs, John, *History of Clubs and Club Life* (London, 1872)

Wilson, Angus, *The World of Charles Dickens* (Harmondsworth, 1972)

Chapter Six

Beeton, Mrs, *Mrs Beeton's All About Cookery* (London, 1900)

Blakeston, O., *Edwardian Glamour Cooking Without Tears* (London, 1960)

Bowden, Gregory Houston, *British Gastronomy: The Rise of Great Restaurants* (London, 1975)

Burnett, John, *Plenty and Want* (London, 1979)

Clark, Lady Catherine, *The Cookery Book of Lady Clark of Tillypronie* (London, 1909)

Ellman, Richard, *Oscar Wilde* (Harmondsworth, 1988)

Escoffier, Auguste, *Ma Cuisine* (London, 1907)

A Few Recipes by M. Escoffier of the Carlton Hotel, London (London, 1907)

Frewin, Leslie (ed.), *Parnassus near Piccadilly* (London, 1965)

Graves, Charles, *Leather Armchairs* (London, 1963)

Hart-Davis, R., *Selected Letters of Oscar Wilde* (London, 1962)

Langley, Andrew (compiler), *The Selected Soyer* (Bath and London, 1987)

Law's Grocer's Manual (London, c.1901)

Leslie, Anita, *The Marlborough House Set* (New York, 1973)

Luke, Sir Harry, *The Tenth Muse* (London, 1962)

McDouall, Robin, *Clubland Cooking* (London, 1974)

Miles, Alfred, *The Diner's-out Vade Mecum* (London, n.d.)
Murphy, N.T.P., *One Man's London* (London, 1989)
Newnham-Davis, Col., *Dinners and Diners* (London, 1899)
Pearson, H., *The Life of Oscar Wilde* (London, 1946)

Chapter Seven
Bell, Quentin, *Virginia Woolf* (London, 1972)
Boulestin, Marcel, *The Best of Boulestin*, ed. Elvia and Maurice Firuski (London, 1952)
Burke, Thomas, *Dinner is Served* (London, 1947)
Dickens, Monica, *One Pair of Hands* (London, 1939)
'Diner-Out', *London Restaurants* (London, n.d.)
Fortnum & Mason, *The Delectable History of Fortnum & Mason* (London, 1982)
Garth, Margaret and Wrench, Mrs Stanley, *Daily Express Book of Home Management* (London, 1937)
Heaton, Rose Henniker, *The Perfect Hostess* (London, 1931)
Johnston, James P., *A Hundred Years of Eating* (Dublin, 1977)
Law's Grocer's Manual (London, *c.*1901)
Lehmann, John, *Virginia Woolf and her World* (London, 1975)
Leyel, Mrs C.F. and Hartley, Miss Olga, *The Gentle Art of Cookery* (London, 1925)
Lowinsky, Ruth, *Lovely Food* (London, 1931)
Noble, John Russell (ed.), *Recollections of Virginia Woolf* (London, 1972)
Peel, Mrs C.S. (ed.), *Daily Mail Cookery Book* (London, 1927)
Price, Stephen, *Eating Out in London: a Social History 1900–1950* (thesis, Brunel University, April 1986)
Scott, Clement, *The Wheel of Life* (London, 1897)
Willey, Simon, *Housework made Easiwork* (dissertation, Edinburgh University, 1989)
Wilson, Jean Moorcroft, *Virginia Woolf: Life and London* (London, 1987)
Wodehouse, P.G., *Something Fresh* (New York, 1915)
Woolf, Leonard, *Beginning Again* (London, 1964)
  Sowing (London, 1960)
Woolf, Virginia, *Mrs Dalloway* (London, 1933)
  A Room of One's Own (London, 1929)
  To the Lighthouse (London, 1927)

Chapter Eight

Daily Telegraph, *Good Fare* (London, n.d.)

Driver, Christopher, *The British at Table* (London, 1983)

Fielding, Helen, *Bridget Jones's Diary* (London, 1996)

Ghosh, Amitav, *The Shadow Lines* (London, 1988)

The Good Food Guide 2005 (London 2004)

Grafton, Pete, *You, You and You! The People Out of Step with World War II* (London, 1981)

Graves, Charles, *Women in Green* (London, 1948)

Heath, Ambrose, *Kitchen Front Recipes* (London, 1941)

Johnston, James P., *A Hundred Years' Eating* (Dublin, 1977)

A Kitchen Goes to War (London, 1940)

London School of Economics, *The Alternative Census 2004* (London, 2004)

Longmate, Norman, *The Home Front* (London, 1981)

Mabey, David, *In Search of Food* (London, 1978)

Marwick, Arthur, *The Home Front* (London, 1976)

Oddy, Derek J., *From Plain Fare to Fusion Food: British Diet from the 1890s to the 1990s* (Woodbridge, 2003)

Perlmutter, Kevin, *London Street Markets* (London, 1983)

Piper, David, *The Companion Guide to London* (London, 1964)

Santer, Dorothy, *The Kitchen Front* (London, n.d.)

Stork Wartime Cookery Book (London, n.d.)

Tims, Barbara (ed.), *Food in Vogue: Six Decades of Cooking and Entertaining* (London, 1976)

Willey, Simon, *Housework made Easiwork* (dissertation, Edinburgh University, 1989)

INDEX

Book titles and names of recipes given in the text are in italics.